POWER AND CONTROL IN MENTAL HEALTH SOCIAL WORK

Research in Social Work

Series Editors: **Anna Gupta**, Royal Holloway, University of London, UK and **John Gal**, Hebrew University of Jerusalem, Israel

---

Published together with The European Social Work Research Association (ESWRA), this series examines current, progressive and innovative research applications of familiar ideas and models in international social work research.

Also available in the series:

Social Work and Social Innovation
edited by **Jean Pierre Wilken**, **Anne Parpan-Blaser**, **Sarah Prosser**, **Suzan van der Pas and Erik Jansen**

Living on the Edge
edited by **Samuel Keller**, **Inger Oterholm**, **Veronika Paulsen** and **Adrian van Breda**

Migration and Social Work
edited by **Emilio José Gómez-Ciriano**, **Elena Cabiati** and **Sofia Dedotsi**

When Social Workers Impact Policy and Don't Just Implement It
by **John Gal** and **Idit Weiss-Gal**

The Origins of Social Care and Social Work
by **Mark Henrickson**

Social Work Research Using Arts-Based Methods
edited by **Ephrat Huss** and **Eltje Bos**

Critical Gerontology for Social Workers
edited by **Sandra Torres** and **Sarah Donnelly**

Involving Service Users in Social Work Education, Research and Policy
edited by **Kristel Driessens** and **Vicky Lyssens-Danneboom**

Adoption from Care
edited by **Tarja Pösö**, **Marit Skivenes** and **June Thoburn**

Interprofessional Collaboration and Service User Participation
edited by **Kirsi Juhila**, **Tanja Dall**, **Christopher Hall** and **Juliet Koprowska**

Find out more at:

policy.bristoluniversitypress.co.uk/research-in-social-work

POWER AND CONTROL IN MENTAL HEALTH SOCIAL WORK

Community Care and Involuntary Intervention

Hannah Jobling and Mark Hardy

First published in Great Britain in 2026 by

Policy Press, an imprint of
Bristol University Press
University of Bristol
1–9 Old Park Hill
Bristol
BS2 8BB
UK
t: +44 (0)117 374 6645
e: bup-info@bristol.ac.uk

Details of international sales and distribution partners are available at policy.bristoluniversitypress.co.uk

DOI: 10.51952/9781447369547

British Library Cataloguing in Publication Data
A catalogue record for this book is available from the British Library

ISBN 978-1-4473-6951-6 hardcover
ISBN 978-1-4473-6953-0 ePub
ISBN 978-1-4473-6954-7 ePDF

Cover design: Bristol University Press
Front cover image: iStock/td7373
Bristol University Press and Policy Press use environmentally responsible print partners.
Printed and bound in Great Britain by CPI Group (UK) Ltd, Croydon, CR0 4YY

Bristol University Press' authorised representative in the European Union is:
Easy Access System Europe, Mustamäe tee 50, 10621 Tallinn, Estonia,
Email: gpsr.requests@easproject.com

For Helen

Contents

List of figures and tables

Figure

Tables

About the authors

Hannah Jobling is Senior Lecturer in Social Work in the School for Business and Society at the University of York. She has researched and written on diverse domains in social work and social policy, including mental health social work and coercive practices, social work in different times and places, and community-based approaches to social support.

Mark Hardy is Honorary Fellow in Social Work in the School for Business and Society at the University of York. He has published widely on social work theory and practice, particularly on the nature and position of risk within mental health and forensic social work.

Introduction: Virtuous authority? Power and control in practice

Questions about the operation of power, and more directly control, are central to social work, particularly in countries where social workers operate within a statutory framework in fields such as child and family social work, youth justice and mental health. As a profession which often claims a deep seated commitment to social justice, power – particularly as it manifests through control – tends to be represented as a negative social force utilised by dominant actors to reduce the agency of service users whose own power is scant and suppressed. In this analysis, social work ought to be an instrument for overturning established power arrangements as a basis for individual and social change. However, when reducing the agency and autonomy of service users, social workers are often seen as perpetuating rather than challenging established power relations, thus deepening existing inequalities and oppressions. They are criticised for assuming expertise that is not necessarily warranted; disguising true motives 'under cover of kindness'; and emphasising control rather than offering care and support. At the same time, they are represented as being entangled in oppressive systems of power which exist to maintain a neoliberal order (Brockmann and Garrett, 2022).

These are the orthodox positions within contemporary social work debates. Wilson (2017, 1312) infers the limits to what these orthodoxies can achieve when she notes their repetitive narrative that 'if we think right and work right, the future will be more than just the past'. For her, canonical beliefs instead represent 'precious artefacts' which provide a reassuring point of orientation in a profoundly destabilising world. Totalising normative critiques of social work thus have the effect of side-stepping the actualities and possibilities of the present. This can be seen in the ways that although a perennial debate exists regarding the relationship between care and control in social work, control in itself is an under-theorised aspect of social work practice. Instead, Wilson (2017, 1312) argues, the social work imagination should be expanded to include the impossibility of knowing the consequences of what are constituted as emancipatory or controlling practices and relatedly 'the fact that it is impossible to act in the world without ever causing harm'.

The position we take in this book is sympathetic with such a perspective, and indeed, we take it further by arguing that the production of knowledge for social work practice is best served by moving from conflictual to constitutional – specifically Foucauldian – models of power. We ground these theoretical considerations by examining the 'case' (Shaw, Hardy and Sommerfield, 2024) of control in community mental health practice. Our premise is that there is significant value for social work in constructing an ethically informed but non-prescriptive approach to understanding the ambiguities of control and how it is made sense of, experienced and enacted by both practitioners and service users. In particular it allows for a more modest, honest and heterogeneous orientation for progressive forms of practice to emerge.

Care and control in social work

Tensions between care and control have been present within social work practice and discourse since its inception (Alfandari et al, 2022). The use of control does not always sit easily with the ethical frameworks social work espouses despite comprising a significant strand of social work, particularly in countries like the UK where social work is mandated by and embedded within statutory systems aimed at responding to both need and risk. The academic literature on control tends to a critical position which associates these measures with the 'depersonalisation' and depoliticisation of social work, and an emphasis on risk management ahead of the realisation of rights within a neoliberal milieu (Hardy, 2015). These narratives position social workers as deskilled 'agents of the state' (Timor-Shelvin, Hermans and Roose, 2023), while at the same time critiquing the professionalisation of social work based on hierarchical formulations of expertise. The current parlous socio-political and economic context has, it is argued, further embedded a control orientation in social work while simultaneously limiting the capacity for social work to act for progressive social change and for social workers to undertake rights-based and relational practices (Murphy, 2021). Indeed, calls for the abolition of social work in various practice domains (Asgarian, 2023; Fox, 2025; Tseris, 2025) are based on the premise that social work is fatally undermined by its capitulation to social control and lack of emancipatory vision and action. As Maylea (2021, 777, original emphasis) evocatively writes in his call for the end of social work, 'Social work has not held back the flood of oppression, inequality, neoliberalism or managerialism. Social work is *stuck* and it has *failed*.'

However, while care and control may be positioned oppositionally, the relationship between them is more complex than this juxtaposition does justice. The boundaries between what may be counted as 'care work', often preventative in nature, and 'control work' where compulsion is invoked, are blurred, raising questions around the nature and spectrum of consent and collaboration (Alfandari et al, 2022). Care and control can operate in complementary rather than contradictory ways; a contemporary example being the emergence of relational approaches to risk management in forensic social work in recent years (Blumenthal, Wood and Williams, 2018). In adult social care, notions of acting in the 'best interests' of service users when capacity is being considered are underpinned by statutory and practice frameworks which operate on the crux between control and autonomy. A more critically informed and systemic analysis of the intersection between care and control comes via the concept of vulnerability, which has been used to underpin what Brown (2024, 289) describes as 'interwoven welfare and penal mechanisms'. Here, approaches to protection and regulation come together in the governance of particular groups and problems, as can be seen most obviously for social work in practice with young people within youth justice and care systems. It is also worth reiterating that as a mediator between individuals and society, social workers are constantly balancing different interests within family, institutional and community systems. The significance of this mediating role in shaping the nature and focus of care/control configurations within different domains of social work practice is rarely acknowledged (Philp, 1979).

Power and its relationship to control

The varying divergences and overlaps which characterise the relationship between care and control also point to a more fundamental question on how control can be understood within broader theorisations of power. It is worth stepping back a little and sketching out some of these theoretical positions; as Han (2019, vii) notes 'when it comes to the concept of power, theoretical chaos still reigns. While the existence of the phenomenon itself cannot be doubted, the concept remains altogether ambiguous.' There is no transcendental essence to power and it therefore cannot be defined in singular terms. Instead, there are a variety of contested understandings reflecting an increasingly complex world in which neither ends or ethos are uncontested. Conceptually it can be argued that power is more akin to a family (Haugaard and Ryan, 2012) with points of resemblance and difference between 'power over' (structural), 'power to' (consensual) and 'power created' (constituted).

'Power over' in simple terms is defined causally and oppressively – the capacity to alter another's behaviour regardless of their will (Weber, 1978). The agentic nature of power is emphasised as a top-down phenomena in which a minority dominates decision-making regarding the majority who themselves lack the necessary power to bring about a different – fairer, more equal – distribution of power within society. Lukes (1974) in his 'third face' of power extends this perspective beyond behaviouralism to incorporate the role of social structures in the operation of power, and in turn the ways that people may become inured to subjection via false consensus to further the interests of elites. In this way, structural theories emphasise the often covert nature of power, including the role played by ideology in promoting and maintaining existing orders of power. Gramsci (1971), for example, highlighted culture as a highly effective vehicle for controlling imaginative possibilities by limiting what people are able to think and say. Thus power takes on a psychological element, both in terms of understanding its nature – if you control what people think and say, you can control what they do – but also how change might be achieved. These conflictual models position freedom as a separate state from power, with power being possessed for particular reasons and by particular groups (Gaventa, 2010).

Critical perspectives on the control functions of social work are embedded in these conflictual understandings of power, with an ensuing tendency to conflate power and control within a narrative of coercion and resistance or acquiescence (Tew, 2006). Perceiving control in these terms can mask the subtle realities of control in practice, and how control is made sense of and experienced by practitioners and those individuals made subject to it in context, risking the creation of a reductive picture of relations and responses. Indeed, the tendency within the extant literature to focus on strategies to limit control rather than interrogating dimensions of control work in practice, means that ideals of emancipatory and collaborative approaches to social work are difficult to marry with some commonplace social work contexts and experiences (Healy, 2000).

In this sense, control work can be understood more fully if it is related to productive as well as repressive theorisations of power, which portray power in recursive, organic and non-linear terms. Power thus can be distinguished from the use of force, as it is mutually enacted through social relations. Arendt (1970, 56) notably contrasts power with violence when she states 'In fact, violence destroys power: it is insufficient to say that power and violence are not the same. Power and violence are opposites; where the one rules the other is absent.' Drawing on classical Greek philosophy, she reconceives power as a vehicle for empowerment rather than subjugation. Key to this is the value of the individual to collective societal decision-making, without which people do not truly develop their full human potential. Consensual models of power thus rely on a politics characterised by pluralism, human freedom and flourishing, using collective communicative mechanisms to sustain themselves (Alexander, 2010). In order to promote a politics of freedom, the state should actively facilitate dynamic interaction among the citizenry, challenging both the apolitical and the oppressive. Only where power is a function of a politics based on active citizenship is it truly legitimate and only where power concerns the self as a political project can it be truly empowering. Han (2019) takes this further in his discussion of power and freedom, where he argues the threat of sanctions undermines power. Power is theorised as a scale with violence and freedom at each end, where unmediated coercion between an *ego* and *alter* leads to fragility in power, and mediated free choice ensures the stability of power. As he notes (Han,

2019, 17), 'power as coercion and power as freedom are not fundamentally different; they differ only with regard to the degree of mediation … At the highest point of mediation, power and freedom coincide. That is the situation in which power is as stable as it possibly can be.'

This in turn connects with a Foucauldian approach to power which similarly does not take a fixed position on power relations and via his theory of governmentality (2011), foregrounds freedom as a signifier of power. Foucault's analysis developed over time, from elite – or sovereign – power to a more nuanced and adaptive analysis of power as a shifting form of dispersed authority, via a focus on the disciplinary microphysics of power. His post-structural analysis was critical of the one-sided picture in Marxist structural theory, which he saw as insufficiently nuanced in its portrayal of how power works. He challenged the idea that power is a possession, instead theorising it as pervasive and productive. Additionally, he was hesitant about grand theories which advocated replacing existing top-down power structures with other, equally hierarchical, systems. Over time, Foucault's analysis shifted to exploring how power is perpetuated through self-work. He was especially interested in the experiences of those subject to formal and informal apparatus of social control, particularly individuals who were prisoners or severely mentally distressed (Luxon, 2019) but also others subject to overt stigma because they did not abide by societal norms. Significantly, these studies demonstrated that even in overtly repressive scenarios, people were able to develop strategies of resistance and therefore retain hope. Rose (1999) has applied these ideas to the 'practices of freedom' associated with the rise to prominence of neoliberal rationalities within the institutions of government over the last 40 years or so. Other post-Foucauldians such as Dean (2013) and Villasden (2024) emphasise the multi-faceted nature of power and thus the complex ways in which power is entwined with different ways of thinking and achieving both control and domination but also empowerment and freedom, a recurrence which Dean (2013, 12) highlights as a characteristic 'bipolarity' of power. The double edged nature of power – its dual mandate – is most evident in domains where traditional sovereign forms of power have been supplanted by 'Foucault's 'social entourage' who define individuals through their relation to institutions that traverse society' (Luxon, 2019, 321) – welfare, healthcare, criminal justice, mental health.

Applying a Foucauldian analysis to control opens up a variety of possibilities for understanding how control is realised and encountered within different configurations of power. Han (2019, 11, emphasis in original) notes that '*the feeling of freedom* on the side of the one who is subordinated to power does not depend on the number of alternatives at his or her disposal'. Control, which by its nature limits choice, can nevertheless result in multifaceted (and non-coercive) consequences. Recognising such complexity means that there is little option for social work but to revert to a practical–moral model of practice which is flexible and plural, so as to do justice to the uniqueness of each situation (Hood, 2018). Taking this approach by its nature necessitates an ascending analysis where localised manifestations of power are prioritised (Foucault, 1980). We return to such points later in this chapter, but first we survey control in relation to mental health practice.

Control as part of mental health practice

Control as a topic of debate and a facet of practice is present in different forms across all domains of social work. However, it is arguably foregrounded in some domains of social work more than others. Furthermore, the ability for social workers to act with discretion when applying control also differs from one domain to the other (Evans, 2014). Mental health social work is one domain where a mandate for control can exist alongside significant discretion in decision-making. Within countries where statutory mental health frameworks exist, individuals who experience severe mental distress can be made subject to compulsory detention and treatment. A range of professionals administer this apparatus of control, making decisions about the liberty of individuals via the interpretation and application of law.

In England and Wales, the Mental Health Act (1983, as amended in 2007 and 2025) forms the basis for legal compulsion regarding treatment and detention alongside the Code of Practice (Department of Health, 2015) which provides guidance on the use of the Act. The UK is distinct from other countries in giving social workers a significant statutory role in assessment and decision-making under the Mental Health Act (Stone et al, 2021), and in England and Wales this is via the role of the Approved Mental Health Professional (AMHP). The AMHP is responsible for coordinating the assessment of individuals who may need detention for compulsory treatment and, alongside medical recommendations, applying for detention to hospital when deemed necessary. As explained in more detail later on they also play a central role in assessing and deciding on the imposition of community treatment orders (CTOs). While the role of the AMHP is open to a range of other mental health professionals (with the exception of medical doctors), it is primarily held by social workers (Skills for Care, 2025). The AMHP is intended to bring a social and independent perspective as a balance to the medical view in legal decision-making; a central element of their assessment is to consider an individual's social circumstances when deciding upon detention and to ensure that any action is guided by the principle of least restriction of an individual's liberty (Department of Health, 2015). However, in practice, AMHPs face ethical challenges relating to systemic constraints, resource limitations and professional hierarchies which can shape an orientation to more restrictive practices (Vicary et al, 2019; Hemmington, 2023).

The longstanding debates on control that have characterised mental health social work are indicative of the tensions inherent to the broader socio-legal field of mental health. Bartlett and Sandland (2007, 71) characterise mental health legislation as 'the most coercive expression of the policy of the state … which licenses some to invade or significantly curtail the freedom of others'. The mental health system – and psychiatry in particular – has faced sustained critical scrutiny since the late 1950s. 'Anti-psychiatry' brought together complementary critical strands which challenged the legitimacy of the power and knowledge possessed by mental health practitioners, including their 'expert' status. Critics such as Szasz (1961), Scheff (1966), Cooper (1967) and Laing (1960) emphasised the disputed merits of psychiatric diagnosis, the under-developed knowledge base of medical mental health, the dehumanising impact of both compulsory hospitalisation and treatment, and the role of psychiatric power in perpetuating stigmatising stereotypes regarding individuals who experience severe mental distress. Foucault's (2006) analysis of the psychiatric regime called into question the very status of knowledge as truth, highlighting the flimsy underpinnings of professional power and the questionable effectiveness of established practices. Instead, 'madness' represents a means of distinguishing the normal from the abnormal, with the ability to make this distinction the defining responsibility of the psychiatric discipline.

With time, some of the orthodoxies of the mental health system have diminished as decades of campaigning for alternative understanding of mental illness have eroded the legitimacy associated with tradition (Rissmiller, 2006; Beresford and Rose, 2023). Relatedly, there is increased recognition of the value of the experiences and knowledge of those who experience mental distress (Bracken and Thomas, 2005). At the same time, however, concerns regarding risk remain central within mental health discourse, stoked by occasional tragedies and a public mood that despite advances remains fearful and safety focused (Stanford et al, 2017). Indeed, Fistein et al (2009) found significant deviation from human rights standards in the mental health statutes of Commonwealth countries with a low threshold being present for their use. There has been a steady rise in the use of compulsion in English mental health services in recent years (Care Quality Commission, 2025; NHS England, 2025) for which there are a number of potential explanations. A widely held understanding is that substantial shifts in the socioeconomic environment have taken their toll. In other words, people with severe mental health conditions have come under increasing stress due to the rolling back of social protection, at the same time as social and health services have been cut back. Trends in legal compulsion also hold implications for mental health provision in the community, and we now come to the focal point of this book, the use of control in community settings.

Control mechanisms in community mental health services

Within the debates and challenges that play out in mental health policy and practice, the treatment and control of individuals with severe mental health distress in the community has long been positioned as a problem in need of a solution. This book investigates one 'solution' in English mental health services – CTOs, enacted under the Mental Health Act (2007). CTOs exist in a variety of forms in different countries around the world. Names vary from country to country and from jurisdiction to jurisdiction. For example, they have been referred to as 'outpatient commitment laws', 'mandated community treatment' or 'community compulsory treatment orders'. For the sake of clarity, we mainly retain 'community treatment order' and 'CTO' in this book.

Despite widespread use across different jurisdictions, CTOs remain a much debated addition to the landscape of community mental health. Modern mental health services, both in the community and in hospital, have always utilised elements of compulsion and coercion from informal persuasion to formally mandated hospital treatment (Monahan et al, 2001). However, a distinction can be made between the discretionary use of coerced treatment in the community and the legislatively defined role of CTOs. As Churchill et al (2007, 20, emphasis in original) state, CTOs are qualitatively different from what has gone before in the countries where they have been implemented because they, 'enforce community treatment *outside (and independently) of the hospital*, contain specific mechanisms for *enforcement and/or revocation* and are authorised by *statute*'.

This means that CTOs give mental health professionals the power to impose conditions on how service users live in the community – especially regarding medical treatment – and provide a mechanism for hospitalisation and treatment enforcement if these conditions are not met or if the service user's mental health has deteriorated to the extent that they are deemed to be a risk to self or others. Opinion on CTOs has been strongly divided, with opponents arguing that an extension of compulsion into the community results in an unnecessary and stigmatising focus on risk, a loss of liberty and rights for service users, and the neglect of alternative, less coercive methods of engagement (Lawn et al, 2015; Maylea et al, 2025). Conversely, supporters of CTOs argue that they help to engage service users who are hard to reach and/or considered a risk, facilitate community-based care, reduce rates and length of compulsory hospitalisation, encourage better treatment, improve clinical outcomes and promote recovery (Ingram, Muirhead and Harvey, 2009; Kisely et al, 2013; Segal, 2022).

As these two positions demonstrate, the reason why debates regarding CTOs remain impassioned is because they act as a crucible for enduring tensions within the field of mental health policy and practice. CTOs have expanded the boundaries of legally mandated compulsion and so have provoked debates about where the balance should be struck between rights or risk, and freedom or coercion for individuals within the mental health system. In this sense, the CTO brings into sharp focus the longstanding moral and ethical balancing acts that frame the use of control in the treatment (broadly defined) of individuals diagnosed with severe mental health difficulties.

CTOs in an English context

The development of CTOs in England has not been immune from such debates, with their inception stimulating controversy and campaign action, including fierce opposition from groups such as the Mental Health Alliance. A Department of Health official closely involved in the introduction of CTOs to the English system was reported as saying, 'it was trench warfare' but 'there was never any wavering … [against] the stakeholders' position' (Cairney, 2009, 681). Given such contention, CTOs took nine years to become enshrined in law as part of a broader reform programme in which the Mental Health Act (1983) was eventually amended by the Mental Health Act (2007). It is worth noting that lobbying against CTOs is ongoing; the review of the Mental Health Act (Department of Health and Social Care, 2018) recommended significant restrictions on the use of CTOs, while several prominent mental health organisations called for their abolition. However, the legislation that resulted from this review, the Mental Health Act (2025), has not changed the CTO regime beyond aligning it with stricter criteria for detention. The Labour Government agreed to a review of CTOs following the introduction of the Mental Health Act (2025), but there is no indication at the time of writing when this will happen.

Social workers play a key role in CTO practice in England not only as AMHPs, but also as care coordinators within NHS Mental Health Trusts (Campbell et al, 2019). While not holding the formal statutory mandate of AMHPs, care coordinators can have significant informal sway over how service users experience CTOs, both via their everyday practice with service users and as informal contributors to decisions on when to put the controlling mechanisms of the CTO into play. An investigation of CTO practice as we present in this book therefore provides an ideal opportunity to destabilise and enrich existing narratives on control practices in social work.

The statutory characteristics, criteria and protocols for CTOs in England

At this point, we think it would be helpful to briefly segue from the discursive to the descriptive by giving an overview of CTO characteristics, criteria and protocols in England including the role of social workers; this will provide a 'reference guide' to help navigate the more in-depth empirical discussion of CTO practice in the rest of the book.

CTOs in England are an example of what is called a 'preventative' CTO (Churchill et al, 2007). This means that they have different criteria – a lower legal threshold – than for compulsory hospitalisation. The function of the CTO therefore is to *prevent* mental health deterioration before it occurs rather than *reacting* to deterioration that has already occurred. Preventative CTOs tend to be aimed at that group of service users sometimes described as 'revolving door patients', meaning they regularly experience relapse, leading to continuous movement between hospital and the community. The large majority of individuals placed on CTOs have been given a primary diagnosis of a psychosis-related disorder, and are on antipsychotic medication (Churchill et al, 2007; Barkhuizen et al, 2020), which the CTO is intended to ensure they adhere to. Table 0.1 outlines the roles and responsibilities of CTO decision-makers, both statutory and informal, and Figure 0.1 gives a diagrammatic overview of the CTO process.

CTOs can only be applied immediately following compulsory hospitalisation for treatment under Sections 3 or 37 of the Mental Health Act (1983). When a service user is in hospital, the Responsible Clinician alongside the inpatient team will decide (usually in collaboration with the service user's community team, Nearest Relative and relevant family/carers) whether a CTO is the most appropriate option, rather than simply voluntarily discharging the service user to the community. Practice guidance suggests that the potential for a CTO should be discussed as soon as the service user is admitted to hospital, in order to allow for proper planning (National Institute for Mental Health in England, 2008). The Responsible Clinician makes the formal application, with an AMHP providing the second opinion. The AMHP must approve the decision for the CTO to proceed, and the Responsible Clinician cannot simply seek the opinion of another AMHP if a disagreement occurs. Although the guidance describes CTOs as a 'kind of contract' (National Institute for Mental Health in England, 2008, 17), and recommends that agreement is reached with the service user, they do not *have* to consent to the imposition of the CTO. At the time the research project this book is based on took place, the criteria for a CTO were:[1]

- The patient is suffering from a mental disorder of a nature or degree which makes it appropriate for the patient to receive medical treatment.
- It is necessary for the patient's health or safety, or for the safety of other persons, that the patient should receive such treatment.
- Subject to the patient being liable to be recalled, such treatment can be provided without the patient continuing to be detained in a hospital.

- It is necessary that the responsible clinician should be able to exercise the power … to recall the patient to hospital.
- Appropriate medical treatment is available for the patient. (The Mental Health Act, 2007 (c.12), s.17A(5))

Table 0.1: The roles and responsibilities of CTO decision-makers

Role	Profession	Responsibilities
Responsible Clinician	Mostly consultant psychiatrists	The lead decision-maker with overall responsibility for a service user's care and treatment under the Mental Health Act. They are typically the inpatient psychiatrist, with the role transferring to the community team psychiatrist once a service user has been discharged from hospital. They decide whether the criteria for a CTO are met at the point of discharge from hospital and at regular community care reviews, set CTO conditions, decide when recall to hospital under the CTO is necessary and give evidence at appeal on the continuing necessity of the CTO.
AMHP	Mostly social workers	The secondary decision-maker who must, following assessment, agree with the Responsible Clinician's assessment that criteria for the CTO are met, both at discharge from hospital and community reviews, and that the conditions are appropriate and necessary.
Nearest Relative	The person highest on a hierarchy of family members as specified in the Mental Health Act	The Nearest Relative's purpose is to be a safeguard for service user rights under the Mental Health Act. While they cannot stop a CTO being imposed, they have a right to be informed about when a CTO is made, renewed and discharged. They also have a right to request an advocate (called an Independent Mental Health Advocate) for the service user. They can discharge a service user from a CTO with 72 hours' notice, but the Responsible Clinician can bar this discharge, in which case the Nearest Relative can apply to the Mental Health Tribunal to appeal the CTO on a service user's behalf.
Care Coordinator	A range of professionals, including social workers, nurses and occupational therapists	Care coordinators are responsible for assessing needs, coordinating care, creating care plans and reviewing progress with the service user and other professionals. While they do not have a formal role in CTO decision-making, in practice care coordinators may be influential in guiding formal decisions – for example in recommending whether they think imposing a CTO, or continuing a CTO once it is in place, would be beneficial or not, and advising on recall to hospital. They also give evidence on a service user's social circumstances at CTO appeals.

(continued)

Table 0.1: The roles and responsibilities of CTO decision-makers (continued)

Role	Profession	Responsibilities
Mental Health Tribunals and Hospital Managers' Hearings	Tribunal panels are made up of a judge, a medical member and a specialist lay representative and are run by the National Court and Tribunals Service. Hospital Manager panels are made up of trained lay volunteers and are facilitated by NHS Mental Health Trusts.	The role of the Tribunal and Hospital Manager panels are to scrutinise whether the CTO criteria are met at regular points throughout the duration of the CTO. They hear evidence from the Responsible Clinician, the care coordinator, the Nearest Relative/family members, the service user (supported by a solicitor and sometimes an advocate) and can decide to discharge a service user from the CTO or agree to its renewal. Alongside these mandatory reviews, service users can choose to apply for appeal to both bodies.

There are two mandatory conditions attached to all CTOs: that the individual made subject to the CTO makes themselves available for assessment to determine whether the CTO should be renewed; and if a service user does not have capacity/will not consent to treatment in the community, for assessment by a second psychiatrist to review their treatment plan. Discretionary conditions can also be attached to a CTO as long as they are necessary to ensure medical treatment, prevent risk of harm to the health and safety of the service user, and/or protect others. In the majority of cases, discretionary conditions will refer to requirements to take medication and to attend appointments with the care team. In some cases, conditions may be attached relating to residence (typically if in supported accommodation) and drug/alcohol use (Lepping and Malik, 2013; Smith et al, 2014).

The power of recall is how the CTO is enforced, and this can be triggered if the Responsible Clinician believes that a service user requires treatment in hospital, and that there would be a risk of harm to the health and safety of the service user or others if the service user was not recalled. A service user can also be recalled if they do not meet the mandatory conditions of the CTO. Typically, a care coordinator who is in closest contact with a service user would alert the Responsible Clinician if and when they think there are grounds for recall, and the Responsible Clinician would decide on the basis of the information given to them by the care coordinator whether the recall criteria are met. Recall to hospital has a limit of 72 hours, at which point the CTO can be revoked and the service user readmitted to hospital under Section 3/37 of the Mental Health Act, the service user can be discharged back to a CTO, or they can be discharged to the community with no CTO in place.

The CTO has an initial duration of up to six months and then can be renewed for a further six months, with renewals being yearly thereafter.

Figure 0.1: A diagram of the CTO process

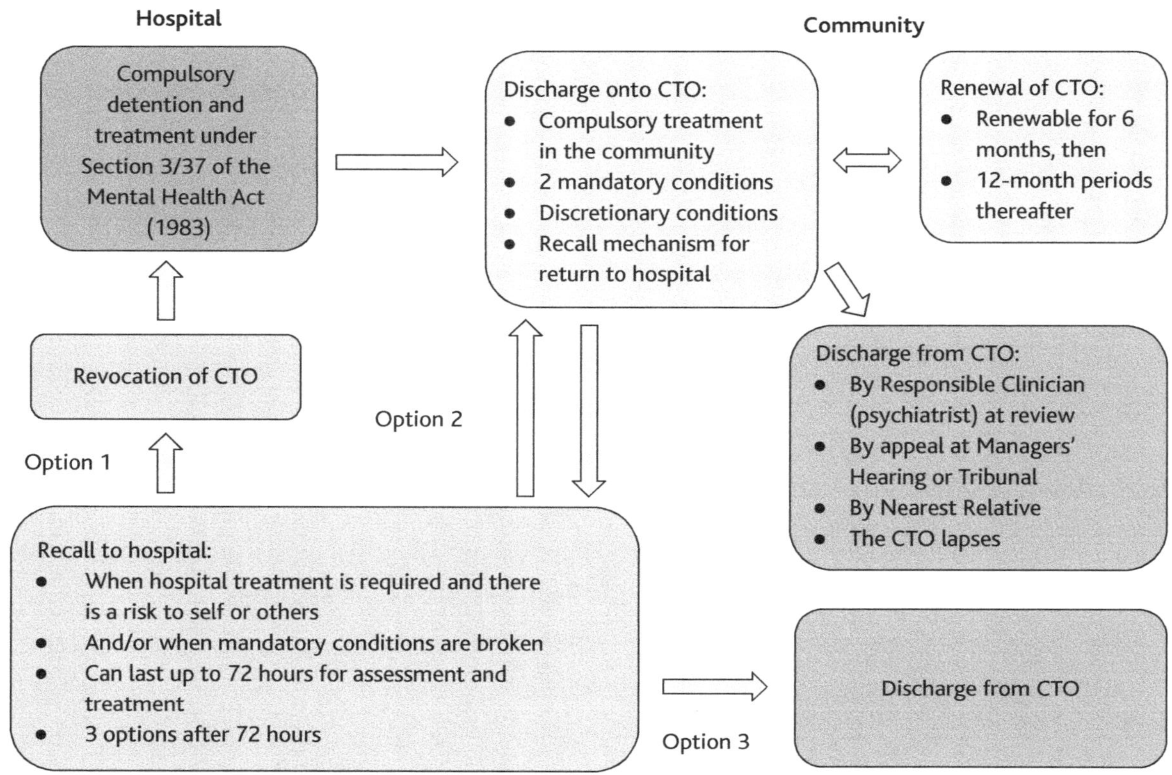

Source: Adapted from the work of Krysia Canvin and Jorun Rugkåsa

Generally the Responsible Clinician will hold a review prior to the end of each CTO period where they will discuss along with the service user, an AMHP, the care coordinator and where appropriate/possible the Nearest Relative and Independent Mental Health Advocate whether the CTO should remain in place. The Responsible Clinician may decide to discharge the service user from the CTO, or with the agreement of the AMHP renew it. If the CTO is renewed, a mandatory Hospital Managers' Hearing is held as an oversight function. Appeals to the Mental Health Tribunal also happen automatically within six months of the initial detention in hospital which led to the CTO and then three years later if the CTO is still in place. A service user also has the right to appeal at a Hospital Managers' Hearing at any point during their CTO and to the Mental Health Tribunal once within each CTO period. The Nearest Relative can also appeal to the Tribunal if their discharge of the CTO is blocked by the Responsible Clinician.

The theoretical orientation of this book

A significant body of international research on CTOs has built up over the last 40 years, much of it based on experimental research to ascertain whether CTOs are effective in relation to a defined set of outcomes, particularly reduced hospitalisation rates. This research yields an equivocal picture of CTO effectiveness, with little agreement on conclusions (Swanson and Swartz, 2014; Kisely et al, 2017; Maylea et al, 2025). Consequently it appears that these studies have contributed to the further embedding of the dichotomous positions that exist on CTOs. Additionally, this research agenda takes a very particular view of how CTO effectiveness ought to be conceived, disregarding complexity in process and outcomes. While there have been exploratory studies of stakeholder perspectives, there have been relatively few studies of everyday CTO practice which may provide a sense of the variable ways they are implemented.

By contrast, the practice-oriented and 'localised' ethnographic account of the CTO process we present in this book helps develop an understanding of how and why CTOs are used, the range of potential consequences they can lead to, and how these consequences are shaped, interpreted and experienced by service users and practitioners at different points of the CTO process. A diversity of research strategies and questions allows for a more holistic understanding of the work that CTOs entail, incorporating multiple aims, agency and both intended and unintended consequences. It also accounts for plurality in how these consequences are balanced, how they can be designated as 'good' or 'bad', and which consequences matter to whom. Through taking such an approach we form a dual analysis; one which both *explains* the paths a CTO might take inclusive of stakeholder influence and *describes* the ways that the CTO affects those who are made subject to it and who implement it. We therefore join the abstract political questions they engender with the concrete practical–moral concerns that surface in their use.

In this sense, although policies such as CTOs are based on certain ideas about human thought and behaviour, as service users and practitioners engage with each other and the broader system they also shape the playing out of policy in differentiated ways. Thus, gaining an idea of the operation of CTOs in practice involves exploration of individual responses and micro-social interactions alongside the contextual factors (cultural, political and institutional) that mediate the CTO process as it unfolds over time. This, of course, needs to be considered as a mutually constitutive process, not only in terms of how the responses of practitioners and service users to the CTO influence the workings of the CTO, but also how the CTO shapes aspects of identity and choice for both groups. The theoretical and functional coherence and integrity of CTOs depends on their ability to ensure some form of conformity to particular goals. Consequently, developing an understanding of CTOs as (intending) change through *compulsion* foregrounds the role of different forms of power within social relations and institutional settings.

This orientation entails the bringing together of empirical and hermeneutic traditions in social research, as envisaged within the social and philosophical approach known as governmentality. Embedded in Foucauldian thought, governmentality is discursive and explanatory in nature, entailing the investigation of organised practices of governing through the lens of power. Given our view that debates regarding CTOs have become unnecessarily polarised, we draw from both the empirical and 'real world' practice orientated strands in social research to elucidate connections between theory, practice and context. At the same time, we emphasise the central importance of the ethical dimension of power in action to a study such as this. This framework, then, allows for a non-deterministic yet ethical analysis of different kinds of power as they operate through the 'conduct of conduct' (Foucault, 2007; Dean, 2010). Governmentality enables us to address both the reasons *why* CTOs may lead to a variety of consequences – the effects of policy – and *how* CTOs work to regulate conduct and encourage self-conduct through coercive, disciplinary and reflexive means – the effects of power.

In this book we demonstrate how we married this theoretical approach with ethnographic research, observing CTO practice over time, within variable contexts in English mental health services and through a variety of methods utilised to capture both meaning and action in their everyday practice. In doing so we believe our analysis has significance for:

- Policy, by explaining how CTOs as an indicative case illuminate the potential gaps between policy and practice rationalities and the variability of consequences that can arise from control oriented policy programmes.

- Practice, by showing the differing uses to which CTOs are put, how they are practiced and the implications of such practice for social work.
- Research, by addressing facets of CTO use which have not previously been fully explored, using a methodology which has been under employed thus far.
- Theory, by bringing to the surface the governmental operation of different forms of power, and how they are manifested through thought, practice and identity work.
- Ethics, by examining the ways in which ethical considerations do and do not manifest in the operation of power in practice.

Outline of the book

In Chapter 1 we continue the discussion of power and control begun in this chapter by expanding on our Foucauldian theoretical orientation. We expound on our rationale for employing governmentality as a framework that supports a rich analysis of power in action, which in turn enables an ethically informed but non-prescriptive account of control practices. We explain how this framework has generated a set of questions we address in the empirical core of the book, and how it coalesces with our methodological approach. In Chapter 2 we give an account of control in community mental health practice, drawing on the policy and empirical literature to illustrate the development of CTOs. There are distinctions between how different countries manage mental health, but for countries which are at a comparable point in development, a broadly similar narrative exists. The treatment (in the broadest sense of the word) of individuals with mental health difficulties in such countries has always been entwined with control practices, and this chapter will survey how these practices have developed ideationally and historically before exploring how the discourses underpinning CTOs have manifested in the research on their use.

Chapters 3 to 6 form the main body of the book, presenting an analysis of the empirical findings this book is based upon. These chapters trace a route through the CTO process from theory to application and discharge. Chapter 3 explores ground level conceptualisations of the CTO. We explore service user identity formation in the face of severe mental health difficulties, and how self-perceptions influence their view of the CTO as either performing an important role in regards to provision, risk, recovery and maintenance, or blocking their ability to reach their goals. Moving to practitioner perspectives, we highlight the disjuncture between policy and practitioner reasoning on CTOs, and in turn how practitioners' reasoning on the CTO as a control measure is based on particular ethical foundations. In Chapter 4 we move onto service user experiences of and reactions to the CTO in practice. We consider the significant mediating influence of the service user–practitioner relationship, with the CTO being both shaped by and shaping relationship dynamics, and the various ways that service users acted upon CTOs. In Chapter 5 we focus on practitioners' ethical balancing acts in the use of CTOs and the factors that shape that use, including relational work with service users but also broader cultural and institutional dynamics. Chapter 6 is orientated around how decisions are made by practitioners on when to end legal control within the contested decision-making arena of CTO reviews, and it illuminates how practitioners in concert with service users deal with considerations of risk, evidence, causality and trust when deciding whether to end or continue a CTO. We also highlight how practitioners weigh up the benefits and costs of continuing the CTO, particularly in relation to change/stasis, dependency/responsibility and engagement/alienation.

Chapter 7 acts as a bridge between the empirical chapters preceding and the final discussion chapter by using Foucault's dimensions of self-work (1997a) to analyse forms of conduct and counter-conduct in six service user case studies. These case studies not only highlight the disparate ways control measures can be reckoned with by service users but also how these responses can lead to complex and unexpected consequences of control work, generating predicaments for practitioners. This points to a more fundamental question about how to judge the value of control work to which we turn in Chapter 8 where we draw together our analysis via a discussion of CTO policy and practice. We explore what the findings mean for an understanding of CTO theorisation, 'ground-level' conceptualisations of CTOs, the operation of agency, interaction and context in CTO practice, and CTO 'ends' – their personal and social consequences. We conclude by elucidating what this discussion signifies for social work practice of CTOs and its broader meaning for the nature and value of power in its various guises within the mental health field.

Conclusion

The care and control debate is not the only enduring tension within social work. Different stances on the value of social work – a critical and conflictual lens or a variegated, reparative lens – are not new (see Healy, 2000). There are ebbs and flows in how these perspectives interact dependent on milieu, and both provide valuable orientations for social work theory and practice which need to be held in critical tension. What we can say is that at this point in time, we believe there is merit in revisiting and rebalancing the ways that power and control are conceived in social work.

To do so in a meaningful way however, attention needs to be paid to the detail of differences. Concerns regarding power and control manifest across domains of social work, but maintain a distinct character dependent on the domain in question. In mental health, debates on power and the use of control are connected to the competing models that are put forward to explain mental health problems and the conflicting approaches to prevention and treatment that ensue. At times such debates have been contentious, characterised by dogmatic adherence to particular models and an insistence that the use of power – usually via forms of compulsion – either in and of itself, or because of imperfect imbalances between care and control – represents ethical failure. Generating knowledge of the complex, contingent and contextual character of mental health practice brings more open-minded perspectives to bear on the use of compulsion in mental health provision and specifically CTOs as a manifestation of that compulsion, Our intention, then, is to get beneath the surface of the contested claims made about CTOs: to illuminate both the thinking that underpinned their introduction and the mechanics of how they work; to explore how and why they are utilised; and to highlight the experiential and ethical implications of their use for both the individuals who are placed on them and for the practitioners who implement them. By doing so, this book provides a methodologically sophisticated and theoretically distinctive analysis of the use of power in community mental health, which is of value in terms of both theory and practice.

Note

1 Since the research project this book is based on took place, there has been a change to the CTO criteria. In December 2025 a revised Mental Health Act was enacted and the CTO criteria were changed to reflect the revised and stricter criteria for hospital detention. The revised CTO criteria are:

- The patient is suffering from a mental disorder of a nature or degree which makes it appropriate for the patient to receive medical treatment.
- Serious harm may be caused to the health or safety of the patient or another person unless the patient receives medical treatment.
- It is necessary, given the nature, degree and likelihood of harm, for the patient to receive medical treatment.
- Subject to the patient being liable to be recalled, the necessary treatment can be provided without the patient being detained in a hospital.
- It is necessary that the responsible clinician should be able to exercise the power … to recall the patient to hospital.
- Appropriate medical treatment is available for the patient.

1

Theorising power and control

We draw upon Michel Foucault's conception of governmentality and an 'analytics of government' (Dean, 2010) in order to theoretically ground an understanding of community treatment orders (CTOs) as an exemplar of compulsory community care within an analysis of power. Through exploring Foucault's theorisation of power we draw attention to the connections he made between disciplinary power, power/knowledge and ethics of the self. We then turn to Foucault's conceptualisation of governmentality as the ideation and operation of different forms of power within the context of the liberal state. Central to this approach to power is the way rationalities are put to work to achieve the 'conduct of conduct', particularly through 'practices of the self' where power and freedom are aligned. We argue that while Foucault decentred sovereign forms of power in governmentality, they are still present in his analysis, particularly in his historical treatment of the biopolitical limits of citizenship. Governmentality thus enables a descriptive analysis of power across a spectrum from sovereign through to disciplinary and reflexive forms of power.

Applying governmentality empirically as a framework necessitates reflection on how researchers deal with questions of value when examining how power is administered. Making such judgements is not straightforward, and we give space to addressing how power and its manifestation via control oriented practice can be analysed in an ethical but non-prescriptive way. This leads onto an explanation of the analytical and methodological approaches we take in this book, and how they enable an analysis of CTOs through the lens of governmentality.

Power, knowledge and ethics

Foucault critiqued the idea of sovereign power in which power is operationalised in a centralised, repressive and hierarchical way. Instead, Foucault contended that 'power is everywhere' (Foucault, 1990, 93), being omnipresent and dispersed. As such, power is not 'possessed' by a few but is a force that is relational in nature and in constant flux within society; Foucault therefore 'challenges the polarisation of such categories as "powerful" and "powerless"' (Pease, 2002, 139). Consequently, Foucault argued that power does not have to be thought of in coercive terms, but can also be productive and indeed necessary – an integral part of how societies work (Gaventa,

2003). Such a conceptualisation of power shifts the focus from an analysis of sovereign power to disciplinary power and how it manifests at a 'micro-political' level.

Foucault regarded disciplinary power as a particularly modern invention, emanating and evolving from the Enlightenment period: ' "The Enlightenment", which discovered the liberties, also invented the disciplines' (Foucault, 1977, 222). Disciplinary power is thus reliant on scientific discourses regarding the nature of human thought and behaviour, and associated techniques and strategies of objectification and subjectification, which are not premised on the use of force. In contrast to sovereign power then, disciplinary power is 'a modest, suspicious power [which] regards individuals both as objects and as instruments of its exercise' (Foucault, 1977, 170). The aforementioned techniques and strategies that underpin disciplinary power consist of various systems of surveillance and categorisation, made possible through the creation of the human sciences and associated expert-based disciplines such as social work, psychiatry, psychology and criminology. In this way a 'disciplinary society' is created, where individuals are measured against normalising judgements, and are disciplined, or discipline themselves accordingly.

As inferred here, Foucault's conceptualisation of disciplinary power is entwined with another of his central ideas, that of 'power/knowledge'. While Foucault did not conflate knowledge and power, he was interested in the complex and inextricable relationship between them, arguing that 'power produces knowledge … power and knowledge directly imply each other' (Foucault, 1977, 27). The formation of a 'disciplinary society' is reliant on particular 'regimes of truth' which as dominant discourses constitute normalising judgements and in turn the regulation of conduct, as Foucault (1977, 27) goes on to say:

> Knowledge linked to power, not only assumes the authority of 'the truth' but has the power to make itself true. All knowledge, once applied in the real world, has effects, and in that sense at least, 'becomes true.' Knowledge, once used to regulate the conduct of others, entails constraint, regulation and the disciplining of practice.

The question that therefore arises is how discourse – via power/knowledge – constitutes the subject, in particular through the human sciences and the accompanying application of expertise. Accordingly, power is locally dispersed rather than centrally coordinated, using small-scale rather than hegemonic means.

Foucault also posits how subjects might interact with and work at their own constitution through ethical 'practices of the self'. Foucault's view of what 'the self' might mean is not easily categorised. He rejected humanism and the idea of an unchanging and universal human nature which allows each of us primacy over ourselves and in a greater sense, our destinies and our world. However, in his development of 'practices of the self', which is based on a 'self–self' reflexive relationship, Foucault does not take a nihilistic position. His focus is not on defining human nature, but as Hacking (2004, 288) posits, on how people become who they are; the 'dynamics of human nature'. This presupposes a flat, rather than vertical relationship between self-government, government by and of others, and government of the state (Dean, 1994, 196). If we accept that particular moral codes have held sway at particular junctures, and in turn interact with how we relate to ourselves and others via ethical practices, then the focus is on how we *choose* to form ourselves through a variety of means and in relation to a multiplicity of moral codes in the present. What this means is that: 'Foucault – most assuredly, not a sociologist – offers us a thoroughly sociological sense of self that does not reduce the self to the social' (Dean, 1994, 216).

In this sense, Foucault is not quite as far removed from an existentialist perspective on the role of agency as has sometimes been supposed (Hacking, 2004). His 'practices of the self' refers to four dimensions necessary for ethical self-work: 'ethical substance' or the focus for moral conduct; the external stimulus that leads to recognition of moral obligation; 'ethical work' or the means by which we attempt change; and the *telos* of such work, the end person that is aspired to (Foucault, 1997a). As we shall see, these four dimensions correspond closely with the key tenets of an 'analytics of government' as developed from governmentality by Dean (2010). Governmentality thus brings together disciplinary and reflexive power, connecting the processes by which we work on ourselves to broader governance processes by which we might be worked on.

Governmentality

Governmentality can subsequently be constituted in three ways: first in the original sense it was defined by Foucault as an evolution in the 'art of governing' by and within the state at a particular historical juncture; secondly as it has been developed as an analytical framework to illuminate the 'how' of governing across a continuum that stretches beyond sovereign power, to a dispersed disciplinary 'microphysics of power'; and finally as a form of reflexive power key to the reformation of identity and regulation of the self. Given that CTOs can be seen as a particular embodiment of power in action, the analytical framework offered by governmentality provides a helpful tool to make sense of their use. Specifically, an 'analytics of government' is focused on delineating various manifestations of the 'conduct of conduct' (Foucault, 2007, 192), which can be defined as 'any attempt to shape with some degree of deliberation aspects of our behaviour according to particular sets of norms for a variety of ends' (Dean, 2010, 10). McKee (2009, 466, emphasis in original) draws out the dual foci of thought and action that an analytics of government explores as:

> Both the *discursive field* in which the exercise of power is rationalised – that is the space in which the problem of government is identified and solutions proposed; and the actual *interventionist practices* as manifest in specific programmes and techniques in which both individuals and groups are governed according to these aforementioned rationalities.

Governmentality then is concerned with both how conduct is problematised and how such rationalities are subsequently put to work through technologies which direct and reform conduct. However, the 'conduct of conduct' is not only in relation to how others are governed, but as highlighted in 'practices of the self', how we govern ourselves. In other words, how 'individuals recognise themselves as particular kinds of persons and ... work upon and transform themselves in certain ways and towards particular goals' (Hodges, 2002, 457). Individuals make choices in how they integrate influences; logically an individual who can respond positively to external mandates and techniques can also respond negatively. Foucault (2007, 75) terms such responses as 'counter-conducts', which he defines as 'the will not to be governed thusly, like that, by these people, at that price'. 'Counter-conducts' therefore are not rejections of government in itself, but an expression of seeking different forms and means of government. Within governmentality, forms of conduct and counter-conduct reflect each other and are interdependent – they both rely on rationalities, technologies and reformation. As such, counter-conduct does not translate to resistance in terms of a revolutionary and emancipatory 'stepping outside' of pre-existing power structures. Disciplinary power operates at the micro-level and Foucault posited that so did counter-conduct. 'Thus there is no grand refusal, only dispersed and shifting points of resistance' (Death, 2010, 239) which draw on 'subjugated knowledges' to form alternative ways of thinking and going about governance. As Dean (2010, 40, 48) argues, through a prioritisation of process in power and of 'how' questions, governmentality rejects the theorisation of power as a 'zero-sum game' and therefore does not 'formulate a set of general principles by which various forms of the 'conduct of conduct' could be reformed'. In other words, through focusing on the descriptive, governmentality avoids the monolithic ideation of power present in critical and conflictual 'grand theories' (Haugaard and Cooke, 2010). If power is seen as fluid and not engrained in particular unchangeable patterns within society and social relations of domination, then the focus of critique shifts from a dichotomous 'either/or' lens to one which accounts for a range of imagined possibilities.

Governmentality as an analytical framework for power

Where governmentality has been empirically applied, such research has been criticised for being overly concerned with the 'discursive' aspect of governmentality and a corresponding neglect of the realisation of rationalities in practice (Parr, 2009; Dean, 2015; Bevir, 2016). This focus on discourse analysis emphasises a view of the '"social as a machine" reforming and constituting everything it comes into contact with' (Hunter, 2003, 331), which does not account for the techniques and technologies of government. As has been suggested, most notably by Stenson (2005, 2008) in his conceptualisation of 'realist governmentality', a full analytics of government cannot ignore questions of 'the real' which involves drawing together accounts and manifestations of power, 'from below' and 'from above' (Lippert and Stenson, 2010). We would take that argument further to suggest that the focal point of governmentality – conduct itself – requires more detailed empirical exposition. The emphasis placed on discourse foregrounds power/knowledge while neglecting power/knowledge/ethics and the relationship between conduct, counter-conduct and 'practices of the self'. Specifically, this would involve study of the complex, unpredictable and contradictory nature of life as it is lived with agency and as embedded in varying and variable social relations and institutions.

Sayer (2012) suggests that Foucault's avoidance of 'the real' was not reflected in his theorisations of how individual and population-wide change is produced. Consequently, Foucault's theorisation of power allows for 'the interdependence of dispersed/capillary power and centralised/arterial power' to be acknowledged (Sayer, 2012, 185). In dismissing the 'false choice' that can be made between dispersed (disciplinary) and centralised (sovereign) power, Sayer (2012, 185) suggests that the separation of 'how' (descriptive) and 'why' (explanatory) questions is fallacious:

> Explaining how power works, that is how multiple causal powers are activated and interact to produce effects, and in virtue of what, tells us why those effects occur; and conversely to explain why they do, we have to explain how the mechanisms work, what the powers and susceptibilities of the relevant elements are and how they work when activated.

Similarly, Dean (2010, 8) argues that his interpretation of governmentality allows for the elucidation of 'sovereign and coercive rationalities and techniques' alongside and in interaction with disciplinary and reflexive forms of power.

Dean (2010) explains how this can be understood, starting with Foucault's (2000) contrasting notions of the 'city-citizen' and the 'shepherd-flock', derived from historical accounts of the Greco-Roman era and the early Christian church respectively. Both notions exemplify particular forms of ethical self-conduct comprising how one sees oneself, and how one sees oneself and acts in obligatory relations with others. The individual as *citizen* can be defined as operating within a juridico-political structure, on equal footing with other citizens in the exercise of freedom and rights. By its nature, this conception relies on there being a boundary between those who could be classed as citizens (due to their ability to exercise freedom and rights) and those who cannot. Within the 'shepherd–flock' concept, the individual can be understood in pastoral terms as 'a *living being* who can be *known* in depth, whose *welfare* is to be cared for as an individual and as part of a population, as one *submits* to integration within complex forms of *social solidarity*' (Dean, 2010, 100, emphasis in original). Such an understanding is based on the belief that *all* individuals should be cared for. While Foucault did not suggest that these concepts can be transferred unproblematically across time, he did argue that their enduring presence in some form holds implications for the administration of contemporary liberal government. Notions of pastoral care and citizenship bring between them inherent tensions because they depend on 'human beings as both self-governing individuals within a self-governing political community and clients to be administered, governed and normalised with respect to governmental objectives' (Dean, 1994, 209).

This brings us to what Foucault deemed the potential 'demonic' possibilities inherent in liberal government, which can arise from the interaction between discourses of citizenship and welfare (Foucault, 1988). It is Dean's (2010, 156) argument that such tensions, if sharp enough, can lead to the paradox of 'liberal illiberality', whereby the subject is managed via 'dividing practices' along the axes of autonomy and responsibility: 'the subject is either divided inside himself or divided from others' (Foucault, 1983, 208). Such divisions often have a strong biopolitical element, which can be seen from extreme manifestations such as forced sterilisation of particular members of a society 'for their own good' and for the perceived good of everyone else, through to pervasive 'whole-population' messages on self-care and well-being. Certainly, CTOs can be seen as an example of a biopolitical intervention, as they are based on a particular understanding of embodied madness and their foundational function is to ensure the management of such madness via medical means.

Dean's development of governmentality thus chimes with arguments (Jessop, 2010; Olssen, 2010) that governmentality in its original incarnation does not disregard institutional and political power relations in the way some more recent approaches to governmentality suggest. At the same time, in his work on ethics Foucault also did not negate the role of individuals in changing themselves and their surroundings. In this sense, CTOs can be theorised as containing both inclusionary and exclusionary elements which in turn are mediated by reflexive, disciplinary and overtly controlling processes.

Power and the fact–value relationship in research

In a broader sense, coming to an ontological reckoning on the nature of power also has epistemological implications for how power can be known about, and specifically what place researchers have, if any, in making value judgements on the operation of rule in society. If critical perspectives on power lend themselves to an 'is-ought' perspective whereby research is inherently emancipatory, where does a governmental perspective on power situate the researcher? As Hammersley (2009, 8, emphasis in original) notes when critiquing the normative stance in the emancipatory paradigm of social research:

> My point is simply that social scientists … have no distinctive expertise to determine what is good or bad about the situations they seek to describe and explain; or what, if anything, should be done about them … even where value judgements rely on research evidence they also necessarily depend upon other factual assumptions *and upon value principles that are plural and often in conflict.*

Additionally, Pawson (2006) argues that criticality should apply to the relationship researchers have to each other, rather than with the world at large. This is a perspective that broadly chimes with that employed within governmentality and is integral to its descriptive focus. Foucault (1997b, 131) takes an implicit stance against scientism when he states 'The role of an intellectual is not to tell others what they have to do. By what right would he do so?' An analytics of government 'breaks the shackles of inevitability' through the avoidance of reductionist and totalising critiques of policy and practice (Marston and McDonald, 2006, 8). However, as Sayer (2009) suggests, the position taken by Hammersley and others on the interaction between fact and value risks being as prescriptive as that which is being critiqued. It is difficult to entirely escape the place of values within the field of social work research, with its applied nature and general emancipatory orientation. Thus, it remains necessary to take a position on how to research the operation of power, with reference to questions of value and specifically to questions of 'flourishing and suffering' (Sayer, 2012, 192). It is possible then to take a more graduated stance which appreciates that developing a 'thick' description of the social world necessitates evaluation and that normativity does not have to consist of 'that short but imperious word *ought*' (Darwin, 2004, 120, original emphasis). The researcher cannot escape their own moral perspective on what they see occurring in their field of study but at the same time drawing critical attention to what happens in society is not the same as 'legislating' on what change should occur.

This accords with a Foucauldian orientation towards making the self-evident seem strange via 'problematisation' (Castells, 1983). While Dean (2010) argues that an analytics of government should not invoke judgement, he also states governmentality is not 'value-free'. Instead, its objective is to excavate the foundations of the 'taken for granted' so that space is opened up to consider 'what is at stake when we try to govern in a particular way and ... the consequences and effects of thinking and acting in these ways' (Dean, 2010, 48). This then implies an approach that involves the destabilisation of pre-existing and apparently well-embedded ways of thinking, doing and being. While much has been said about the *general* 'rightness' or 'wrongness' of CTOs, it is therefore not our intention to make such a judgement here. In taking the 'middle ground' through conceptualisations of truth, value and power, we hope to avoid the entrenched positions that have come to characterise CTO discourse. As we explore in more detail in the next chapter, the dichotomous position on CTOs has been reinforced by the majority of research on their use being instrumental in nature and lacking critical engagement with questions of power. In contrast, by exploring the plural ways that CTOs are understood, justified and exercised, the research presented in this book illuminates their 'greyness' and – specifically – the various ethical compromises and balancing acts which make up their use. In this way, mapping *how* and *why* CTOs *are* used and with what consequences, may help *others* consider how and why they *should* be used.

Drawing up an analytical map for the study of CTOs

To do this work, we distil governmentality into a useable framework for researching CTO practice, and to this end we turn to Dean's (2010) analytics of government which enables the elucidation of the various dimensions in which 'regimes of practice' and their associated programmes manifest. 'Regimes of practice' possess four distinct yet reciprocal dimensions: *visibility*, *thought*, *practice* and *identity*. An analysis of these dimensions allows for associations to be made between CTO discourse at national and local level, as well as how these discourses are played out in techniques and strategies of power: 'those ... assemblages through which we ... cure, care, relieve poverty, punish, educate, train and counsel' (Dean, 2010, 40) and at an individual level via 'practices of the self'. In doing so, it brings a critical and destabilising framework within which to understand how power operates in *social* terms.

Analysing the field of visibility refers to examining how a problem to be governed is framed as a problem and pinpointing 'who and what is to be governed, how relations of authority and obedience are constituted ... what problems are to be solved and what objectives are to be sought' (Dean,

2010, 41). The evolution of policy is both a 'rational and thoughtful' process and an 'intensely moral activity' (2010, 19), in that it involves a clear and systematic explication of 'how things ought to be'. In this sense, the art of government necessitates the belief that the world can be made a better place, and therefore contains a Utopian element. Undertaking an analytics of government should include working to 'extract this Utopian aspect' (Dean, 2010, 44). In terms of CTOs, then, the initial task is to trace how and why CTOs came to be seen as necessary and exist in the form that they did; and to consider how particular 'kinds' of individuals became constituted as the focus for intervention through the CTO.

Moving from the macro (policy) to the micro (practice), it is necessary to also understand the starting point of those individuals at 'ground level' – practitioners and service users – in response to a policy programme. This, the second dimension of a governmental analysis – thought, or rationality – requires that the forms of knowledge, expertise and know-how that are drawn upon to realise the conduct of conduct are excavated. To this end, the second task is to examine the motivations of practitioners and service users in relation to CTOs: what purposes they do or do not see CTOs meeting; how these purposes align or not with policy-level conceptualisations; and for practitioners in particular how they formulate CTO practice based on these purposes.

The third point of investigation shifts again, this time from thought to practice in considering how CTOs are 'interpreted and acted upon in different ways by different participants in different positions' (Pawson and Manzano-Santaella, 2012, 180). The governmental approach includes an analysis of the technical aspects of government – the 'means' by which governmental 'ends' are reached. As Dean (2010) states however, this practical element is a condition of governing, 'a means to an end', but also can act to constrain what is possible to achieve. The third task therefore is to investigate the workings of the CTO, specifically: how the techniques incorporated within the CTO regulate behaviour; the ways programme participants act on the central components of the CTO; and the contextual factors which impinge on this process.

The final focus takes theory, thought and practice to their conclusion – the consequences of the CTO, both intended and unintended, and the way these consequences are weighed up by those who have some stake in them. Potential consequences are not necessarily limited to changes in behaviour and yet hoped for behaviour change is at the heart of policy programmes such as CTOs. A governmental analysis thus considers reflexive and ethical 'self-work' in response to governmental practices. Governmentality sees this in both internal and external senses – how individuals are encouraged to identify with new subjectivities that cohere with governmental rationalities. It is necessary then to reach an understanding of how individuals go about 'practices of the self' the ways we think about and act on ourselves – and how these practices relate to the process of governance. Accordingly, the fourth and final task is to investigate the transformative powers of the CTO; how they bring about individual change; and in what ways they might be implicated in forms of conduct via the development of various 'capacities, qualities and statuses in particular agents' (Dean, 2010, 44) as well as forms of counter-conduct.

To sum up, an analytics of government enables us to come to a variegated understanding of power in practice via the different dimensions of 'regimes of practice', and we apply these dimensions to CTOs via the following questions:

1. How have problems been framed for the CTO to solve?
2. In what ways are CTOs conceptualised by practitioners and service users? For practitioners, how do they formulate CTO practice based on these conceptualisations?
3. How do CTOs work to regulate behaviour, and what factors – inclusive of participant action – influence why they work in those particular ways?
4. What are the varying consequences of the CTO that result from these practices and how are these consequences thought about by practitioners and service users? How do CTOs work to produce change in service user identities and conduct, and in what ways are the transformational potentials of CTOs realised or resisted?

Drawing up a methodological map for the study of CTOs

The final element of our theoretical approach to consider is how the ontological and epistemological work on power in this chapter relates to methodological concerns. In this last section, we explain our turn to ethnography as an 'under-labourer' for an analytics of government.

This book draws upon a study in which varying forms of data collection have been used in a complementary way, with differences that arise put to use in clarifying rather than confounding the questions at hand. An ethnographically informed methodology has thus been adopted which draws on diverse sources and methods in order to form a deeper understanding of the social world. Ethnography is well suited to an analytics of government. Sayer (2000, 21) describes an ethnographically oriented approach to depth level questions in his explication of 'intensive' research designs where questions might be asked such as 'how does a process work?', 'what produces a certain change?' and 'what did the agents actually do'?

Hammersley and Atkinson suggest that ethnography fits such questions, particularly because of its focus on 'meanings, functions and consequences of human actions and institutional practices, and how these are implicated in ... wider contexts' (Hammersley and Atkinson, 2007, 3). Maxwell (2012) concurs that intensive, long-term involvement in the field can help researchers to gain a clearer picture of process by allowing for the testing out of theories and interpretations. In sum, ethnography allows for experiences, actions and events to be considered together; it has an intrinsic focus on context; and it allows for social processes to be examined over time.

There is a strong foundation therefore to suggest ethnography can provide distinctive insight into the workings of CTOs in ways more general qualitative research has not. Ethnographic studies of how policy is translated into practice are relatively rare. 'Policy ethnography' as Povall (2006, 1) calls it, 'provides for lessons at the macro level, looking upwards to shed light on and deepen understanding of the processes there'. This chimes with the shift in governmentality from discursive to more grounded studies. In Foucault's early work on the relationship between knowledge and power he problematised the utility of practice accounts which he felt would inevitably reflect inculcation into dominant professional discourses. Our view is that while discursive constraints are indeed real, the impact they have is diffuse rather than direct, and so there is merit in incorporating practice accounts as one of an array of sources in research, which we extend to incorporate the experiences and perspectives of services users as a necessary source of 'ground level' knowledge within an analysis of pluralistic power. Indeed, ethnography is suited to the premises of governmentality as it allows for attention to be paid: 'to the messy actualities of the empirical world; the multivocal nature of governing practices and their consequences; the experiences and perspectives of "targeted" populations; and the tensions and conflict between shifting modes of power' (McKee, 2009, 482). Here we have set out in a broad sense how an ethnographic study of CTOs maps onto the landscape of governmentality. For a more detailed and concrete description of our research practices, the reader should turn to the Appendix.

Conclusion

The integrity of CTOs depends on their ability to ensure some form of conformity to particular goals. Consequently, developing an understanding of CTOs through the lens of power holds relevance in two ways: in a broad sense CTOs are an intervention intended to bring about change; more specifically, CTOs are about change through *compulsion* and thus foreground the role of different forms of power within social relations and institutional settings. Governmentality offers us one particular and helpful perspective on how CTOs might be thought and made into being for the 'conduct of conduct' via disciplinary, reflexive and coercive means (Foucault, 2007).

It is worth noting that despite the historical utility of Foucault's ideas and concepts to progressive politics, his work has also been subject to accusations of a lack of critical and practical 'bite'. Garrett (2020), for example, questions the utility of Foucault's theoretical and conceptual armoury – his 'tools' – for social work as a radical emancipatory activity, as providing cover for the ongoing coercive use of 'soft power' in the interests of dominant hierarchies. Dean and Villasden (2016) characterise such views as 'state phobia', a reluctance to acknowledge the positive potential within state activity. While remaining ambivalent about the potential motives and effects of power, their view is that this critique is appropriate in some cases of the operation of state power but inappropriate in many others. As such they advocate for a reinvigorated understanding which incorporates ambiguous perspectives regarding the role and function of state power, including the positive contribution civil society makes to social order. In this study we try to do justice to this ambiguity so as to enable a broader analysis of the ways in which experiences of being subject to power are multi-faceted rather than necessarily or characteristically disempowering in intent or effect.

Such an analysis does not conflate power with a hegemonic and conflictual exercise in domination, but instead elaborates a more productive model, which is relational, fluid and dispersed. Our account of CTOs encompasses causation, but avoids determinism by focusing on the decentralised relations and settings within which the CTO plays out. Governmentality emphasises the need to address both the reasons *why* CTOs might lead to a variety of consequences and *how* CTOs work to regulate conduct and encourage self-conduct. It allows for a flexible yet anchored analysis of power in action which accounts for, but is not bound by, theories of power as either inherently structural or devolved. In the next few chapters we bring governmentality to bear on the CTO as a 'regime of practice', exploring its rationalities, means and ends.

2

Control and community mental health practice

Over 60 years, community treatment orders (CTOs) have evolved in various ways and in different times and places as a purported solution to a problem. In this chapter we trace how dominant discourses in mental health policy and practice informed the underlying rationalities for CTOs, framing the problem of particular 'kinds' of individuals in the community so that they were seen to require a state-mandated response. There are distinctions between how different countries manage mental health, but for countries which are at a comparable point in development, a broadly similar narrative exists. The treatment (in the broadest sense of the word) of individuals with mental health difficulties in such countries has always been entwined with control practices, and we survey how these practices have developed over time, with particular reference to the context in England. We begin with an overview of the historical drivers and precedents to contemporary control practices in community mental health. Here we discuss the part played by deinstitutionalisation in shifting the control of individuals with mental health difficulties from boundaried institutions to the open community. Specific attention will be paid to policy discourses such as risk and recovery, based on biomedical formulations that have underpinned the inception of CTOs. This contextualises our following exploration of how these policy discourses play out in the empirical literature which documents the perspectives and experiences of practitioners and individuals made subject to CTOs.

The rise of compulsory community care

CTOs internationally have taken a number of different forms over the last 60 years. Ironically, given the human rights protestations they now engender, CTOs were initially developed as part of the patient rights movement in the USA during the 1960s and 1970s, as a way of maximising individual liberty by minimising involuntary hospitalisation (Hiday, 2003). This 'first wave' of CTOs have been classified as 'least restrictive' (Churchill et al, 2007), as they effectively allowed for compulsory community care under the same legal criteria as compulsory inpatient care, thus creating an alternative to detention. However, 'least restrictive' CTOs were little used as it became evident that it was politically and practically unviable to treat people in the community who met the risk criterion for detention in hospital.

In response to constraints on their use, a new kind of preventative CTO became prevalent from the 1980s (Churchill et al, 2007). Preventative CTOs have lower thresholds for use, and instead of being an alternative to inpatient detention, became a way of compulsorily treating individuals in the community either following their release from hospital, or before they reached the threshold for involuntary hospital treatment. Preventative CTOs thus have different legislative criteria from involuntary inpatient treatment and are often aimed at specifically targeted individuals, usually those defined as 'revolving door' service users who have a history of non-compliance and who go through rapid cycles of release from hospital, deterioration and re-detainment. In this sense, preventative CTOs are more explicitly concerned with risk management both for the individual and for society rather than the earlier aim of promoting civil liberty (Hiday, 2003). It is this type of CTO that has become most widespread and formed the foundation for the development of CTOs as they are used currently.

CTOs are in place in around 75 jurisdictions, including in most US states by 1994 (Torrey and Kaplan, 1995), in all Australian states by 1999 (Power, 1999), Israel in 1991 (Bar et al, 1998), New Zealand in 1992, Canada in 1994, Scotland in 2005, almost all US states by 2006 (Churchill et al, 2007) and England and Wales in 2008. CTOs, then, seem predominantly to be enacted in countries with similar cultural backgrounds, and in the case of the Commonwealth countries, legal heritage. Less widely reported is their use in European countries; Norway has had preventative CTOs in place since the 1960s but became a rare example of a state revising the law to enable least restrictive CTOs in 2001 and Sweden legislated for CTOs in 2008 (Sjostrom, Zetterberg and Markström, 2011). Switzerland and the Netherlands have also been reported to have CTOs (Dawson, 2005; Kortrijk et al, 2010).

Although the majority of countries where CTOs are present have aligned with the preventative model, within that broad category CTOs encompass a shifting range of legal and medical mechanisms reflecting the cultural and societal norms of the jurisdiction in which they are enacted. However, despite differences between countries, it is still possible to highlight broad trends that have instigated a 'domino effect' in the global spread of compulsory community care. Delineating the possible policy 'drivers' for CTOs helps us to understand how different jurisdictions may develop similar rationales for their use. This is necessary to contextualise policy making, because as Hall (1993) suggests, the role of ideas and ideology need to be accounted for in policy formation as the normative structure that is taken for granted by the general policy-making community, but which nevertheless shapes what are viewed as policy problems to be solved. The expansion of CTOs in developed countries has arisen from an array of interacting factors, beginning with the process of deinstitutionalisation, the ensuing increased focus on risk and community safety in mental health services, and what can be described as the associated dominance of a neurobiological approach, which emphasises the use of drug treatment as a 'solution' to mental disorder. CTOs can thus be described as a consequence of the burgeoning movement towards community care in the last 60 years, combined with the perceived need to maintain some form of control through treatment over individuals deemed as posing a risk to themselves or others (Brophy, 2009). All of these factors can be related to themes which have framed the growth of CTOs, and which reflect the concerns of mental health policy in general. As Moynihan (1996, 13) states, the enduring challenge for policy in mental health has been to balance 'the state's interest in protecting the well-being of its citizens; the traditional value placed on medicine as a means of addressing issues of illness; the normative demands of citizens for the elimination of danger; and the recognition of rights of individuals'.

It could also be argued that a constraint on mental health policy and services, as within any welfare domain, are questions of resources, such as to whom and in what ways they should be made available. CTOs can be viewed in one respect as the latest means to manage areas of pressure in the system, such as bed shortages.

Deinstitutionalisation and its consequences for compulsory community care

To fully understand this coalescence of policy drivers for CTOs, we need to understand the central role deinstitutionalisation has played. Deinstitutionalisation refers to the process in a number of Western societies from the 1960s onwards, whereby the focus of mental healthcare moved from the 'total institution' of the asylum (Goffman, 1961) to care in the community, driven by a combination of the growth of patient rights movements, the advent of antipsychotic medication and the rising costs associated with inpatient care. While community care has provided many people with a better quality of life (Černe Kolarič et al, 2024), it has also been critiqued for letting down those service users who have characteristics that mean they struggle to survive in society and consequently have been left 'rotting with their rights on' (Appelbaum and Gutheil, 1979; Novella, 2010). Thus, particularly in countries such as the USA where healthcare is more fragmented, CTOs have been framed as a way of obligating services to provide quality care (Van Dorn et al, 2010). While not articulated in the same way in England, changes in resources did play a part in policy reasoning. The number of beds in inpatient units in England fell from 154,000 in 1954 to 33,000 by 2005 (Joint Committee on the Draft Mental Health Bill, Session 2004–2005, HL 79-1/HC 95-1: Para 183) and continue to fall (Gilburt and Mallorie, 2024). The Government explicitly linked CTOs with this phenomenon when drafting the legislation, with Lord Warner, a

Minister of State in the Department of Health stating, 'supervised community treatment is probably the key change in the Bill … It is important not just from a patient and public safety angle but because clinical practice itself has changed' (Hansard, House of Lords Debates, 28 November 2006, vol. 687, col. 656). Indeed, the impact assessment carried out by the Department of Health (2007) predicted that CTOs would save the NHS approximately £34 million per year by 2014–15, due to a presumed 10 per cent reduction in admittance to hospital.

Troubled or troubling individuals?

As well as concerns about service users being abandoned to their fate, community care has become associated with public fears about insufficiently controlled individuals presenting a risk of harm to the community at large. While the evidence of a link between violence and mental disorder is contested, it has become increasingly accepted that a co-occurrence of substance misuse and/or dependence with diagnoses of severe mental illness can lead to an elevated risk of violence (Fazel et al, 2009, 2010; Whiting et al, 2022). However, it is also the case that substance misuse, and other environmental factors associated with mental illness and violence, such as socioeconomic status or experience of childhood abuse, are also correlated with general population levels of violence, regardless of the presence of mental illness (Youn et al, 2025). Consequently:

> it is simplistic as well as inaccurate to say the cause of violence among mentally ill individuals is the mental illness itself; instead … mental illness is clearly relevant to violence risk but … its causal roles are complex, indirect, and embedded in a web of other (and arguably more) important individual and situational cofactors. (Elbogen and Johnson, 2009, 159)

However, it could be argued that this 'expert' view is not deemed as important as the public view on mental disorder and violence by policy makers. As Madden (2003) states, large-scale statistical studies do not address 'catastrophic' events when they do occur. It is clear that even though the majority of violence committed by individuals with a diagnosed severe mental illness is towards people they know, such as family members, the public, 'most fear violence that is random, senseless, and unpredictable and they associate this with mental illness' (Stuart, 2003, 121). Surveys of attitudes towards people with severe mental illness have shown that a large proportion of the public, while holding sympathetic attitudes, also experience feelings of uncertainty and fear, particularly towards individuals with a diagnosis of schizophrenia (Pescosolido, Manago and Monahan, 2019).

Rose (2002a) describes how the focus of this debate has shifted since the 1980s. Increasingly, instead of service failure being discussed in terms of the 'plight' of service users, it is now 'posed in terms of the failure of assessment, prediction, and management of risky individuals and the minimisation of risk to the community' (Rose, 2002a, 216). CTOs as a tool for regular monitoring and medication compliance can therefore be posited as a political response to public concerns, most obviously in the North American practice of naming their introduction after the victim of homicide by a mentally disordered individual (for example, Brian's Law in Ontario, Kendra's Law in New York and Laura's Law in Florida). A similar narrative was evident in England, beginning in 1998 when the then Secretary of State for Health, Frank Dobson proclaimed that 'community care has failed' (Department of Health, 1999). As with the USA and Canada, a spate of much reported homicides committed by individuals in contact with mental health services provided impetus for policy reform, with the Home Office as well as the Department of Health shaping policy based on public safety. The public inquiries that arose attracted substantial media attention, particularly in relation to their key findings, which drew attention to common service failures and made a range of recommendations, including that legislation should be examined, particularly in regards to compulsory treatment and supervision in the community (Blom-Cooper, Hally and Murphy, 1995; Sheppard, 1997). The Government made it clear that they believed the existing legislation for community supervision was outdated, and had failed to either benefit service users or to protect the public (Department of Health and Home Office, 2000). As the then Minister for Health Services, Rosie Winterton made clear, the argument for CTOs was closely linked to risk:

> There are 1,300 suicides every year and 50 homicides by people who have been in contact with mental health services. We believe that supervised community treatment is vital to helping patients continue to take treatment when they leave hospital and to enable clinicians to take rapid action if relapse is on the horizon. (Hansard, House of Commons Debate, 18 June 2007, vol. 461, col. 1193)

As Pilgrim (2007) noted, the purpose of the reform and the contention it created were not unique to present times; an enduring feature of mental health law-making has been debate over balancing issues of rights and liberty with those of risk and constraint. Even so, commentators suggested that 'an illiberal stance and an obsession with risk minimisation did dominate ministerial deliberations about legal reform' (Pilgrim and Ramon, 2009, 284). In this sense the reforms could be viewed as evidence of a general policy shift to the realm of 'the social' under New Labour, which constituted an interventionist 'culture of control' (Lawton-Smith, 2005).

The will to empower

However, it would be simplistic to suggest an overriding concern with risk was the sole driver behind policy making. CTOs have also been associated with a somewhat paternalistic version of the recovery approach in mental health, where it has been surmised they can provide a secure foundation for individuals to operate from and to encourage self-efficacy. The debate on whether CTOs enable or constrict self-determination has been central to both CTO policy making and resistance to CTOs. In turn, this has led to deeper questions on the concepts of choice and free will in mental health. A New York campaign group arguing against the introduction of CTOs made the point that 'people recover when they have a choice among alternative treatments and services, when they are empowered to make their own decisions … and when they are offered hope. These conditions are impossible under outpatient commitment' (Swanson, 2009, 183).

The centrality of medication within CTOs is an especially problematic issue in regards to choice, where it has been suggested by campaigning groups that medical treatment combined with the compulsory power of CTOs will result in its inappropriate and unreflective use by clinicians, a further decrease in choice and involvement in treatment decisions by service users and a lack of consideration of non-medical approaches.

Conversely, Dawson (2009, 29) argued that an understanding of CTOs as enabling self-direction and choice is grounded in the concept of positive liberty (Berlin, 1969) which refers to 'our capacity for self-governance … our ability to set goals and have some chance of meeting them, and to maintain important relationships, without being dominated by internal constraints that prevent this occurring'. The framing of CTOs as a conduit for individual growth and empowerment was most evident in assertions that CTOs are reconcilable with the recovery model and indeed, can act as an opportunity for individuals to become 'well enough' through long-term medication adherence to start the recovery process (Munetz and Freze, 2001; Kinderman and Tai, 2008). In this way, they suggest longer-term outcomes of being on a CTO could include service users sustaining meaningful activity in the community, experiencing better quality of life and holding better relationships with significant others. The result of this thinking is that arguments for individual freedom are constructed as morally hazardous, as it is not enough to simply offer services and medical care which service users are free to reject (Kinderman and Tai, 2008). Similarly, Sjostrom, Zetterberg and Markström (2011, 425) comment that even though adverse incidents provided the 'window' for CTOs to be introduced in Sweden, 'where the official rationale for the policy was eventually spelled out, it is striking to observe how reducing risk was pushed to the background by an agenda oriented towards treatment and rehabilitation'. Although less prominent as a rationale in England, CTOs were nevertheless defended with recourse to recovery in parliamentary debates: 'Supervised community treatment ... will allow patients, so far as possible, to live normal lives in the community. This will reduce the risk of social exclusion and stigma associated with detention in hospital for long periods of time or with repeated hospital admissions' (Roll and Whittaker, 2007, 21).

The biomedical foundation for CTO use

The foundational argument for using CTOs for both risk management and recovery purposes has been their ability to ensure medication compliance. Policy debates around the use of CTOs have mostly been based on a view of mental illness as primarily a medically treatable concern. CTOs thus reflect the common culture of mental health policy and services, where biological explanations for mental illness are given causal precedence, and medication is consequently the dominant intervention with medication compliance the primary aim (NICE, 2014).

The role of insight in the justification of CTOs

Not adhering to treatment is commonly attributed by CTO advocates to a lack of insight by individuals into their disorder which makes them unable to make rational treatment decisions (Cossu et al, 2024). Research has suggested that people diagnosed with severe mental illness who have poor levels of treatment compliance tend to display worse psychotic symptoms, relapse more quickly and are hospitalised more frequently (Perkins et al, 2023). Insight in these terms is defined as an individual's ability to see themselves as mentally unwell and to frame their experiences in pathological terms (David, 1990). Further, defining insight in such a way is associated with the view that lack of insight is a 'neurological deficit' which manifests as a clinical symptom of mental disorder (Arango and Amador, 2011). Insight is therefore framed as a specific, measurable entity which is likely to be missing in individuals diagnosed with a severe mental disorder, especially schizophrenia.

Focusing on a lack of insight as the cause of noncompliance, particularly as a neurological symptom of illness, provides greater justification for enforced treatment as it is based on the premise that it is the individual who needs to be acted upon rather than the external factors impacting on their engagement – a biopsychological stance which omits 'the social' (Tew et al, 2012). It also means that the individual's view of their own experiences may be underplayed. Taking this stance may limit the practitioner's ability to explore an individual's explanations of their experiences, which could yield valuable knowledge and lead to different conclusions on treatment pathways. Dawson and Mullen (2008) suggest that if a service user does not hold the same view as their psychiatrist, capitulation may be required from the service user for discharge from the CTO to occur. More specifically, insight as a concept can foster tautological reasoning, where resistance to treatment is automatically equated to a lack of insight.

Accordingly, the routine conflation of a lack of insight and noncompliance has been challenged. As Chakrabarti (2014) points out, the rate of compliance with medication tends to be similar across physical and mental illness, which challenges the theory that noncompliance is due to an inherent inability in individuals diagnosed with psychotic disorders. Noncompliance with medication can be seen instead as a complex process, dependent on social and service factors, life circumstances, resources, priorities and available information (Chakrabarti, 2014). Social factors that can contribute to noncompliance with medication include the stigma attached to being a mental health service user, the availability and closeness of a support network, housing instability, employment status and levels of substance misuse (Wade et al, 2017). If a service user fears that compulsion may arise through maintaining contact with services, or feel that they are not included in treatment decisions, then levels of compliance can be affected (Sweeney et al, 2016).

The well-documented potential side effects of antipsychotic medication (Calton and Spandler, 2009) and the possibility of treatment resistance (NICE, 2014) can also contribute to individuals deciding to reduce dosage or stop medication altogether. As Wales and Hiday (2006) point out, the arguments in favour of CTOs as a medication enabler are the consequence of assumptions that are rarely critically examined in the CTO research literature, about both the typical characteristics of individuals diagnosed with a severe mental illness and the usefulness of medication, specifically antipsychotics. NICE (2014) suggests that up to a third of people do not respond to antipsychotics, and if an individual displays treatment-resistance to one type, it is unlikely that they will respond to others. There is a general consensus that the evidence base for antipsychotics across a range of outcomes is ambiguous and partial at best (Leucht et al, 2017; Leichsenring et al, 2022).

A common response to treatment resistance by psychiatrists is to combine different types of antipsychotic medication, or to increase the dosage beyond the standard dose recommended. However, neither of these strategies have been proven effective (Taylor, 2010), and in the case of 'over-dosing' can lead to worse outcomes due to the escalation of side-effects. Consequently, it could be concluded that if medication non-response is beyond the ability of psychiatrists to control, it could lead to relapse and hospitalisation for a proportion of service users, which partially challenges the claim that noncompliance is the primary cause of mental deterioration. Studies on service user opinions around medication management in mental health suggest that practitioners may not always listen sufficiently to concerns around treatment side-effects, or try and act to alleviate them, which may lead to medication self-management in the form of reduction or ceasing of medication (Li, Hsieh and Liu, 2023).

In and out of the community: the language of CTOs

Given the assumptions around risk, recovery and biomedical causality that underpin the discourse on compulsory powers in the community, CTOs can be understood in terms of biopolitics and biopower, offering a way of ensuring both 'optimisation' and control of 'biological citizenship' (Rose, 2007). Dean's (2010, 156) conception of 'illiberal liberality' is helpful in how CTOs differentiate 'low-risk' individuals, who are 'empowered' to become responsibilised, autonomous and self-regulating members of society, from 'high risk' individuals who require external regulation. In this sense, mental disorder is not only framed in biomedical terms, but as a problem situated outside of societal norms that requires management. Bentall (2004, 176) describes this latter perspective in the following terms:

> The distinction between the pathological and the non-pathological inevitably involves some kind of implicit reference to human values … it is not enough that a … characteristic is shown to be statistically unusual in order for it to be regarded as pathological; it must also be perceived as undesirable, or at least to have consequences that are undesirable.

As Rose in his development of freedom in psychiatric care (1996, 12) emphasises, 'professionals … are not so much required to cure as to teach the skills of coping, to inculcate the responsibility to cope, to identify failures of coping, to restore to the individual the capacity to cope'. If this is not possible, then the generation and sharing of risk knowledge through professional networks of communication and surveillance enact 'circuits of exclusion' in which the threat that 'high-risk' individuals pose within the 'territory of the community' is managed (Rose, 1999, 262). Policies and practices that develop to meet this requirement are, by their nature, preventative in their aims and objectives.

CTOs, then, can be viewed as a mechanism which contains both inclusionary and exclusionary facets so as to both manage risk and bring individuals into the fold of citizenship. This enables reformation of individuals and their conduct if possible, but also control and separation from society should this transformative optimism prove unwarranted. The terminology of CTOs reflects these dual objectives. They have a highly contractual flavour, most specifically in the use of the term 'conditions' which service users must 'agree' to. Behaviour control in this sense is concerned with a relatively abstract conceptualisation of risk, where prudent individuals are expected to make their own way in society while complying with complex rules and requirements, or as Rose (2002b, 19) puts it, ''play the game' of community care'. Citizenship is therefore defined conditionally, and 'irregular citizens' (Zedner, 2010) are expected to earn their way to full citizenship through conforming to prescribed expectations. As Zedner (2010, 397) describes, the use of 'contractual devices', specific to the individual, subvert 'the universalism of the … law and [delegate] considerable quasi-legislative powers to the public officials who determine their precise terms'. In this way, CTOs change the state of play in regards to the rights that those who are placed on them hold, as compared to 'regular citizens'.

CTOs can also be viewed in a more concrete way as a preventative and potentially punitive 'early detection' system for events that have yet to, and may never, occur. Indeed, CTOs in England were acknowledged by Lord Hunt, the then Minister of State for Health for the Government as a 'psychiatric ASBO' (Hansard, House of Lords Debates, 2 July 2007, vol. 693, col. 842), thus firmly situating them within the wider discourse of public order policy. Defining the CTO as a preventative community intervention means that it can be used for a broad range of risk-related reasons and thus encompass a large number of service users. In England, the definition and categorisation of the 'revolving door patient' has become a signifier for who has been 'made knowable' for CTOs to work on, through the formation of such individuals via both professional knowledge and research expertise into a homogenous group who share similar characteristics and patterns of behaviour. Within the legislative process, the Government overturned amendments attempted in the House of Lords which would have limited the use of CTOs to those individuals who fell within a 'hard' definition of revolving door such as having a certain number of previous compulsory hospitalisations, as happens in other countries. Instead they stated that clinical expertise on who does, or more importantly *may in the future*, belong to this particular group should take precedence. As Lord Hunt argued, to legislatively limit who was placed on a CTO would 'immediately risk excluding patients who might benefit … and would fetter clinical judgment' (Hansard, House of Lords Debates, 2 July 2007, vol. 693, col. 843). Thus the accompanying Code of Practice for the Mental Health Act 2007 (Department of Health, 2008) advised that CTOs be aimed at the 'revolving door scenario' but did not state what this might mean.

Therefore, CTOs in England are not legislatively targeted and can be applied to any inpatient facing discharge, including those on their first admission and those who may agree to voluntary treatment. Indeed, shortly following their implementation, the Care Quality Commission (2010) analysed 208 CTO cases and found 30 per cent of them did not have a history of noncompliance or disengagement and therefore could be classed as having the potential to be treated voluntarily. Here then we can see how particular issues became identified as problems for CTOs to solve; more specifically tracing the way CTOs were explained at policy-level highlights who is being made 'visible' in order to be governed and how ideas on individual reformation via CTOs have developed.

Risk and recovery in practice: perspectives and experiences of practitioners and service users

How do these policy narratives play out at practice-level? It is evident that practitioner views on CTOs are largely context-dependent, and involve balancing potential benefits and harms. Many practitioners value CTOs for their potential for stability in the community, but are also concerned about the less easily quantifiable effects resulting from coercive experiences (de Waardt et al, 2022). Similarly Mullen, Dawson and Gibbs (2006) reported the uncertainty involved for practitioners in deciding whether CTOs would be helpful and the difficulty in considering the broad range of factors at play in individual cases. In this study, justification for the use of CTOs was linked by practitioners to the role they felt CTOs could play at the start of a long-term process of rehabilitation. By contrast, concerns were also reported that being placed on a CTO may remove an individual's sense of autonomy and foster dependency, as the CTO acts to 'bind' service users to services. From a legal perspective, Approved Mental Health Professional (AMHPs) interviewed by Stroud, Doughty and Banks (2013) thought that CTOs gave more legal protection and structure for service users than pre-existing legislative provision. What is also evident here is that practitioners' views on why they valued CTOs did not always cohere. For example, in contrast to the well-reported views that CTOs were seen as positive as they could allow for stability in the community, Stroud, Doughty and Banks (2013) report the key purpose given for CTOs by psychiatrists was to facilitate fast and preventative recall to hospital, as a risk management exercise.

An overarching theme in qualitative studies that include service user participants is considerable service user ambivalence regarding the use of CTOs, with benefits like security being described alongside references to CTOs' stigmatising effects and the loss of freedom they entail in relation to medication, travel and residence. The focus on medication was particularly resented, as it was seen as displacing other forms of support (Corring, O'Reilly and Sommerdyk, 2017). Other themes that arose were uncertainty about what service users felt they were allowed to do, and strong views on the coercive element of CTOs, which were described as limiting genuine involvement in decision-making and carrying an underlying threat (Corring, O'Reilly and Sommerdyk, 2017). Some service users were also concerned that being made subject to a CTO placed an additional label on them, which might serve to differentiate them within services, and consequently negatively affect the way they are treated by practitioners (Brophy, 2009; Mfoafo-M'Carthy, 2014).

However, these same studies also highlight that service users could also appreciate the safety net CTOs provided, believing they allowed for quicker access to hospital if necessary and to higher quality, more attentive services (Gibbs, Dawson and Mullen, 2006; Lawn et al, 2016). CTOs could also be viewed as helpful in providing structure and stability in the community through difficult periods in service users' lives (Stensrud et al, 2015). If the CTO had been experienced as helpful during difficult periods, then service users could become 'volunteers for compulsion' (Gibbs et al, 2005, 365). Similarly, research suggests that if CTOs were believed to be effective by service users, they also tended to be perceived as fair (Swartz et al, 2004; Pridham et al, 2015). Service users were also likely to prefer the freedom of CTOs to hospitalisation (Stroud, Doughty and Banks, 2013). Swartz et al (2003) used vignettes to ascertain which outcomes would be least acceptable to different stakeholder groups and found that for the service user group, being placed on a CTO was significantly more acceptable as an outcome than experiencing re-hospitalisation.

Comparing CTOs positively to hospitalisation does not necessarily tell us about the feelings of disenfranchisement that may result due to the CTO in itself or allow for a deeper understanding of service users' lives while on the CTO. In this sense, Light et al (2014) make the point that the experience of CTOs is not as simple as a choice between freedom and control, and that ambivalence towards CTOs points towards deeper, more complex aspects of living under compulsion. Instead, being on a CTO can accentuate metaphysical questions of what it is to be in the world as an individual within the mental health system. Indeed, exploration of compulsion in the community and its corresponding potential to affect self, identity and belonging require further attention. Newton-Howes (2010, 218), in describing how compulsion should be dealt with ethically in practice, notes that:

> When considering the 'harms' of coercion and compulsion it is the requirement to do 'good' that acts as a counterpoise … In other words the consideration of any … coercive 'loss' is outweighed by the potential for 'good' to come … There is an increased burden on the professionals involved to be clear what that good is.

Decision-making and reasoning on CTOs

Therefore, an important element of cooperative working is a shared understanding of what the CTO is for and how it works. Understanding can vary between different stakeholder groups and there can be associated uncertainty for professionals in making decisions. Research into decision-making and reasoning on CTOs tends to focus on how they work 'downstream' particularly in relation to the central interlocking mechanisms of conditions and recall, and in regards to the legal oversight of CTOs, specifically the appeals process. Various studies (Mullen, Dawson and Gibbs, 2006; Riley, Hoyer and Lorem, 2014; Stuen, Landhei and Rugkasa, 2018) have highlighted the dilemma practitioners faced in deciding whether to discharge a CTO or not. A broadly recognised theme is that decisions involve the weighing up of probabilities and making a judgement on whether any positive progress made will continue following discharge. Deciding on discharge was dependent on the level of risk a practitioner was willing to accept, given their past experiences of CTOs and the profile of the individual they were making the decision about.

It can be inferred from this that although CTOs may for some individuals prevent 'short, sharp' compulsion via involuntary hospitalisation, they may result instead in 'defensive' decision-making in the community, resulting in individuals being under compulsion for much longer periods of time. Nevertheless, risk management understood in terms of the protection of others is not necessarily viewed as being a significant element of practitioner reasoning in deciding on the use of CTOs. An interesting finding is that CTOs were supported by psychiatrists on clinical grounds rather than in relation to risk management (Manning et al, 2011; DeRidder et al, 2016). Both surveys described how psychiatrists rated supporting treatment adherence, provision of authority to treat, contact with professionals, identification of relapse and protection of service users from consequences of relapse as their 'top five' decision-making factors for using CTOs, with reduction of risk of violence to others given lower importance. This also suggests that practitioner reasoning follows a particular chain of logic, with emphasis being placed on enabling mechanisms (for example, authority to treat) and 'foundational' outcomes (such as treatment adherence) rather than secondary outcomes.

Service user responses to the CTO process

Central to practitioner decision-making on CTOs is how individual service users respond to compulsory activities and events. Newton-Howes (2010) defines coercion as a potential, but not inevitable, product of compulsory intervention. In these terms compulsion is the objective 'event' that occurs, and coercion is the possible subjective reaction experienced in response. This research highlights the complex range of informal and formal leverages that can be used on service users and provides evidence that a significant minority of voluntary inpatients experience feelings of coercion. This demonstrates that the relationship between compulsion and coercion is not entirely straightforward. What he and others (Olofsson and Jacobsson, 2001; Haglund, von Knorring and von Essen, 2003) suggest matters in mediating experiences of coercion are the 'interactive processes' that occur between service users and practitioners. The seminal MacArthur coercion study (Monahan et al, 1999) used the concept of procedural justice to suggest that perceived fairness in the process of decision-making by practitioners can lead to lowered feelings of coercion. In particular, important factors for service users included feeling heard by practitioners, being respected and treated with dignity, getting clear and honest explanations for decisions in favour of compulsion and of the future steps necessary for compulsion to be lifted.

A foundational element therefore for service users formulating a response to the CTO is how they respond to practitioners' explanations of what the CTO is and what it entails. Research suggests that service users are not well-informed about the CTO, the CTO process, or about their rights in respect of the CTO (Pridham et al, 2015). Rolfe, Sheehan and Davidson (2008) conducted a survey of service users in Western Australia, and found that a sizeable minority stated that the CTO and associated care plan had not been discussed with them, and that they were not made aware of the right to a tribunal and the process for reviewing the CTO. This suggests there is a need for information-giving to be carried out in a more meaningful and enabling way. Stroud, Doughty and Banks (2013) found that even when practitioners stated that written information had been provided, service users did not remember receiving it. Assimilating and understanding information is the first step to being actively involved in a process and they also found that service users were not clear about discussions on the CTO, and reported not playing a part in them. In England, the practice guidance for CTOs (National Institute for Mental Health in England, 2008; Department of Health, 2015) suggests service users should be as involved as much as possible in the CTO process. However, the process via which a CTO is made and maintained, whereby CTOs can be drawn up by the inpatient team but implemented by the community team, may militate against such involvement. Perhaps unsurprisingly then, service users in Stroud, Doughty and Banks (2013) described that they felt little sense of choice and control in the CTO process.

In regards to dealing with the everyday reality of the CTO, it seems likely that individuals who are placed on them may take different approaches, dependent on interpretation of the CTO and involvement in the CTO process, but also based on perception of self and others, and previous experiences. Van Dorn et al (2006) examine the relationship between CTOs and perceived barriers to seeking support. They suggest that the complex interplay of personal and environmental factors that can lead to noncompliance means that those individuals who tend to be put under the greatest pressure to comply with medication via leverage such as being placed on a CTO, can also face the greatest barriers in being able to do so. In addition, they hypothesise that the CTO as a tool that should facilitate treatment and engagement may instead act to further estrange individuals, making it less likely that they will engage voluntarily. In finding a relationship between low level usage of services and CTOs, they considered that this may either be because practitioners were targeting those individuals who would not otherwise participate, or because CTOs have had the effect of 'further alienating some individuals and strengthening the internal barriers that keep them from participating voluntarily in treatment' (Van Dorn et al, 2006, 504). Social support networks were a positive mediating factor in individuals' perceptions of barriers to support even if they were on a CTO, and Van Dorn et al (2006) propose that practitioner support which focuses on quality of life may lessen the likelihood that individuals will avoid services and treatment. Given these findings, and that CTOs 'may constrain autonomy in multiple ways … [but] the heart of the matter, for proponents and critics alike, is the scope of the individual's autonomy to make medication choices' (Wales and Hiday, 2006, 459), an argument can be made that how treatment is negotiated in the context of the CTO is central to their functioning.

This is particularly the case considering the association of CTOs with the use of depot, which is an injectable form of antipsychotic medication with long-acting effects, often used as a way of managing noncompliance. Service users on CTOs are more than twice as likely to be prescribed depot rather than oral antipsychotics (Lambert, Singh and Patel, 2009; Barkhuizen et al, 2020). While the use of depot is not as widespread in England as oral antipsychotics, Patel et al (2011) suggest that the introduction of CTOs may lead to a rise in their use, as the status of being on a CTO could lead to greater consideration of such methods to manage noncompliance. However, it is not clear whether this treatment pathway is chosen as part of the decision to use a CTO or is more a reflection of the type of cases where CTOs are being applied. Depot injections can be viewed by service users as more stigmatising due to the method of administration and painful side effects (NICE, 2014). Just as importantly, the long-acting nature of depot and the passive experience of receiving it are likely to result in increased feelings of coercion and a lack of control for service users. As Patel et al (2009, 1486) state 'the power of others that is lack of true autonomy is more notable for those on depot than those on oral tablets … As depots are "given" rather than "taken" this sense of power may be seen as more potent'. Using CTOs and depots in conjunction raises questions around how medication conditions are formulated by practitioners and how a dual-action approach of legal and 'proximal' compulsion (Watts and Priebe, 2002) is considered in relation to least restrictive principles.

The therapeutic relationship

Practitioner concerns about the coercive impact of CTOs on the therapeutic relationship are well documented (Manning et al, 2011; de Waardt et al, 2022). As Churchill et al (2007, 188) state, problems in the relationship between practitioner and service user may arise because 'The implementation of CTOs requires that mental health professionals fulfil potentially incompatible roles, becoming both "game-keeper" and "poacher", providing treatment to unwilling patients, and monitoring and enforcing compliance with this treatment.'

This may place practitioners in an uncomfortable position where the power disparity inherent within their relationship with service users is further emphasised by the legally mandated use of compulsion outside the prescribed boundaries of hospital and the extension of their role as supervisor. Consequently, research on the practitioner–service user relationship within the context of the CTO has tended to focus on what effect practitioners and service users believe the CTO has had on the relationship, and as can be expected, findings are mixed.

A common response of service users on CTOs is ambivalence towards their psychiatrist, resenting the perceived paternalism of coercive measures taken under the CTO, but at the same time understanding why such decisions were made (Corring, O'Reilly and Sommerdyk, 2017). Psychiatrists in a study by O'Reilly (2006) described having to accept that they were going to be viewed negatively because of the CTO, but also the importance of knowing an individual well before placing them on a CTO, in order to have a therapeutic foundation to work from. Likewise, McMillan, Lawn and Delaney-Crowe (2019) highlight the concern of practitioners that if the use of authority to mandate compulsion occurs at the beginning of the relationship between them and a service user, it may influence how the service user perceives future action by them. Indeed, they go on to state that practitioners held the paradoxical belief that a compulsory intervention can only be effective when the service user collaborates within the context of an engaged relationship. However, the view of practitioners in Jansson and Fridlund's (2016) study was that a combative relationship at the beginning of the CTO was not necessarily insurmountable, because damage to the relationship can be ameliorated over time, as the service user may become accustomed to the CTO and change their attitude to its use. In this way, practitioners held the view that the CTO could act to improve the relationship through the framework it provided for consistent engagement (Sjostrom, Zetterberg and Markstrom, 2011). As a consequence, the general consensus was that the negative influence the CTO might have on the therapeutic relationship could, with careful attention and perseverance, be outweighed by the benefits it would bring (Jansson and Friglund, 2016).

Stroud, Doughty and Banks (2013) also reported on specific elements of the CTO that could cause particular tension. Although service users in their study generally reported good relationships with professionals, both service users and practitioners felt that the requirement for regular appeals could bring to the surface disagreement and undermine the supportive relationship practitioners might have with individuals. Similarly, practitioners reported that the process of recalling an individual to hospital highlighted the importance of having the skills necessary to maintain a positive connection within the context of coercion. The challenges of sustaining a therapeutic alliance seemed to be of more significance for care coordinators, rather than for the psychiatrist who may not see an individual very often. More specifically, some care coordinators in the study reported feeling concerned that they now had to take on 'formal' legal aspects of work that they hadn't previously, which they felt affected both their sense of role and the nature of their practice with service users.

The research reviewed here tells us much about how concerns regarding the practitioner–service user relationship have manifested. It seems that practitioners believe the state of the relationship can be important to the working of the CTO, in that positive interaction signifies collaboration with the CTO. The influence the CTO has on relationships is dependent on timing, the nature of prior relationships and changing responses to the CTO in itself. The structure the CTO may provide can also have a positive influence on the relationship between practitioners and service users. Particular tensions may surface through elements of the CTO process and this can mean skilled work has to be done by practitioners in order to maintain a good working relationship with service users. Different groups of practitioners have a range of perspectives on the relational effect of the CTO, depending on their proximity to the service user and possibly, because of their role. These findings reinforce the point that more importance needs to be placed on the experiences and perspectives of those practitioners who carry out the everyday work of the CTO.

Conclusion

In this chapter, we have traced the evolution of CTOs through policy discourse to on the ground experiences and practices. Through doing so, we have highlighted the contested nature of control in community mental healthcare. There are alternate and on the surface contradictory discourses that have fuelled the creation and ongoing use of CTOs. Risk and recovery are two sides of the same coin, highlighting both the inclusionary and exclusionary nature of controlling practices in mental health community care. Underpinning all conceptions is a focus on biomedical explanations and solutions for the control and rehabilitation of service users in the community. The ambiguities that are inherent in such discourses and ways of understanding mental health distress are echoed in the empirical literature on CTOs. In particular, research highlights the variable purposes that CTOs may be put to, the weighing up of benefits and risks by both practitioners and service users, the dilemmas inherent to decision-making on CTO use and the complexities of maintaining therapeutic engagement within the context of legal and medical compulsion.

This research provides the context for four interconnected themes which form the basis for the approach taken in our study: first, in order to gain a fuller picture of the nature and significance of compulsion in community mental healthcare, an approach that takes into account the multifaceted ways CTOs are understood, implemented and with what implications is necessary. Second, such an approach will at least in part involve a deeper exploration than has occurred thus far of the everyday practice of CTOs and the mechanisms through which they work. Third, central to the analysis of everyday CTO practice is a consideration of the diverse motivations and actions of practitioners and service users in the context of the CTO; in particular, their responses to the CTO, the mediating influence of their interaction with each other and the way such responses affect how the CTO unfolds. Finally, in order to understand how practitioners and service users approach CTOs, it is also necessary to get a sense of where they are coming from, particularly in regards to the exercise of power the CTO represents. For practitioners this refers to the underlying beliefs that influence their stance to CTOs and underpin the various ways they balance the tensions that may arise in the use of CTOs. For service users, this would involve an exploration of how the CTO interacts with their identity and sense of self in the world within the context of consistent 'background' and sometimes foregrounded compulsion. This would enhance understanding of both the workings of the CTO but also how the CTO may shape those individuals who experience it, both practitioners and service users alike.

In what follows we expand on these themes via an exploration of 'on the ground' practice; as Dean (2010, 88) suggests studies of governmentality can gain critical traction from analysing the connections and disjunctures between policy rationalities and the internal and implicit logic of governmental practices. Moreover, we posited earlier that a neglected aspect of governmentality as empirically applied has been how conduct and counter-conduct are mediated through 'practices of the self'. Given that the use of CTOs in England depends so much on practitioner discretion, this further reinforces the argument we have made that our study provides fertile ground for an analysis of ethical self-work by both practitioners and service users in relation to CTO use. In this way we formulate an understanding of how and in what ways CTOs are theorised and used by those constituents who are affected by them.

3

A virtual asylum? The various meanings of compulsion in the community

In this chapter we highlight the various ways community treatment orders (CTOs) are conceptualised by both service user and practitioner study participants, paying attention to the distinctive yet variable interview accounts of each group, which need to be taken on their own merits as whole narratives. The chapter title refers to a quote from a practitioner in relation to CTOs which illustrates their ambiguous nature as a form of control. A 'virtual asylum' can be viewed as both a source of safety and constriction – an invisible sanctuary or a prison without walls. We illustrate this ambiguity by emphasising that control measures such as CTOs engender a spectrum of often conflicting thoughts and feelings for those made subject to them and those who implement them.

We begin by discussing the various *beliefs* that shaped service user ideation of the CTO and the different *purposes* that service users felt CTOs might have. We incorporate an overview of service users' experiences of mental distress and instability, including how they negotiated a sense of self in the face of adverse circumstances. Participant beliefs regarding CTOs did not arise from nowhere; the varying ways service users viewed themselves and their experiences had a strong influence on how they perceived and responded to the CTO. To fully understand the effects of control measures on individuals, and why it is that they may respond to such interventions in differentiated and complex ways, where those individuals 'come from' must be accounted for. Our subsequent discussion links this exploration of the self to how service users viewed the various purposes of the CTO – provision, risk, recovery and maintenance – and it is fair to say that perspectives on these are mixed. We therefore include reflection on how the CTO might act as a kind of 'anti-purpose' by creating additional barriers to the realisation of goals and aims, and also accentuate 'cross-purposes' between users and professionals.

The guiding rationalities service users and practitioners employ for CTOs both coalesce and diverge and in the second half of the chapter we focus on the practitioner perspective, examining how they thought about CTOs as they related to their individual practice. We consider the ethical underpinnings of their views, focusing first on the gaps the practitioners felt existed between policy and practice rationalities. The claims that have been made for CTOs were received with some scepticism by practitioners and both the effectiveness and ethicality of CTOs were challenged. At the same time, practitioners constructed narratives around the use of CTOs that highlighted their beliefs about what 'kinds' of practice they valued and the associated 'ethical balancing acts' they navigated in weighing up CTOs. Despite the ethical discomfort many practitioners felt about CTOs, similarly to service users they all saw some value in CTOs across a variety of purposes including in the shorter-term protection and risk management and the longer-term stability and recovery.

Self and the CTO

As with any intervention, service users did not come to CTOs with a blank slate, and much of the discussion in interviews focused on their experiences of mental distress, medication, services and how their sense of self had developed in relation to all three. We cannot fully detail the service users' hinterland of experiences here, but it is important to sketch out such 'self-work' as it underpinned how service users then went on to form perceptions of the CTO.

On shifting ground: the consequences of mental distress

All of the participants had lengthy histories of mental distress, and associated periods of time where they had felt out of control of their lives, or had control taken from them. Behaviour associated with psychotic or manic states, and the subsequent response of services, had made it difficult for many of the participants to maintain stability. Patrick told me how the constant repeat hospitalisations he was subjected to meant that *everything stops*, and this seemed to sum up the paradoxically dual sense of instability and being 'stuck' that numerous participants described.

Being unable to maintain an uninterrupted life in the community could be described as an indirect consequence of severe mental distress, mediated by the institutional factors inherent in the process of hospitalisation. However, perhaps the most poignant accounts service users gave related to the direct impact of mental distress, especially loneliness, isolation and associated fracturing of relationships that they had experienced because of their situation and the responses of others to it. Less than half of the participants' had someone in their life who they described in terms of non-professional support, and in these cases, relationships were generally discussed as complex, precarious and difficult. Exploring the various individual and social impacts of mental distress on participants highlighted the sense of flux a majority of them had experienced. Subsequently, the additional challenges mental distress brought to constructing a cohesive and settled identity and integrating dissonant aspects of self was present as a theme in most of the participants' narratives.

Identity formation in the face of adversity

One way in which participants tried to assert control over identity was in how they explained their experiences of mental distress. Respondents reported a variety of causal explanations for their current circumstances, some more aligned with the language of diagnosis and biomedical models of illness than others. Often it would be the case that participants believed drugs (both illicit and legally prescribed) they had taken in the past were what had triggered their difficulties, as with Gwen: 'I started on anti-depressant medication and it progressed from there you see. So I'm convinced it's the medication that's done it whereas everybody else believes it's psychosis.' Or they might offer alternative diagnoses to the one they had been given. Simon explained that he felt he had trapped himself into a diagnosis of schizophrenia by lying to professionals about what he was experiencing in order to get help. He described what he experienced in terms that were differentiated from diagnostic criteria: 'it's more like I'm restless, I'm on the edge of life'. Similarly, Sarah took the diagnosis 'schizoaffective disorder' out of the medical domain by using the 'affective' part to explain her situation: 'I think schizoaffective disorder sums it up, because one thing affects another thing … affects your family, affects your relationships, the fact that your family and relationships are affected affects you again and there's … there's social consequences to having this illness, it's not just a medical thing.'

In general then, many participants resisted or reshaped the meaning of their diagnosis to help them make sense of who they had become. Participant sense of self was also often explained in terms of who they felt they 'should' be, particularly in terms of self-efficacy, in contrast to their actual experiences. Graham described the sense of institutionalisation that was present in some participants' stories when he said he: 'Wanted to start taking my life into my own hands a bit. Start doing things for myself.' This desire for independence contrasted with the reliance Graham felt he had on professionals. Resentment about the involvement of services in certain aspects of life could follow, as Irene described when discussing her last experience of being hospitalised under the Mental Health Act: 'I've shown self-reliance and so I haven't needed all that big type approach. And I've resented it, yes. That's all.' However, this self-conception sometimes contrasted with the described effects of participants' life experiences and associated stories of fragility. Sarah, who had been in and out of hospital over a period of 20 years, felt that her age meant that: 'I'm more frightened now than I was about the possibility of being in hospital again … it's knocked the stuffing out of me. As it happens more often, it's making me … less and less able really.' This illustrates the ongoing struggle that many participants went through to retain self-belief despite challenging circumstances. Repeated experiences of compulsion here led to a resigned acceptance of dependence in the face of authority.

Alternatively, an acceptance of dependence could be caught up in an individual's view of themselves as subsumed in a 'deficit' identity. Simon had been in contact with mental health services and the criminal justice system since very early adolescence. He described himself in 'professionalised' terms: 'because I am a poly drug user … And so for me it is like most people who have mental health problems and are on drugs, hospital is a safe environment, away from society, away from everything.' A similar process could be seen for those participants whose identity was shaped in response to others' beliefs about their abilities to cause harm. Michael drew a contrast to the gentle demeanour he presented when he responded to the question of who he thought CTOs were for: 'I don't think it's something for everyone, it's something that is good for violent, psychotic people like me.' In this sense, 'dangerousness' was a category that appeared to have been accepted by some participants as applicable to themselves, but which understandably could also be difficult to assimilate.

As can be seen here, participant narratives segued between wellness/illness, independence/dependence and safeness/dangerousness. The overarching narrative, however, was that of being or becoming 'normal'. The concept of 'normality' was one referred to across participant accounts, either directly or indirectly. In comparison to those participants who saw their identity at least in part through the lens of professional concerns, being 'normal' was used by others as a way of distancing themselves from and questioning the attribution of mental illness to their experience. Although Brendon was accepting of the diagnosis he had been given, he still struggled to accept what this meant: 'The doctor has suggested giving me some stronger medication. I was agreeable to it, although I was a bit … after he left I thought, "I'm a normal lad really", I *am* a normal lad, and I don't really need it.' In stronger terms, achieving what was deemed a normal life could be linked to rejection of professional involvement as the emblem of difficult and 'abnormal' experiences. For some individuals a wholesale rejection of what the mental health system had to offer seemed necessary in order to preserve a certain sense of self. However, more typically a complex relationship existed between participant's view of themselves and their stance towards services in general and CTOs in particular.

Service users' perceptions of what the CTO could do for them

Talk of struggles with security and identity resonated through service users' descriptions of what the CTO meant for them. The relationship between compulsion as an objective event and coercion as a subjective experience is not straightforward; as we noted earlier, the former does not necessarily lead to the latter (Newton-Howes, 2010). For service users who saw the CTO as a positive development, it offered a range of purposes which connected to how they felt about their lives and themselves.

Provision

'Provision based' accounts included references to the higher quality of service provision some participants believed they received due to the CTO. The function of CTOs in reciprocally 'binding' community services to service users is not as central in England as it is in countries like the USA. It could be argued, however, that the very legal framework of the CTO, particularly in terms of regular appeals, may prompt more scrutiny and regulation of care plans. In observations of appeals for example, the panel members habitually questioned the care plan as a whole, rather than focusing solely on the legal status of the CTO.

Accordingly, participants referred to the CTO providing a clearer structure for what they should expect in terms of service response and subsequently more leverage for them over services. This was especially the case in regard to repeated admissions to hospital. The 'revolving door' cycle is typically attributed to the behaviour of the individual and the CTO is aimed at ensuring compliance and thus prevention. However, participant narratives of their movement between the community and hospital also highlighted the systemic forces that could influence this cycle. Common experiences were related to professionals not having the time to try and avert involuntary admissions, as in Sarah's case: 'They've wanted to keep me out of hospital but every time something happens they're either short of time, they can't really see me very long, they just do it [involuntary hospitalisation under the Mental Health Act] for the sake of "better be safe than sorry".' A number of participants had previously had to wait until crisis point before being admitted, usually involuntarily. The CTO meant participants felt services would respond much faster to relapse, thus preventing a spiralling out of control. Difficulties with access to crisis care are a longstanding problem within English mental health services, and it may be that participants viewed the obligations the CTO represents via recall as a means of ensuring they could get help when they needed it, rather than when best fits the system. For these participants, the idea of being recalled to hospital was not viewed in a punitive sense, but as a reassuring safety net should things go wrong.

The CTO also represented access to legal protection in other ways. James felt that the CTO framework limited practitioner discretion and therefore acted to protect his freedom:

> It's there to protect you again … under the rulings that are on it they've got to abide by that CTO. They can't just keep you in indefinitely. It's there to say, 'look, he's back on his meds, he's listening to us okay, he's responding well, send him back out'. It's kind of two-fold.

More broadly, participants also expressed the view that the CTO could act as a 'passport' to ensure their access to support was protected in other arenas.

Specifically, participants referred to access to benefits and being able to use the CTO to demonstrate their need for financial support. Participants felt that the CTO helped their chances by signifying the level of their difficulties.

Risk

Risk was discussed by participants in terms of 'staying safe' (Stuart), with the CTO offering a preventative framework to protect self and others. For Michael, the CTO was not linked to his level of engagement. Nor did he link the CTO in a direct sense to maintaining his mental stability: 'I don't get the injections because of the psychosis.' Michael's view of himself as being dangerous when unwell meant that he saw the CTO as primarily being of benefit to others: 'It's required by law … because my mental health affects other people, not just myself. I think they did it for the benefit of the community. Well, the name says it all, community treatment order. Protect the community from me.'

The main aim of the CTO for Michael was to manage his behaviour when he felt he could not do so himself. In similar terms, Nick described how the conditions of his CTO provided him with firm and clear boundaries which he had found reassuring both for himself and others:

> It's given us a structure … I've got to attend probation, I've got to get my injections, I can't refuse them. In the past I've had nothing like that, I've just refused and I've been taken in on Sections, but being on a CTO if the truth's known, I know deep down I'll never ever get to the point where I've totally lost control like I've done in the past.

The compulsory nature of the CTO brought boundaries which acted to keep individuals on what they perceived to be the right path. This was also the case for self-protection, as Christine describes: 'You've got an order and if they want you back in you've got to go back in. And you've got no choice have you, really? But I think it's good, because you could harm yourself or …' The theme of delegating choice to an external force was significant for a number of the participants. Belief in the power of the CTO was as important as the actual power of the CTO.

The CTO could be seen by participants as leverage for positive risk-taking by professionals, as Patrick explains, 'I can't see them not changing my medication, because if I am on a CTO it's much safer than not being on a CTO … If things go wrong, it's much easier for them to react.' In this sense, the CTO could be viewed as a safe space within which to try out different approaches. However, the CTO in itself could also present a personal risk. For those participants who believed the CTO had 'worked' for them, taking steps toward stability could be disconcerting, as Nick explains:

> But all these feelings are coming back and I don't know how to cope. And it just builds up and builds up and I just lose it, I just lose my temper. And I find it really hard. Really hard. I need to sort my head out. I just want to carry on the way I'm going. Hopefully these feelings will go away, I don't know.

The fear of things going wrong could become more anxiety-inducing when things were going right, and yet at the same time established patterns of coping strategies (in Nick's case the triggering of admissions to hospital) were disrupted by the CTO. It is indicative of the symbolic power the CTO can hold that even though recall was not actively used in Nick's case he still saw the CTO as a significant mediator of his actions.

Recovery

Enabling recovery has not played as large a role in the empirical or discursive literature on CTOs as managing risk. Furthermore, while promoting stability in the community has been cited as a reason to use CTOs (O'Reilly et al, 2006), it is only one aspect of recovery, and recovery as a broader, future-orientated concept has not been fully addressed. Recovery refers to living a fulfilling and hopeful life alongside personal difficulties, with support from significant others through an on-going process (Anthony, 1993). Recovery was seen by participants as a process of positive change, leading from the opportunity the CTO provided for stability. In this sense, stasis and change were entwined in participant narratives.

When participants talked about the CTO as promoting recovery, this tended to involve looking to the past and comparing where they were now favourably with where they had been, and then looking to where they wanted to be in the future. James felt that the CTO gave him a sense of responsibility for safeguarding his future, which he related to the contractual nature of the CTO: 'You're responsible for yourself. That's what the CTO is about, isn't it? So the responsibility for taking your meds, for coming to your appointments, for seeing your doctor, I mean, yes, it's a huge responsibility.' Additionally, participants spoke of sharing purpose and trust with the professionals working with them. Brendon expressed this clearly: 'they wanted to safeguard a good, steady future, and a better quality of life … that was their reasons for the CTO really.'

There was a sense of precarious hope about these narratives, as Brendon went on to illustrate: 'I suppose being on a CTO and the right medication I'll conquer it, hopefully I'll get over things, but we'll see.' In this regard, participants viewed the CTO as helping them navigate through difficulties that might cause previous patterns of events to be repeated. The CTO then was 'the next process in an ongoing process' (Sarah), and participants talked in staged terms, with stability bringing change. Being able to stay well led to maintenance in the community, which could in turn lead to incremental differences in quality of life: 'I don't think it's instantaneous help. It's a long slow process and lately in the past few months I started … making friends but forming a relationship … yes, it has helped' (James).

Given the entrenched nature of the majority of participants' difficulties, like James, they talked about change as a slow, gradual process, but nonetheless change which went beyond engagement with services and medication, and that affected various fundamental aspects of their life.

Maintenance

Furthermore, maintenance in the community in and of itself was viewed as a valuable aspect of being on the CTO as a way of avoiding traumatic admissions. Participants thus did not only talk of being at home but also staying out of hospital. In this latter regard one of the participants, Sarah, suggested that the CTO should be weighted more towards keeping individuals in the community:

> Well I think it would be better if the community health team had more powers to help keep us out of hospital because … if you're brought into hospital against your will, there's a lot of panic there, there's a lot of feeling there … I don't know but from my point of view it's good for me to stay out of hospital.

For a number of participants, the CTO had come at a time when they were at a crossroads, with the hospital team deciding what level of compulsion they should be subject to. For example, Christine illustrated how when an inpatient, the decision for her future was between sending her to a secure unit or placing her on a CTO:

> I saw the doctor without Sharon [her care coordinator and AMHP]. And I says, 'I'm looking forward to being discharged.' And he says, 'Well we'll see about that.' He says, 'I'll ask Sharon to come to the meeting next week.' And Sharon were reluctant to get me discharged you know, she kept saying, 'Oh no, I'm sending her to a secure unit' because she said that all the time, 'I were going to a secure unit.' But the doctor piped up and he says, 'Christine's very well now on lithium, on this tablet and we don't see no reason why she should go to a secure unit.' Well I were smiling, you know (laughs), and then a couple of week after that I got discharged on the CTO.

Being discharged onto the CTO was therefore not always straightforward, and could involve negotiation across a surprisingly broad spectrum of options, from secure compulsion at one end, to community compulsion at the other. For participants, the possibility of the CTO gave them an opportunity to avoid being sent to more specialist 'heavy-end' services.

Similarly, for those participants who had experienced lengthy stays in hospital, getting out of hospital signified a return of hope, as Brendon describes: 'When I was in hospital I felt … I don't know, I felt condemned.' Being at home even if still feeling 'fragile', was widely perceived to be more conducive to recuperation than hospital, and the CTO was perceived by some to help with that immediate goal: 'they said I can appeal against the CTO but I never bothered. I felt it was needed to help me to recover easier living at home' (Graham).

The CTO as a barrier: accounts of ambivalence and resentment

Ambivalence could feature in those accounts; views on the CTO were not usually articulated in straightforwardly negative or positive terms. For a small number of service users, ambivalence meant having no strong feelings about the value of the CTO at all. Particularly for those individuals who expressed resigned attitudes towards control, the CTO was seen as simply another unremarkable manifestation of their treatment. Gwen for example, said: 'I've not got any feelings about it. It's there because it's there. I never looked into the ins and outs of it. I've just accepted it.' For such participants, the CTO was of no particular consequence and they saw no reason to actively engage with it. However, ambivalence in terms of mixed views was quite common, and there were participants who displayed some degree of resentment towards the CTO. Again, as with more positive conceptualisations of CTOs, strong connections can be made to participant self-conception, particularly in relation to hopes of recovery and 'normality', and the framing of mental distress and how it is treated.

'Anti-purposes'

For those who were ambivalent ranging to negative about the CTO, it took the form of a coercive 'anti-purpose' for them, blocking or disrupting their attempts at accessing provision, achieving recovery, maintaining stability and taking control of their lives. The Damoclean sense that the CTO was 'hanging over' them was described as being difficult to deal with, as Sheila suggests: 'life would be so much better. So much more freedom and getting rid of this horrible heavy weight of waking up every morning and thinking "I'm on the CTO".' Sheila's view of the CTO was strongly grounded in her experiences of services over the years and her rejection of a biomedical model of mental illness. She had been on and off a CTO since their introduction, and displayed real anger and distress towards it. In this regard, the CTO could be seen as being iatrogenic, as Sarah describes: 'lots of decisions get made out of my control and it causes other mental health problems, the fact that my life is out of my control'. Ambivalence about the CTO could therefore be complex; for example Christine, as described earlier, appreciated the way the recall to hospital mechanism of the CTO would be activated to protect her if necessary, but at the same time expressed a consistent fear that recall would be used even if it wasn't necessary, meaning she felt she was always under scrutiny.

Indeed, ambivalence often arose in response to participants feeling that the purposes of the CTO were in tension with their long-term aims. Individuals could struggle to reconcile where they were with where they wanted to be. For instance, Michael stated:

> I could relapse so I'm quite happy with the way it is, but I do find it a bit of a burden because I do want to go to university to study and they said under the CTO they'd still need to visit me and give me injections. I want to live a normal life and be able to work and study but the doctors said stress is a major issue.

At the heart of Michael's ambivalence about the CTO was a struggle with how he saw himself; on the one hand, he felt strongly that the CTO provided him with control over his actions that had been lacking; on the other, he felt that it hampered his plans for the future. For many, a sustained period of wellness could shift their view of what was necessary to keep them well. Being told that they had a chronic and recurring condition did not always extinguish hope for participants that they would one day have a full clinical recovery and become medication-free. Michael encapsulated this when asked about his future: 'I have to take medication for the rest of my life probably. I hope though that I'll make a recovery of some sort miraculously and then I wouldn't have to take medication anymore.' In recovery terms then, coming off the CTO could be seen as the point at which progress could be made, as Simon states when asked if it was significant to him when he came off the CTO: 'it was actually, so I can move on and go in the army, it was the next step to doing that'. In both Michael's and Simon's accounts we can see that the CTO may be viewed as antithetical to dreams of 'normality'.

Perhaps unsurprisingly, such discussions were often associated with participants' views on the stigma attached to their status in society. Craig framed his diagnosis in terms of punishment, stating: 'I mean the stigma of being labelled mentally ill, once you're labelled nobody believes a word you say. Once they label you, that's it, you're mentally ill and you always will be.' This sense of having their personhood devalued and pathologised resonated in the majority of participants' experiences of discrimination and harassment. While participants who viewed the CTO in a more positive light felt that it contained and over time diminished stigma, for others the CTO enhanced the 'outsider' status they already keenly felt. How participants constituted their pathway towards 'normality' was therefore central to how they viewed the CTO.

Cross-purposes

Resentment about the CTO could also be related to feeling at cross-purposes with professionals. As discussed later, compliance with medication was viewed by all practitioners as the primary aim of the CTO and could be seen not only as a means to an end but as an end in itself. This was unsurprising, given that CTOs provide a framework for treatment in the community, and 'treatment' although defined very broadly, tends to be viewed in medical terms. However, for service users it could be a cause of tension if first, they wanted the focus of the CTO to be on secondary goals, and second if they believed that practitioners disregarded ways to achieve those secondary goals that were not necessarily about medication, such as social and psychological support. A concern raised when CTOs were first introduced was that they might lead to further restriction of treatment options and certainly service users have expressed resentment at the focus within CTOs on medication (Brophy and Ring, 2004). This was a concern shared by some participants, as Sarah summed up when she stated, 'if the purpose of the CTO is to keep you out of hospital then I'm all for it, but it does seem to come down to medication which over the years I've sort of gone against'. Indeed, medication compliance in and of itself did not strongly feature when service users talked about their own aims for the CTO.

Contrary to participants who saw practitioners as trusted allies, those who manifestly disagreed with the CTO viewed it solely as a mechanism for coercion. Patrick gave an account of how agreeing to the CTO was an additional barrier to surmount before discharge from hospital could become possible: 'They kind of forced me to do it. They said, "look you're not getting discharged unless you get on the CTO". So, I was between a rock and a hard place.' It was a common theme that the CTO served professional interests, in that it allowed for defensive decision-making. Practitioners were viewed as using the CTO as a way of managing risk to their reputation. An associated, perceived purpose was to enable surveillance, or as Andrew noted, 'just so they can keep an eye on me, so I can't operate'. Craig was perhaps the most vocal participant about having his rights denied through the CTO:

> Nobody has written that my life or anybody else's was in danger, you don't need more than that. I think it's highly unfair, there's no choice. You should have choice over your own health. If you've never hurt

> anybody else there's no justification for you to be medicated against your will.

Potential aims of the CTO were also explained in more systemic, abstract ways. Irene believed that she was put on the CTO because: 'they have a procedure … and instead of me feeling that I'm taken as an individual I'm treated like the run of the mill'. The CTO was viewed as a de-individualised and routinised occurrence. Similarly, resources were raised as a factor, driven at a macro policy level. Patrick reflected on this: 'I think it's a much used thing now … I suppose it costs a lot of money to keep a person in the hospital. I'm sure it's cost driven.'

Coming to a view on CTOs: practitioner perspectives

Similarly to service users, practitioners expressed scepticism as to what they saw as the aims policy makers had for CTOs, which they did not see as aligned necessarily with their perspectives. Accordingly, we start this section with practitioners' views on the framing of CTO policy, before we move onto a discussion of practice beliefs and practitioners' ethical 'weighing up' of CTOs.

Policy and practice

Although many practitioners thought that CTOs were beneficial, there was still a gap between how they thought about the purposes of the CTO, and their introduction as a policy. Practitioners were particularly critical of how CTOs had been presented in regards to risk and public safety, while at the same time acknowledging their role in risk management. Policy makers emphasis on risk was believed by practitioners to be influenced by public opinion, as a psychiatrist put it:

> I'd like to think that somebody thought that there was a group of patients who deserved a better deal, but I think I'm realistic and old enough to realise that actually one of the policy drivers behind that was this idea that there were homicidal maniacs who were being lost to services, and they needed a framework to contain them.

There was also a widely held view that policy makers did both service users and practitioners a disservice in how they 'sold' CTOs. Furthermore, and similarly to other areas of policy and practice where risk is at the forefront, practitioners felt that policy makers did not account for the limitations of risk management in how they represented CTOs (Stanford et al, 2017). Hence, practitioners generally saw at least some value in the CTO, but this did not necessarily align with its presentation by policy makers as a panacea to longstanding problems in community care.

In contrast to the broadly therapeutic reasoning practitioners articulated, there was a widespread belief that policy reasoning for CTOs was also premised on reducing resources. Consequently, cuts to services, ongoing staffing constraints and restructuring in community teams figured in practitioner concerns about CTOs. Resource management was here understood as not only keeping people in the community but also using the CTO to discharge from hospital more quickly in the first place. Resource management was connected to 'surface' practice (Howe, 1996), in that it was believed that community compulsion might lessen the need for 'deep', potentially more resource-intensive work with service users. As one AMHP commented in relation to 'typical' CTO cases:

> You have psychosis, you're difficult to engage, you've had this number of admissions, therefore CTO for you, and actually all that involves is maybe that you get your depot every fortnight, it's going to keep you to a level of wellbeing where you're not putting yourself or others at risk, but maybe that's all people are going to get.

While CTOs were viewed critically as part of this shift to residualised services, they were also seen as a pragmatic way of supporting service users in such a climate: 'if it was an ideal world we would possibly be able to manage people in a different way. We haven't got those resources, and we have to think about the best ways of managing people without them' (Care coordinator).

In contrast to concerns that CTOs would lead to restricted care, this pragmatic view was premised on the basis that CTOs might channel resources to those who were deemed to need the most support, due to the obligations CTOs placed on services.

Practice beliefs and the CTO

Practitioner views on the significance CTOs might have on their practice had an ethical dimension, related to what 'kind' of practice they valued. When practitioners talked about the ethics of the CTO, they broadly considered what constituted ethical practice, and also the ethical implications of CTOs for the individuals they worked with. Taking ethical practice first, practitioners discussed CTOs in relation to what they thought was 'good practice' within an Assertive Outreach Team (AOT). Assertive Outreach is premised on working with individuals in their environment, meeting frequently over a sustained period of time and using a needs-focused approach (Graley-Wetherell and Morgan, 2001). Consequently, Assertive Outreach work has a particular ethos and focus which practitioners drew upon, specifically in relation to how they defined 'skilled' work; the difference between 'assertive' and 'coercive' engagement; and the difference between tailoring services to individuals rather than individuals to services. Respondents emphasised relational engagement:

> assertive means … without necessarily being coercive. Rather than blaming the individual, it's about what services can do to engage. So we're finding what we've got in common with patients, working with that, and finding what it is that they want, what's going to be the currency that engages them. (Psychiatrist)

Within this approach, 'skilled' work was defined in relational terms:

> We always try and use interpersonal skills, use therapeutic risk taking … I think we have a way of being able to encourage people to do the right thing. Not always, but a lot of the time … it's not any special powers that we've got, it's just because we know people so well. (Care coordinator)

Alongside this, practitioners talked about being used to working with a high level of risk and 'crisis' in Assertive Outreach work, which meant they had become accustomed to working with incremental change and handling uncertainty when making decisions in complex situations. In contrast, many practitioners saw CTO practice as a 'quick fix' with little need for theorising, understanding or relating. Within this context, one psychiatrist who was very 'pro-CTO' still worried that CTOs 'can be deskilling for the team, because it can make us lazy, we don't have to try and engage or we're less creative about how we try'. In this sense, it may be that CTOs have the potential to change practice configurations as well as service user experience, with more of an emphasis on 'surface' level practice emphasising legal leverage. It is worth noting that practitioners viewed such practice changes via the CTO as potentially detrimental to them personally as well as service users, in that some felt their work would become less rich, complex and interesting as a result.

An ethical balancing act

Despite practitioners' qualms about the possible effects of CTOs on practice, none of them expressed an outright negative attitude towards CTOs. Instead, and as with service users, practitioner perspectives on CTOs ranged across a spectrum. How they felt about CTOs was very much grounded in practice and tailored to individual cases. Consequently, practitioners took a 'balancing act' approach, weighing up the pros and cons of CTOs for each service user in ethical terms and taking a consequentialist position on the implications of their use. Sometimes, practitioners did not feel they had the 'answer' as to whether CTOs were harmful or helpful, as this care coordinator explained:

> If we look at outcomes we may well say it's of benefit, but if we look at human rights you might say this person should have the same right as myself to choose not to accept services. Or does the CTO mean that people have more human rights because if they're unwell it means that we have more of a responsibility to them? … the jury's out.

Concerns about unnecessary coercion and the reduction of choice and autonomy for service users were expressed by many of the practitioners, particularly in regards to CTO conditions on medication, where it was felt CTOs could lead to side-effects being ignored and service users not being given the opportunity to try a different medication regime. On this basis, practitioners referred to the dual dominant discourses of recovery/choice and risk/control in mental health policy and the 'mixed messages' they could engender:

> It's really difficult to … say 'I want you to have control, I want you to recover at your pace, I want you to set your goals … oh and by the way, if you don't stick to these conditions, we're going to whip you back into hospital, you're going to stay on this medication, you can't have a choice in what you take'. It just feels … a bit odd. (Care coordinator)

Relatedly, it was felt that the short-term gains of the CTO in managing engagement could undermine the potential for lasting change: 'If you can work with somebody and help them to understand their needs … to stay well, that becomes a much more powerful protector in the long term than the coercive, "you have to take this because the law says you have to take it"' (Care coordinator). In a similar sense, some practitioners talked in terms of using their knowledge of individual service users and how they responded to intervention in order to weigh up whether the potential damage to engagement and the therapeutic relationship the CTO could cause was worth it: 'The dynamics of the CTO for some people … they don't see us as people who are working with them, often they see us as people who are working against them which makes a big difference' (Care coordinator).

If practitioners felt that engagement could be managed without the CTO, they could also question its usefulness: 'Sometimes I question the CTO because mine and Andrew's relationship is reasonably strong that I think that he would still engage with me, there would still be hiccups with appointments, you know but … sometimes you question whether or not it works or not' (Care coordinator).

Deciding whether the benefits of CTOs outweighed such ethical difficulties was talked about by practitioners in terms of best interests and risk. In relation to best interests, and contrary to the previously discussed perspective, some practitioners took the view that CTOs meant 'short term pain for long term gain', in that they could help service users reach a point of stability: 'We want to work with people rather than against them, but sometimes … you're almost saying "okay well there are two opinions here, yours and mine but we'll go with mine". But just keep in the back of your mind that this is for the greater good' (Manager).

In regards to risk, the majority of practitioners felt that they could justify the CTO when more 'gentle' approaches would not be feasible and also in utilitarian terms for the wider benefit of society: 'As much as we are about helping vulnerable people and social justice and all that good stuff, we're also about protecting the public from some people that are potentially quite dangerous, but that's hidden away, isn't it?' (Care coordinator).

Where practitioners placed themselves ethically in relation to CTOs affected whether they felt the CTO should only be used when absolutely necessary for tightly defined reasons, or for a wide range of circumstances and people. If practitioners took the view that CTOs had the potential to cause harm to the service user, and/or they thought in the majority of cases positive outcomes could be achieved by less coercive means, they tended to see it as a 'last resort'. For these practitioners, CTOs were believed to hold a great deal of power and not to be used lightly:

> We're selective because we reserve it for when we think it's really needed, rather than for when it might be helpful. As soon as we get somebody on a CTO, we're always aiming to get them off it as quickly as possible. Because there's a terrible danger of using it purely because you can and you've got that power and you can use that power then to affect somebody's life.

In contrast, for those practitioners who did not feel the CTO would have much of a negative effect, CTOs were seen as a tool to be used proactively, preventatively and often:

> At the time when they first started to be talked about, I think very quickly you were thinking 'oh that would be great for Mr X or Mrs Z'. And the first lady I put on … and straightaway I thought that would be perfect for this lady for … reducing the distress around admissions. (Care coordinator)

Such practitioners might be more likely to believe in CTO efficacy, broadly defined. In this sense, judging that CTOs are a success could have a low threshold; for some and in keeping with service user views that practitioners prioritised 'first-order' purposes, as long as medication adherence was being achieved then positive outcomes would automatically follow:

> In my view each and every CTO has worked at least to some extent. I don't think there have been any kind of big failures, because under the CTO the authority is given to us, we are able to keep them in treatment and that cannot be a bad thing. (Psychiatrist)

The purpose of the CTO – what outcomes it could achieve – is therefore interpreted positively for a range of individuals and situations.

Conclusion

The foundational narratives service users held about their experiences of mental distress and hopes for the future strongly influenced how they perceived the role of CTOs in their lives. Questions of vulnerability and strength, dependence and independence, (self) control and riskiness, and above all difference and 'normality' were central to how they interpreted the CTO. Those individuals who came to the CTO as a positive development in their life, felt the CTO met some self-perceived need that had previously not been met. Conversely, ambivalence or more clear-cut resentment could ensue when service users felt the CTO enhanced the differences between them and professionals, deepened their sense of powerlessness and lack of control, and added to the barriers they had to surmount in reaching their goals. The complexity of these narratives and the pathways service users saw to a future self led to a spectrum of ambiguity on CTOs with very few service users expressing wholly positive or negative perspectives. In turn, service users' feelings and beliefs about the purposes of the CTOs relating to provision (the CTO as enabling access to services and reciprocity or being procedurally and resource driven), risk (the CTO as supporting safety or managing institutional reputational risk), recovery (the CTO as a foundation or barrier for change) and maintenance (the CTO as a way of maintaining stability in the community or getting 'stuck' in community compulsion which reinforces stigmatisation) filtered down to how they understood and experienced it in their daily lives.

Similarly, practitioners did not approach CTOs as an abstract 'problem'; their views of the CTO and why, how and when it should or should not be used, were very much embedded within their prior practice experiences and associated beliefs and values. Their perception of the CTO and what it could offer was coloured by their beliefs regarding 'good' practice, particularly within the context of Assertive Outreach, which was aligned with skilled, complex, relational work. Practitioners therefore engaged in a form of situated ethics, carefully weighing up benefits and harms when considering the consequences of CTOs for individual service users. For some practitioners this ethical balancing act was less problematic than for others, and it is here that we can see a difference in when and for whom practitioners felt CTOs should be used. How practitioners dealt with their varying levels of ethical discomfort is in turn connected to how they formulated the purposes of the CTO.

By contrasting service user and practitioner perspectives we can see the ways that they mirror and diverge from each other. The findings presented here highlight how CTOs have been conceptualised in two relatively distinct ways by both groups. The first way relates to mutually aligned accounts of risk management and protection of various kinds. Putting CTOs to these kinds of purposes is characterised by: a consideration of the present, the CTO having immediate effects; active use of the functions of the CTO; and not requiring the exercising of self-control by service users. The second way refers to the use of CTOs as a vehicle for a staged process of maintenance, recovery and change. This can be characterised by: a consideration of the future; the CTO as enabling longer-term effects; the psychological use of the CTO to shape behaviour through boundaries; and requirements for service users to display self-control. Particularly within this latter way of thinking about CTOs there were some differences in emphases between service users and practitioners. While service users referred to recovery as a shared, interdependent endeavour between service users and services, practitioners gave more weight to the CTO developing service users' autonomy and responsibility. It should be noted, however, that the principle of reciprocity was referred to by practitioners as well as service users; there was a sense that the CTO should provide a *quid pro quo* of some kind. The practitioner data therefore does not straightforwardly support the exclusionary/inclusionary, risk/responsibilisation policy narrative for CTOs described by policy analysts. While present in practitioner accounts, it was undercut by, or coexisted with a narrative of care and a sense of contractual obligations, which was set within the context of the current service landscape.

4

Experiencing control: how service users navigated CTOs

In this chapter, we move on from the way community treatment orders (CTOs) were thought about to how they were experienced and acted upon by service users. The process of understanding and integrating the CTO into their lives was strongly influenced by the service user-practitioner relationship, and we draw attention to how service users constructed beliefs on professional expertise and motivation. Both elements together are key to whether a trusting relationship is formed, which in turn plays a constitutive role in how service users approached the role of the CTO. At the same time, the advent of the CTO can affect this relationship, and we go on to explore what these effects might be.

In the latter part of the chapter our emphasis shifts to service user experiences of the everyday practice of the CTO, where we examine service user experiences of the CTO process and components. We start with discharge onto the CTO, before moving onto navigation of CTO conditions such as mandatory engagement with practitioners and treatment, and finally recall to hospital when mandatory conditions have been breached and/or the Responsible Clinician believes a service user needs medical treatment in hospital and there is a risk of harm to health and safety if they are not recalled. In each section, we highlight the reflexive connections between service users' overall beliefs about the CTO, their understanding of how the CTO works and their responses to it. As will become apparent, service user actions in response to the CTO were not straightforwardly channelled through the relationships they held with practitioners, and so we also explore the various ways service users demonstrate agency in relation to the CTO. In doing so, we highlight the effect the CTO can have on the individual but also the effect the individual can have on the CTO. The focus on service user experience means this chapter primarily draws upon data from service user interviews but also refers to practitioner accounts as well as observational and documentary data.

The service user–practitioner relationship

Underpinning service user sense-making on CTOs was their perception of professional knowledge and motivation in its use. Thus as we explore in this section, alongside service users' prior experiences and beliefs about self, their beliefs around professional intervention were also significant in how they approached the CTO, while perceptions of expertise fed into the development of trust. Subsequently, we turn more directly to the CTO and consider how it might affect the relationship between service users and practitioners.

What do they know? Professional expertise and the making of trust

Service users drew upon variable constructions of expertise and professional judgment when they considered the path their treatment had taken thus far. Much has been made of the breakdown of trust in authority in late modern society, where changes in forms and sources of knowledge have undermined existing hierarchies. However, the majority of participants, and in particular those who were older, could be said to inhabit a world which did not reflect this societal change. Holding a belief in professional expertise could therefore involve taking a 'leap of faith' into the unknown, as with Irene whose understanding of her medication was filtered solely through professional explanation: 'and I'm told, so I presume it's true, that they help to stabilise your mood'. Trust is in part about making a choice to be dependent on another (Brown and Calnan, 2012), and underpinning these views on expert knowledge was the sense of how individuals 'should' respond in the face of an authoritative action when they have delegated their understanding of their situation to a professional. James summed this up when explaining why he adhered to the CTO:

> And the CTO, if you're not compliant to it, you're wasting people's time. You're abusing the system. They've got you well, you're on your meds, you're on a CTO, you know it works and then, if you don't do it, you end up back in hospital. It's like, you're insulting their intelligence. They're saying, 'look, if you do this, we'll get you better', and if you don't do it, you're knocking yourself but you're knocking the system as well.

In this scenario, the individual is part of a larger system, in which they have to be responsive in the right way to guidance. The expertise of professionals here relates to beliefs about professional motivation. The thought that a professional must know what they are doing can be linked to the belief that they are acting benevolently. Glenn, for example, felt that the CTO was a positive development because: 'the mental health are there to help. They're not there to ruin my life, they're just trying to make it better.' At the other end of the spectrum were participants like Craig, who had little belief in the knowledge or motives of professionals, as he says: 'I don't know what qualifications these people get, because they don't have a clue what they're doing. I mean the brain is the most complicated thing on the planet which nobody has a clue how it works and they're just throwing drugs at you like they're Smarties.'

Participants combined their view of professionals' general expertise, with their beliefs about the knowledge practitioners had specifically about them as individuals, in order to judge the ability of practitioners to manage their situation. The extent to which participants felt practitioners *knew* them helped them to weigh up how much they trusted practitioners to predict, and intervene in, what is happening to them. James believed that when he relapsed, his care coordinator 'just saw it coming', and that with the CTO it was a case of her and the psychiatrist thinking, '"we've got James on a CTO; we know what we'll do for James; we'll get him well" and that's what it's done'. In contrast, participants who believed that professionals had approached them in an impersonal way had little faith in the power of professional prediction, as Sarah suggests when talking about her first experience of being placed on a CTO: 'because something's happened in the past, they just assume something's going to happen in the future and you know there is prejudices, there is habits of behaviour among staff just as much as there is among patients'.

When practitioners acted in ways that service users did not agree with, those participants who viewed professional knowledge and motivation favourably appeared to differentiate individual practitioners from the mental health system, or in other words, give practitioners the 'benefit of the doubt'. Nevertheless, at times it could be difficult for participants to make sense of painful experiences while at the same time holding on to an underlying trust in professionals, resulting in a kind of dissonance which participants could struggle to manage. James, who highly valued professionals' abilities and motivations, reflected back on when he was put on an injection to administer his medication for the first time: 'At the time, there was a bit of negativity towards my nurse. There wasn't a bond; there wasn't a friendship. It was like, "no, you're the nurse and you're the injection and that hurts, I don't like it and I'm tired of it".' The care coordinator's role in providing injections created a professionalised distance and conflated her as an individual with the painful intervention she administered.

The nature of the service user–practitioner relationship and the CTO

From these accounts, we can see not only that perceptions of professional motivation and expertise influenced beliefs about the CTO, but also that the CTO may have some mediating role to play in the relationship between practitioners and service users. Indeed, as we refer to in Chapter 2, one of the questions that has often been asked about CTOs is in what ways, if any, they might affect the relationship between practitioners and service users. For some participants, the CTO did not particularly affect their pre-existing feelings – whether positive or negative – towards practitioners. For others, the CTO appeared to erode the therapeutic compact they held with practitioners, by introducing a new focus for conflict and enhancing the differences in the views they held on treatment, support and future goals. Statutory obligations under the CTO could encroach on the relationship and reinforce any distrust that already existed; for example, Sheila felt strongly that the presence of the CTO meant her care coordinator was *not on my side* due to the role she took in supporting the continuation of the CTO at review meetings and appeals. Respondents reported that the compulsory nature of the CTO acted as a barrier in forming the collaborative relationship with professionals that they wished to have.

Conversely, the CTO could signify a welcome shift in the relationship service users had with practitioners. Participants did not just view the CTO as a depersonalised safety net. It was also the relational aspects of the CTO that made participants feel secure and 'taken care of', as Glenn explains: 'If I become unwell with my mental health I'll get looked after won't I … People will help me sort it out rather than me trying to do it myself and make a mess of it.' A significant element in keeping relationships and regular engagement working within the CTO framework was finding a point of agreement, however small. Practical help with day-to-day living could support service users to find a way through the CTO. For many of the participants, their care coordinator was valued as a person who they could talk to, who was consistent and available, who would help them navigate various systems and who would advocate for them with other professionals. As Brendon stated when asked if he would stay engaged with services if his CTO was ended: 'I think I would yes, because I feel like my care coordinator is a friend now, you know what I mean, whereas before I didn't.'

Service users' accounts of CTO interactions included references to professionals relating to them in both 'depth/care' terms (relationship and personhood) as well as 'surface/control' terms (compliance and risk). A focus on broader support rather than solely on medication and two-way rather than didactic communication were the two central aspects which influenced service user's views of both practitioners and CTOs. As we shall see when we turn to practitioner accounts, integrating surface and depth practice could be difficult, such as judging when and how to refer to CTOs in interaction with service users, and how to use the CTO as a tool in facilitating compliance through reminder and explanation. At different points in the CTO, the socio-legal nature of practice (McGregor and Dolan, 2021) was more apparent and it is clear that practitioner approaches were integral to how service users experienced the central legal components of the CTO.

Service users' experiences of discharge from hospital onto the CTO

Service users' understanding of the CTO in legal terms, specifically what it allowed them to do or not to do, constituted the foundation for how they engaged with its boundaries. A sense of procedural justice (Lessard-Deschênes, Pariseau-Legault and Goulet, 2024) was significant in how service users related to the control placed on them by CTOs. Understanding and involvement in decision-making go hand in hand; how much service users felt able to have a voice and be listened to in the early stages of the CTO also influenced their attitude towards and subsequent engagement with the CTO.

Early understanding and involvement in the decision-making process

The initial explanation given by professionals was the starting point for most of the service users when beginning the process of understanding the CTO. Participants gave varied accounts of how and what they were told when preparing for discharge from hospital onto the CTO. Observations of hospital discharge meetings reflected this variability, with a wide range of practices observed. For example, in Julie's discharge meeting, the paperwork was completed very quickly and Julie and her partner were invited in once the decision to use a CTO had been made. The psychiatrist addressed Julie three times about her *conditions of discharge* but did not explain what this term meant or ask if she understood. The CTO was only briefly mentioned at the end of the meeting, with 'when you get discharged we will put you on something called a community treatment order' being the sum of explanation provided. Professionals using jargon could make understanding difficult as Irene describes: 'I would have liked it explained on a very ordinary level so that I could understand it.' As well as being clear, having the time to think and digest the information and being able to ask questions were viewed as important aspects of being positively discharged onto the CTO.

Participant understanding in the early stages also affected involvement in initial decision-making. Participants variously described feeling involved or marginalised, listened to or ignored, and talked to or with by professionals during decision-making. Practice guidance (Department of Health, 2015) suggests that decisions should be collaborative, even if not consensual. In reality it was more common for individuals to be informed but not involved. It should also be noted that although all individuals on a CTO are entitled to support from an Independent Mental Health Advocate (IMHA) who can help them understand and navigate decision-making points, none of the service users in the study had used them. Participants explained this in some cases as being down to inherent suspicion of any professional who was thought to be 'part of the system', or because they felt able to speak for themselves, or because they were not aware of this provision. Indeed, only one participant, Glenn, felt that he had played a relatively equal role along with professionals in the decision to use the CTO, as he states here when asked about the process of his discharge from hospital:

Interviewer:	Do you know why they started talking about the CTO at that early stage?
Glenn:	Because I wanted to … It was my decision. It wasn't mine … obviously it can't be my decision but it was me that wanted to be on it

Given that when being discharged from hospital, individuals tend to focus on returning home, the initial explanation of the CTO by practitioners could also lack meaning for participants. As one practitioner pointed out to me after a discharge meeting: 'They're getting off the ward so you could say, "you have to wear your underpants over your trousers" and they would agree to it.' All participants reported being given leaflets on the CTO but these did not appear to be a particularly effective way for them to gain understanding of the CTO, as the majority reported not reading them. The experience of 'just signing' was common among participants, but this did not necessarily reflect a lack of interest in what the CTO would mean for them. Participant understanding of explanations tended to reflect their feelings more generally regarding compulsion and coercion. Michael felt powerless in the face of authority, believing that the implementation of the CTO was a judicial rather than clinical decision: 'It's a compulsory law order, it's signed by the law courts of some sort and it's done by the law without my rights.'

Changes in service user understanding of the CTO over time

More in-depth discussion could be helpful both for the service user and for the progress of the CTO, particularly in mitigating coercion and encouraging acceptance (Canvin, Bartlett and Pinfold, 2002). In some ways the CTO is best seen as a process rather than an event, and it is not always helpful to constitute individuals' feelings about it in binary or 'fixed' form. While some service users appeared to maintain a consistent stance towards the CTO throughout, others did not. Although those who were more positive about the CTO from the start tended to stay positive, some participants who had started from a negative viewpoint shifted over time to a positive perspective. This shift was often due to practitioner influence on service user understanding of what the CTO actually entailed, which affected service user ability to form purposive meaning for the CTO.

Those participants who started out feeling negative about the CTO before changing their view reported feeling initially quite anxious about how restrictive the CTO would be. For example, Patrick thought at first that 'it was quite a drastic thing you know, like house arrest'. As an AMHP described, the semantics of the name 'community treatment order' did not help counter punitive impressions:

> There is a problem with the naming of it, because a community treatment order actually sounds like it is a legal order, it's like a probation order you know? So I think there's an immediate assumption by the patient that this is something that they have to do or be punished for.

Turning points for participants whose view of the CTO had shifted from negative to positive, partly related to the CTO being 'reframed' in a more beneficial, less restrictive light, which chimed with their sense of self, identity and place in the world. Explanation which went beyond legalistic description of what the CTO meant could help participants understand it more. A significant event for Nick was a conversation with the community psychiatrist following discharge from hospital where the aim of the CTO was described as to keep him well, which was a different approach than the hospital psychiatrist had taken, which was to tell him the CTO was being used because he was considered, in Nick's terms, 'a danger'. His view changed:

> I thought well I might as well just go to jail. But then I had time to think about it and I thought, well, he's explained why I'm on it and then all … everything just come to us, and you're not going to get as bad as what you were.

Even though Nick felt he had behaved unacceptably in the past, he still found it difficult to be described in such a way, and having the CTO explained in 'softer' terms helped him to accept it.

How service users felt they had been treated by professionals during the decision-making process was also significant in changing attitudes. Sarah felt that she had been 'talked to' in a rather dictatorial, inflexible way by the hospital psychiatrist when placed on her first CTO: 'The doctor who put me on the CTO, I'm very wary of him because he didn't seem to take into account anything I said. He seemed to sit there and already have an idea of what he was going to do and he was going to do it regardless.' This CTO was an especially coercive experience for her, as the conditions meant she was made to take medication that she had a particularly adverse reaction to: 'I begged them not to, I didn't really want it at all, the side effects were really bad.' The way this decision was made – being informed after the fact, not allowing her input and prescribing medication which she hated due to the side-effects – affected Sarah's ongoing view on the CTO.

In contrast, when Sarah was placed on a CTO a second time, the discussion was more open: 'It was still out of my control but I was more agreeable to it.' Additionally, her concerns about medication were listened to and she was given options. This CTO was based on a 'mutuality of accounts' (O'Neill, 1995) developed through ongoing explanation, discussion and reassurance about what the CTO would mean. This interplay between contextual experiences and the way in which the CTO was explained and negotiated by practitioners in the present was a significant aspect of the pathway a CTO might take. Hence even though there were disagreements, a joint recovery-focused aim of creating stability was emphasised, which made the CTO acceptable to her. In Sarah's experience of two CTOs it is evident that being informed and involved in decisions made a significant difference to her stance.

However, it should also be noted that, for some, acceptance of CTOs could be despite practitioners not because of them. Becoming accepting of the CTO generally involved some movement to shape the CTO in a way which was coherent with participants' understanding of its purpose in their life; active engagement could shape this meaning-making. James illustrated this iterative process:

Interviewer:	And that's how the CTO was explained to you at the time?
James:	Well, not–, that's how I explain it; that's how I took it on; that's how I understood it. I started formulating my own ideas about what a CTO meant and what it would do for you.
Interviewer:	Right. Okay. So to make it make sense to you.
James:	Yes. That's how I got round it.

The telling phrase here of 'getting round' the CTO denotes some activity on James' part. James shaped the CTO by taking 'ownership'. At his care review, the psychiatrist wondered whether the CTO was a 'security blanket' for James, and James after a long pause, carefully responded: 'it's like a ring (pointing to his finger). I've made a promise and it was a choice for me to do that.' James did not see the CTO as being 'done' to him, and he demonstrated considerable agency in making the reality of the CTO fit with his conception of it, which revolved around him taking responsibility for his recovery as part of a trusting partnership with professionals.

The key issue for James had been feeling that he lacked control over his medication under the CTO. He particularly disliked it being administered by his care coordinator. In response he made a unilateral decision to have his medication given via his GP surgery instead. An element of the CTO which practitioners view as intrinsic – compelled medication – was viewed very differently by James as being in opposition to how he saw the purpose of the CTO. He explained:

> I felt that part of my Community Treatment Order and part of my injections were in conflict because I didn't feel in control of my injections … It was in the hands of the nurses here and the doctors here and I thought, well, that's not fair because my CTO says I've got to be responsible; I've got to be in charge and then, when … they [the GP] started doing it, I settled down a bit better.

James' resolution of the tension between his perception of the CTO and how it was practised also highlights the importance of meaningful medication choice within the CTO framework. For James, making this choice was a recovery-orientated step which supported him 'settling down' and achieving stability. In this sense, acceptance entailed taking some control over the process, thus shifting negative views.

Understanding the CTO process: conditions

We now move on to consider service users' understanding of the day to day mechanics of the CTO, specifically in relation to their understanding of CTO conditions. We begin with an overview of how service users understood (or misunderstood) their conditions with (or without) the help of practitioners before exploring how service users negotiated the most significant condition for many of them – the requirement to take medication.

Beliefs about conditions

Some participants expressed significant ambiguity about what was expected of them under the CTO and either could not say what their conditions were, or held beliefs about their conditions which were not the case. A broad view of what conditions entailed – particularly around drug and alcohol use – was relatively common among participants and seemed to reflect a belief that the CTO was not just focused on their engagement with services and medication but on other aspects of their life and behaviour as well. Despite these beliefs, case file analysis demonstrated that although conditions might include, for example, that individuals see a dual diagnosis worker, none of the participants in the study had specific conditions on abstinence or reduction in substance use as part of their current CTO. Such ambiguity about expectations of behaviour meant that service users could feel that they had to watch everything they did, giving the CTO a sense of pervasiveness, as with Ian who admitted: 'actually I don't even have a clue what I've got to do but I do everything right in here, go for my medication, don't sleep out, don't take drugs, keep away from women (laughs)'.

The perceived encroachment of the CTO into areas beyond its actual legal remit also manifested in a physical and literal sense in the belief that the CTO constrained movements via coercive means. Sheila, for example, held the belief that she would not be allowed to go on holiday, despite her care coordinator explaining this was not the case. As a logical follow-on, 'escaping' from the CTO could be viewed as quite a radical step, which Craig described here when asked what he understood by travel restrictions: 'Because you're breaking the CTO [by moving], and you're not technically allowed. But no one can stop you going to Scotland, but if you wanted to emigrate for real you break everything don't you.'

It appears then that the power of the CTO could lie equally with the psychological impact it had on service users as much as how it actually affected their lives. However, as with the CTO as a whole, practitioners could at times reshape service users' interpretation of the 'workings' of the CTO. Revisiting the CTO at different points with service users could help develop shared viewpoints. Glenn, for example, had been actively involved in working out what he would and would not have to do on the CTO:

> We sat down and did a lot of talking about it. Because you want this person to comply you see, so there could then be a split second where I disappear and I'm not taking my meds and I'll go stop in somebody's house say in London or something. I'll go live there. You've got to sit down with them and make sure it's a mutual understanding and agreement.

This sort of communicative intervention was not always what participants experienced, however. This was particularly the case with conditions around drug and alcohol use, where service user ambiguity around such conditions could be reinforced by practitioners. On the one hand, practitioners expressed the view that the conditions of the CTO had to be clearly understood because it was unethical to expect an individual to adhere to boundaries otherwise. Having the capacity to understand what the CTO means is not part of the criteria for its use in England. Nevertheless, if service users demonstrated little or no ability to understand conditions, the CTO was generally seen as not viable by practitioners. On the other hand, not being entirely clear about conditions could be seen as part of making the CTO work for some practitioners, in terms of reinforcing the power of the CTO and mediating certain kinds of behaviour, as this Approved Mental Health Professional (AMHP) describes:

> I suspect patients are not being told in very clear straightforward terms that while these are conditions, if you breach these conditions,

> it will actually have no effect in terms of you being recalled back into hospital. If you explain that, then it weakens the order and it weakens the boundaries.

Certainly, observation of interactions between practitioners and service users turned up examples of obfuscation by omission, as shown here in a home visit following the renewal of a CTO:

Care coordinator:	So this is about why you're on a CTO, what happens when you're on a CTO, what happens if you don't keep to the conditions. Though I have to say you don't have many conditions. So can you tell me what they are?
Stuart:	Keep taking medication, not smoking cannabis, not drinking heavily and seeing you.
Care coordinator:	And do you know what happens when you don't keep to them?

The practitioner did not go on to explain to Stuart that his conditions did not make any reference to drug or alcohol use. When Stuart was asked later what his conditions were, he replied: 'no overly excessive alcohol drinking, no weed and that's about it'. In this sense, service user understanding and subsequent level of certainty about conditions and what would happen if they were broken, was dependent to a certain extent on how definite, clear and honest practitioners were about the process.

Medication and consent

One condition that all participants were clear about was compliance with medication. As we have seen, there could be many complex and interlinking reasons why individuals did or did not adhere to medication, relating to both internal and external drivers. For some participants, however, internal drivers to take medication were not as important as the external factors which compelled them to adhere to medication regimes, regardless of how they felt about it.

As Brendan explains, 'the very strict rule of being on a Section and a CTO is that you conform and comply with medication'. For all but one of the participants this meant medication being administered with a depot injection rather than taking oral medication of their own accord. For a very few participants, such an imposition of control by professionals over medication administration was accepted, as they did not feel able to maintain medication adherence by themselves. However, oral medication was the preferable choice for most participants and medication via injection was the condition that most encapsulated the loss of control the CTO can mean for individuals, as Sarah makes clear:

> I think it's only the injections that make it more control … because there's times in the past when I've hid the tablet … and spit it out afterwards, there's loads of times when I haven't taken medication. So the injection is the only way that the staff know that the patients get the medication.

Being on a CTO might be preferable to a long admission in hospital, but one of the potential consequences of long-term compulsion in the community for individuals like Sarah was the continuing loss of self-efficacy over the path their treatment might take.

This raises a broader point about the nature of consent. Legally, individuals can only be given treatment in the community if they consent to that treatment (except where capacity is an issue). In practice this was much less clear-cut and indicative of the ambiguous nature of the term 'consent'. Irene understood the medication condition for her CTO as highly coercive:

> I was being forced to take medication. I understood that … I had no say in it. So I thought that wherever I was on injections I would be on a community treatment order, whereas if we mutually agreed on a different strategy that would mean I would be off the community treatment order.

Irene did not appear to be aware that medication could not be 'forced' on her in the community. Even so, although the psychiatrists observed in discussion with service users at reviews tended to be resistant to requests for changes to oral medication, they were more open to trialling reductions in medication, or trying different kinds of medication. Christine was given the choice to try lithium for the first time by the hospital psychiatrist, and as it worked for her it was written into her conditions with her agreement. This supported her belief that ongoing decisions about her medication were a joint endeavour: 'If it needs changing, we'll cross that bridge when we come to it.' It appeared, then, to make a difference to the service user experience if practitioners elicited service users' views on medication and made clear that some negotiation on medication conditions could be possible from the outset.

Understanding the CTO process: recall

Medication was the most tangible manifestation of coercion under the CTO. However, when participants talked about the CTO as a coercive force in their lives, it was in psychological as well as experiential terms. Participants who were ambivalent or negative about the CTO were especially fearful of 'quick and easy' recalls to hospital even if they had not experienced recall while on the CTO. Holding a firm belief that they could be recalled at any time, but at the same time not knowing what would cause them to be recalled, caused participants considerable anxiety. Hence, the coercive impact of the CTO was not necessarily related to the active use of compulsion, but about more incorporeal effects, specifically in relation to feelings of powerlessness and loss of control over what *might* occur.

Beliefs about recall

If participants believed that they could be recalled at any time regardless of their mental state, then this would mean they also believed it could happen for no discernible reason. Patrick's belief that the recall process could be evoked at the whim of practitioners was grounded in his understanding that he could be taken back to hospital on ill-defined grounds: 'I don't really understand the CTO … I know if I do anything they think is wrong I'm straight back in there. I can't afford to take chances like that.' Such fear could also be dependent on previous experiences of hospitalisation, as illustrated by a conversation with a care coordinator about a recall he had just instigated:

Care coordinator:	Well Bob has been picked up by the police
Me:	Was he at home?
Care coordinator:	He must have just got the recall letter because he rang up sounding absolutely terrified saying he'd be in until 1 pm, but no one was here to take his phone call.
Me:	Why do you think he was so frightened?
Care coordinator:	He's been in hospital five or six years, he doesn't want to go back in. I don't think he understands that it's only recall for treatment. I think he thinks he'll be taken in for another five or six years.

Extreme anxiety could lead to avoidance tactics; when recall did occur, service users who were particularly anxious sometimes absconded. Craig disappeared for a number of days when he was issued with a recall and told practitioners he would 'rather commit suicide than go back to hospital' (Case note).

Conversely, participants who were more positive about the CTO expressed an optimistic view of the recall process, which related back to their underlying sense of trust in practitioners. Gwen, who perhaps had the most 'passive' stance towards the CTO out of all the participants, felt that with recall: 'You'd have to listen to them because they're professionals. So, I would be quite happy to go back again.' Similarly, Brendon held the belief that he would not be recalled unless it was deemed absolutely necessary: 'But I don't really see any reasons why I would get recalled back to hospital so it's hard to really tell you how I would feel … But if I was, there would have to be a good, solid, strong reason behind it.' For Brendon, the aim of the CTO was to keep him out of hospital and he trusted practitioners to keep to that aim, so the recall part of the CTO held the least personal relevance for him. Brendon's account highlights that the key mechanism of the CTO – recall – which gives the CTO structure and which is aimed at ensuring behavioural compliance, may not be of particular importance to individuals who accept the CTO. The very value of the CTO for practitioners and service users alike could lie in not putting it to use.

However, recall could also be seen by service users as one of the main benefits of the CTO in ensuring quick treatment. Such participants tended to express the view that recall had a particular remit. Recall is limited to a 72-hour period, and a particularly common belief was that participants believed recall was intended to stabilise the situation before a quick discharge back into the community. None of these participants considered that recall might lead to a longer stay in hospital through the CTO being revoked, as Glenn explains: 'it's not going to be forever is it? It's not as though I'm going to spend another three and a half years in hospital, it just remind you a bit … It's just to get everything sorted out and get back out again.' Consequently, participants generally varied between those who thought they would only be recalled if they started to become very psychotic, as with Stuart who said to be recalled he would have to: 'think the TV were watching me again, or saying something to the staff, like if I started talking psychobabbly bullshit', and those who believed that they would be recalled at any time if they did not 'stick to the rules'.

Interaction and action in the recall process

Such beliefs were mediated to a certain extent by practitioner description of what would happen during recall. Observations suggested that practitioners tended to try and manage service user anxiety with a mixture of levity and reassurance, as seen at Christine's review:

AMHP:	So does the CTO make any difference to you?
Christine:	Oh yeah, I'd be much freer without it. I wouldn't be looking over my shoulder all the time.
AMHP:	Do you understand the CTO doesn't make any difference to if you come back into hospital? It's only if your mental health deteriorates that you will have to

	come back in. We can't just come and go [clicks fingers], you're in.
Christine:	Yeah, yeah … I'd just feel better if it was lifted
Psychiatrist:	Why is that Christine?
Christine:	Because I've always got that fear about someone banging on the door.

This exchange was typical of interactions observed, where practitioners would reassure service users that the CTO should act like an 'insurance policy', in that recall would not be used unless needed. It should be noted, however, that practitioners themselves did not always have a clear handle on when to use recall or not. Indeed the actual use of recall did not always match formal explanations. Hence, service users' responses to practitioner reassurance were variable, and again, pre-existing trust in practitioners and the system played a large part in how they approached recall. In Christine's case, she had experienced recall before and so reassurance did not change her fear of the possibility of recall. At the other end of the spectrum, in order to try and instigate compliance, practitioners could use the threat of recall even if it were not likely to occur. For example, Andrew rarely came to reviews with his psychiatrist but would meet with his care coordinator and take his medication. At the review, the psychiatrist pointed out:

> The other thing about your order is that you need to see a psychiatrist, and you haven't seen me have you? You've seen me once since you left hospital. Now if you're not keeping to your conditions, that means I would have to see if you have to be back in hospital.

Even though the belief that recall would happen if conditions were broken was common, the level of latitude service users displayed within that remit demonstrated subtle yet significant differences in the amount of power they felt they had in the process. Service users could know which boundaries they might and might not push; in relation to drug/alcohol use, even when individuals erroneously thought that abstention was a condition of the CTO, it seemed unlikely to stop or limit their substance use. But finding ways around the CTO could also occur in relation to medication. As stated earlier, participants understood medication conditions to be absolute, but they could also demonstrate some control over their medication intake. In this sense, a tension between choice and control underpinned service user narratives on medication. Simon described how even on the CTO he sometimes missed his appointments for medication, so that, 'the CTO doesn't affect when I get my depot. It just means that if I turn around and say "No I am not going to take it full stop", then they can section us and give us it.' Conversely, the only way other participants felt they could take some control over medication was to force the hand of professionals, as in Graham's account when he described how his medication regime was changed:

Interviewer:	So you got your medication changed recently?
Graham:	Yeah, I took myself off Risperidone and got recalled.
Interviewer:	Oh is that how it happened?
Graham:	Yes, I wanted a different tablet, different dose of medicine.

In situations where medication was not being negotiated, acts like Graham's where recall was manipulated to meet his medication needs can be seen as a way of regaining some proximal integrity.

Moreover, service users at times 'played the CTO game' in order to meet other goals, with varying success. This involved triggering recalls through non-compliance as a way of getting access to hospital for respite in the absence of other alternatives, or as an escape from social pressures. While practitioners did not always respond as service users hoped to these actions, attempts to subvert the recall process could still undermine the efficacy of the CTO by creating uncertainty for practitioners about when recall was 'truly' needed. It should be noted, however, that service users' demonstrating agency was not necessarily about taking action but could also be about *not* taking action in order to regain some sense of control over their lives. For some service users, protesting against the CTO was seen as hopeless, and passivity resulted from resignation. For others, a passive response was a way of subverting practitioners' expectations for the CTO. A few participants described how they did everything they needed to for the CTO without complaint so as to not trigger use of recall, but without opening up to practitioners or engaging in any deep sense with what practitioners wanted regarding internal change and motivation. Surface compliance and 'doing the right things' while at the same time not losing sight of their own goal (discharge from the CTO) was seen as a way of gaining control without losing integrity. Sarah described this in relation to the first CTO she was placed on:

> No I was complying, although I really didn't want to. I was very unhappy about that decision but I wasn't fighting it. I know some people try to avoid the person coming to give them the medication and all sorts of things but I wasn't doing anything to avoid it. So … because I was complying they saw no need to have the CTO, you know compulsory, so in the end they decided to take me off it.

Finally, it should be noted that outright resistance in the face of recall was also the route taken by some service users. This was certainly the case for

Craig, where the CTO prompted a breakdown in engagement with services. As his care coordinator explained:

> It completely wrecked any trust he had in mental health services and his whole focus and his whole interaction with mental health services became about the CTO rather than him recovering. It just became a personal crusade and a battle and I think that's the same with a lot of clients really.

Craig would avoid appointments and medication which in turn triggered recall, from which he would run away, thus causing a drawn-out process involving his family, mental health services and the police. In Craig's view, this was the only option he had in terms of engaging with the CTO. Although Craig's motivation in such actions was to manage his anxiety about hospital admission, a side effect was that continued recalls followed by lengthy searches for him when he went missing could cause significant strain on services.

Dawson et al (2003, 253) suggest that the CTO has the capacity to 'both advance and limit [an individual's] freedom, in different respects and at different times in their lives'. This complex and fluctuating interaction between compulsion – as characterised by the CTO – and freedom was certainly reflected in participant accounts. The CTO is a compulsory measure, but how much room for manoeuvre participants believed they had within the CTO varied, both individually and in relation to different aspects of the CTO.

Conclusion

Three main conclusions can be drawn from these findings. The *first* conclusion is related to the psychological effects CTOs could have on service users, with real-world consequences for how they lived their lives. Particularly if the view is taken that CTOs act as an 'insurance policy' – being present in the background but not used unless necessary – it can be argued that CTOs have very little concrete effect on individuals. However, this disregards the central and contested place of medication in service users' lives – especially given their varied conceptions of their mental distress – and the blurred lines of consent that CTOs could contribute towards. Furthermore, what these findings suggest is that coercion is not necessarily linked to the 'concrete' manifestations of compulsion. As demonstrated by some service users' understanding of what their conditions entailed, and when and why recall would happen, the CTO has the potential for potent and stigmatising psychological effects, causing iatrogenic feelings of shame, restriction, insecurity and anxiety. At the same time, it would be wrong to say that the psychological implications of CTOs were necessarily correlated with negative beliefs about the CTO. Attitude and understanding were interlinked and mutually reinforcing, and this was also true for those service users who had accepted the CTO as a signifier of care.

The *second* conclusion relates to the practitioner–service user relationship as a mediating factor in the CTO. Service users were not as involved as they could be with the initial stages of the CTO and this lack of involvement can influence their on-going attitude to the CTO. For those service users who were actively involved in decision-making and where time was spent explaining the CTO in terms that chimed with their sense of self and hopes for the future, feelings of coercion could be mitigated. Furthermore, it seems that when practitioners were willing to negotiate and work with service users to create a sense of mutual enterprise, the CTO could be 'reframed' in positive terms. The earlier this relational work took place, the more likely it was to have an effect. Earlier intervention as a whole could help reshape its meaning, but reassurance further down the line about specific aspects such as conditions and recall could be more variable in its effects, particularly with service users who had engrained beliefs about the CTO as a whole. It should also be acknowledged, however, that practitioners' could reinforce coercion during the course of the CTO through what they did or did not tell service users about how conditions and recall worked. It appears, then, that what supports more positive CTO experiences is not necessarily direct mitigation of the CTO itself, but the relational context it resides within. The practitioner–service user relationship did not only influence the CTO; there was a simultaneous process whereby the CTO could influence pre-existing dynamics between practitioners and service users. As noted, beliefs on practitioner expertise, motivation and the consequent level of trust service users felt towards practitioners, could trickle down into how they understood the CTO. Conversely, the presence of the CTO could magnify such beliefs about practitioners, thus engraining relationships of trust or distrust.

This leads us on to the final and *third* point – the varying ways that service users displayed agency towards the CTO. Policies such as CTOs that are based on control are often discussed rather dismissively, without taking into account the ways that individuals affected by them can respond to them or shape the path they take. However, the ways service users act and interact through the course of the CTO are central to questions of CTO 'value', both in relation to ethics and effectiveness. Despite the powerlessness expressed by some service users, they could act on the CTO in a variety of ways in order to gain a sense of control, relating to either acceptance, rejection or subversion of the CTO and its ends and means. Acceptance of the CTO involved mutual work on the part of service users and practitioners – a co-construction of a positive relationship within compulsion and a shared narrative of the aims for the CTO. However, active acceptance was not only about acting in response to practitioner instigation. It could also be a process very much led by the service user, as a way of making the practice of the CTO conform to what they saw as its purpose. Alternatively, for service users who actively resisted both any purpose for the CTO and how it was operationalised, it became a point of conflict characterised by cyclical power struggles, particularly regards adherence to CTO conditions and the use of recall. Subversion of the CTO can be seen as somewhere in between rejection and acceptance, in that it involved service users turning the CTO against itself in order to reach their own ends, which did not correlate with agency aims. All three of these approaches have been described thus far in terms of action, but service users also used more passive tactics relating to avoidance of deeper engagement in order to negotiate the CTO on their own terms. This in itself could be seen as a form of subversion. All three stances – acceptance, rejection and subversion – have implications for CTO practice and cause dilemmas for practitioners, both in terms of everyday CTO use and the shaping of discharge outcomes.

5

Enacting control: the purpose and practices of CTOs

In this chapter, we focus on the various ways practitioners enact community treatment orders (CTOs) and the practical–moral lenses they apply while doing so. In describing service users' experiences of the CTO in the last chapter, our focus was very much on their individual journey through the CTO. The focus in this chapter is more varied in covering both how control becomes realised in practice and the various factors that impinge on that process through the different phases of the CTO. Hence, while we provide the 'other side' of the story by detailing how practitioners deal with the ethical challenges of the CTO, and go about relational work within its bounds, we also weave in the influence of other contextual and systemic factors. These include the effects on CTO practice of: team and interprofessional dynamics, the relationship between inpatient and community services, the role of other agencies in the CTO process and resource issues. This context could play both a constraining and enabling role in how practitioners and service users attempted to negotiate the terms of the CTO. We also highlight how the internal logic of the CTO itself may encourage particular defensive patterns of practice which could be at odds with practitioners' views on how it 'should' be used. We end with a consideration of cases where the activation of the CTO via recall might not be possible, which raises questions about its potential limitations. In this sense, we highlight the spectrum of power present in CTOs from 'surface' practice focused on superficial compliance to 'deep' practice' focused on relational, persuasive and change-oriented work. The chapter foregrounds data from practitioner accounts, but also draws on observational and documentary data.

Putting CTOs into action: practitioners' experiences of their use

To begin, we cover the discharge process and how decisions to impose a CTO are made. There are various formal and informal actors involved in this decision-making and we elucidate how these actors engage with each other to come to the CTO, focusing particularly on the social work role of the Approved Mental Health Professional (AMHP). Subsequently, we explore how practitioners both interpret and use conditions and recall, with emphasis placed on how they negotiate practical–ethical dilemmas throughout the CTO process and attempt to fashion a mutually acceptable meaning and form of control with service users during the course of the CTO.

The practitioner perspective on discharge from hospital onto the CTO

Discharge decisions onto the CTO are relatively complex, involving a number of actors, both formal and informal. The formal decision-makers – the ones who sign off the CTO and decide its details – are the inpatient psychiatrist acting as the Responsible Clinician and the AMHP. The community team who oversee the everyday care of service users have an important informal role in decision-making. Complicating contextual factors include interaction between community and inpatient services in shared decision-making on the CTO, the systemic factors that could cause communication breakdowns between decision-makers and the potential outcomes when decisions are made unilaterally.

As highlighted previously, discharge onto the CTO could sometimes be experienced as an unplanned event by service users, and rushed discharges often meant last-minute CTOs. As secondary decision-makers who have to agree the CTO with the inpatient psychiatrist, AMHPs could find last-minute CTOs particularly difficult to manage. There could often be an expectation that they 'rubber-stamped' CTOs, particularly if they were called in to sign a CTO off on the day of discharge, as described here:

> I still think the involvement of the AMHP is quite tokenistic … just sort of a paper exercise, something to jump through. I've heard lots of AMHPs complain about that as an issue, where they've been asked to attend on the day and the CTO is pretty much signed, sealed and delivered, bar their signature.

AMHPs reported challenging this practice, asking for time prior to discharge from hospital to hold a planning meeting and to speak to the individual, their family and the professionals involved in their care. However, refusing to attend a discharge meeting to sign off a CTO last minute could be uncomfortable, especially if the service user was pushing for discharge as well. More generally, while all the AMHPs emphasised their independence and the responsibility they had to consider the CTO 'in the round', none of them recalled ever disagreeing to a CTO. This fits with the national picture where AMHPs have been shown to agree with 93 per cent of CTO requests (NHS Benchmarking and ADASS, 2018). The momentum of discharge was part of the reason why CTOs had a certain inevitability, but the broad legal criteria for CTOs also made them difficult to oppose:

> An AMHP goes in independently to look at a CTO, but often the criteria really do fit them, it can be applied to pretty much anyone and it's difficult because if you've got a weight of evidence from a number

> of people it's quite hard to be a lone professional and say, 'well let's take that risk' [to discharge from hospital without a CTO]. (AMHP lead)

This is a particularly important point to consider given that it has been suggested that social workers (as most AMHPs are) can act as a counter to the overuse of CTOs (George, 2011). Where AMHPs saw their role as having importance was more in deciding the detail of the CTO, particularly the conditions that were placed on a CTO, which will be returned to later.

The influence of team culture on discharge

While the AMHP and the inpatient psychiatrist are the formal decision-makers on the CTO, the community team play a key informal role, as they are the ones making a CTO work in practice. Team dynamics within community teams were thus an important factor in deciding whether to put in place a CTO. This was particularly in regards to the relationship between the community team psychiatrist and care coordinators. In one of the Trusts, the whole Assertive Outreach Team (AOT) team, including the manager and the psychiatrist, agreed that CTOs should only be used in very limited circumstances, which meant that they did not tend to advocate for CTOs and indeed would decline them. This contrasted with another AOT with a large number of CTOs; the psychiatrist there was very keen on CTOs and would take the lead in arguing for them, which some of the care coordinators could at times find problematic: 'He loves them. It's quite easy to recall. Plus it's protecting him just in case something goes wrong. He's using it for protecting the public, protecting him and his professional practice.'

Conversely, in another Trust, the community psychiatrist was much less active in pursuing CTOs, which could also cause frustration for care coordinators. Consequently, those care coordinators were more instrumental in asking for and securing CTOs at discharge. Thus care coordinators were more likely to take the view 'better be safe than sorry' than the psychiatrist. Thus the decision to advocate for a CTO relied to a great extent on the dispositions, influence and interactions of the different actors involved. Psychiatrists were not always at the forefront or the driver of such decision-making.

Shared decision-making

Shared decisions across inpatient and community services tended to be the norm, whereby the community team would lead in advocating for the CTO and the inpatient psychiatrist and AMHP would agree to it on that basis. It was often the care coordinator – as the person who knew the service user the best in the community – who would make the initial suggestion for the CTO (or indeed argued against the CTO) and who carried the decision through different forums. One care coordinator explained their role as being at the crux of decisions: 'So, if the AMHP asks us, "no I don't think they should be on a CTO", if the psychiatrist asks us, "I don't think they should be on a CTO". And the likelihood is by me saying that they probably wouldn't.'

The involvement of the community team was not always clear-cut, however. In both study sites, we observed inpatient teams overseeing discharges without authorising a CTO when the community team had been advocating for a CTO, or the reverse situation where the inpatient psychiatrist made the CTO against the opinion of the community team. Discharge onto the CTO against the advice of the community team was not only disapproved of as unnecessary; it could also make post-discharge care difficult. Not involving community practitioners in the discharge decision could damage existing relationships. This was one of the ethical 'balancing acts' practitioners carried in weighing the benefit of the CTO against retaining trusting relationships with individual service users, based on what they knew about how different service users responded to compulsion. Here it seems that process – whereby practitioners might recommend a CTO not be used – could be bypassed. Indeed, one care coordinator referred to a woman with whom she had worked for years, who had been placed on a CTO against the care coordinators advice, and the damage she felt this had caused:

> The recommendation from the consultant was she would go home on the CTO, and I said to them 'I don't think she needs the CTO, I'm sure I'd be able to deal with it' but I think because she was still very poorly ... Well I knew she would accept medication off me, I *knew* she would. I thought 'oh god she's going to hate this ... And it was horrendous – 'I don't want you in my house' – you know this was such a long relationship that had completely broken down ... It was quite traumatic for me as well because it really did upset me ... I don't feel that we've got the same rapport at all, I think it's completely broken, we're just playing at being nice to each other, that's how it feels to me.

It is worth noting here that like service users, practitioners could also feel out of control and powerless, being placed in the position of implementing coercion against their own will.

Practitioners' use of conditions

As with the initial decision to use the CTO, the legal criteria for imposing CTO conditions are broad, which means professionals have a great deal of latitude in deciding what conditions to include. Despite this, it became evident that most practitioners were typically careful about what conditions they included, and used their discretion within particular boundaries, although as discussed in the last chapter, how this was interpreted by service users was variable. Similarly to findings elsewhere (Lepping and Malik, 2013; Smith, Branton and Cardno, 2014), the three main conditions placed on service users in this study were variations on: adherence to medication, attendance at care reviews and consultant appointments, and allowing access to members of the care team. There were three aspects to practitioners' boundary-setting when they considered conditions: lawfulness, feasibility and ethicality. Formulating 'ethical' conditions also involves considerable work with service users in order to make the conditions acceptable, and so we also consider the relational work practitioners do with service users within the remit of the CTO. Such relational work has limits however, and we conclude this section by elaborating on how practitioners handled medication compliance as part of the CTO.

Lawfulness, feasibility and ethicality

With regards to lawfulness, the AMHPs especially had a view on human rights and possible challenges that could be made to conditions. Subsequently, while they rarely disagreed with the imposition of a CTO in itself, the majority of the AMHPs talked about sometimes having to play a mitigating role in countering the more 'extreme' conditions that might be suggested by inpatient psychiatrists. In making those arguments however, AMHPs relied more on questions of feasibility rather than legality. In Julie's hospital discharge meeting, the psychiatrist was planning on including drug/alcohol abstention as a condition, at which point the AMHP intervened: 'there's no point putting anything about drugs or alcohol, we're just setting her up to fail and she'll never get out of here otherwise'. This concern was widely held; conditions which service users could not be expected to keep to might result in continuous breach of the CTO and subsequently risked repeated hospital admissions. At the same time, including 'unworkable' conditions which admission to hospital would do little to rectify also risked rendering the CTO 'toothless', as highlighted in Nick's case notes:

> Nick is subject to a CTO which originally included a condition on abstention from illicit drug use, but this was removed by his psychiatrist due to the difficulties in enforcement and that recall to hospital could not occur as treatment for his illicit use cannot be provided on an acute inpatient bed.

Making CTOs feasible was closely connected to making them ethical – a kind of 'practical ethics'. Conditions were separated into 'hard' conditions which are easily monitored and enforceable (such as seeing professionals and medication) and 'soft' conditions which are not (such as abstention from drug/alcohol use and attendance at talking therapy). 'Soft' conditions were viewed as unusable not just because they were unenforceable, but also because of practitioners' expressed beliefs about when and where individuals should be 'allowed' choices in how they lived their lives. Such beliefs could be related to perceptions of social norms, especially regarding personal autonomy:

> I know that using cannabis is illegal but lots of people do it you know, and would the police be allowed to use the same power if you didn't have a mental illness, say 'right that's it now, we're sick of arresting you for smoking cannabis and we're going to lock you away'? They're not allowed to do it, so why because you've got a mental illness? (Care coordinator)

Similarly, practitioners broadly held the view that service users had a 'right' not to take part in talking therapies and forms of social rehabilitation in a way that did not hold true for medication. Therapeutic and social activities consequently did not feature in CTO conditions, as if the service user was amenable to such interventions then it was viewed outside the compulsory remit of the CTO, and if service users did not want to take part, practitioners did not feel comfortable or able to 'make' them. Service user groups have raised concerns that CTOs could limit professional involvement with service users to medication and negate other forms of treatment. It was certainly the case in the field sites that talking therapies for example, could be hard to access; during appeals we observed that practitioners were sometimes asked by panel members why talking therapy was not included in the broader care plan and were told that suitable therapy was not available for those service users. However, it was also the case that practitioners responded to service user concerns around overreach, by limiting conditions to the 'bare minimum' of medication and access, as this care coordinator explains: 'it almost feels like maybe you're giving people all these conditions to live, it just doesn't feel very human'.

Even in relation to the 'hard' condition of allowing access to practitioners, respondents described negotiating how such access would be enacted, to allow for ethical acceptability for the practitioner and to try and respect service user preferences within the boundaries of compulsion, as exemplified here:

> There's a requirement that we see him weekly but it's not specific that he engages. We've agreed in the care plan that if he doesn't turn up every second appointment, we can more assertively chase him. He doesn't like to see professionals at his home so we agreed to meet him in a city centre cafe which was more agreeable to him, because we didn't think it would be ethical or a good way to engage him, to insist to use the CTO to see him in his own home. (Care coordinator)

The conditions of CTOs tend to be set out very definitively and briefly; what this example suggests is that there is a lot of 'behind the scenes' work in both making conditions feasible, and in making them acceptable, particularly in ensuring the care plan provides contextual guidance for the CTO. As a psychiatrist noted, such an approach was not only about ethical practice, but also about making the whole CTO viable: 'that's the sort of things that need to be done to make the CTO work, redesign the conditions to fit that patient better somehow'.

Relational work within CTO conditions

Reaching a point of ethical equilibrium on the CTO was therefore often correlated with being able to maintain some kind of working relationship with the service users who were on them. As noted previously, this might be achieved through flexibility and compromise on the specifics of access via the CTO. Practitioners also described how they drew on their personal attributes in order to make visits a more affirmative experience:

> Irene did allow me to visit, but it had to be very tentative. She didn't want me mentioning medication, she didn't want me mentioning illness and it was more about building relationships so … I gradually built up a relationship with her over maybe 6 months or so and it started to get easier. It becomes more of an interpersonal thing rather than 'I must comply, I must attend the reviews, I must do this'. Maybe when it becomes seeing me as a person it's more, 'Rebecca is coming, that's okay because I know her', rather than an agent of the hospital is coming to check up on me and get me if I don't comply. (Care coordinator)

Alongside this general relationship-building, practitioners talked about trying to keep the CTO positive, by providing hope and being optimistic about change. This could take the form of therapeutic work, looking backwards and forwards to review where the individual had been and wanted to be, as this practitioner described:

> You can't change the CTO but you can work through it. You can reflect back with them and get them to understand the reasons you've had to do that. It's about how you use the CTO in a bigger sense, it's not how you use it at a time of crisis. When they're well you can start to introduce things like 'what do you think happened there?', 'how could we change that in the future?', so that there's a longer-term process to becoming well. It's about putting things in place so it's not a forever sanction. (Care coordinator)

The CTO, then, could be used as a starting point for this kind of conversation. It was not simply or only the case that practitioners used relational means to 'work around' the control aspects of the CTO. The CTO could also encourage constructive engagement. The necessity of regular visits had the potential to 'kick-start' relationships by providing a structure and boundaries to work within. Michael's care coordinator commented on how this had worked for him, with a client who had avoided contact with services:

> I think it's given us the space to work with him, to see if we can overcome his resistance. It's about building that relationship up where you can actually challenge in a gentle way, it doesn't have to be confrontational. The CTO can be a good starting point because the clarity and the consistency are there.

More specifically, the conditions – and explaining why service users had to adhere to them – could give practitioners a 'way in' to conversations about risk, which they might otherwise struggle to have, thus supporting collaborative working on risk management:

> Stuart understands that the reason he's on the CTO is because he's considered to be a higher risk … with lots of our clients, obviously we talk about recovery and we talk about meeting their needs and maintaining their independence and that's what you'd rather be talking to people about. But the CTO it allows you to have more conversations about risk as well, about people's offence, about their risk triggers. (Care coordinator)

'Routinised' practice via the CTO in the form of conditions could therefore encourage as well as discourage engagement with service users. In this case, relational and risk focused work reinforced each other, rather than being in opposition. While practitioners were sceptical about the CTO enabling effective monitoring of risk, it was still felt that using the CTO as a tool to get service users to talk more openly about the struggles they were having would help signal if difficulties were ahead.

Echoing some of the service user accounts presented in the previous chapter, practitioners described that some service users tried to maintain control over the CTO and their lives more broadly by choosing to restrict their relationship with practitioners to a superficial connection. Ian's care coordinator explained how this limited what meaningful contact he could have with him:

> Because he doesn't want to engage, he's concordant in the very narrowest sense of the word. He knows that he's adhering to the

> conditions of the CTO by having his depot and engaging … I don't think we do much more than monitor him and make sure he takes medication, but I think that's what he wants.

A focus on monitoring and risk management could therefore be shaped by the service user as well as by the CTO regime, and suggests that risk-focused practice is not always shaped from 'above' and in this sense is not clear-cut. In contrast to the example of collaborative risk management given earlier, only being able to act in a monitoring and compliance role meant practitioners sometimes struggled to 'read' service users and find out what was really going on with them, ironically making effective risk management more difficult.

Medication, adherence and risk management

Medication adherence was more complex for practitioners to negotiate with service users than access and visits. As we have seen, medication could be the most significant 'concrete' coercive aspect of the CTO, and as such it could act as a stumbling block to service users engaging with practitioners but also alternatively as a 'way in' for practitioners if meaningful choices on medication were encouraged. Care coordinators described how they sometimes used their role (specifically not being a psychiatrist) to distance themselves from medication conditions in order to try to maintain progress with service users who were resentful at being compelled to take medication:

> I tried to step back away from the medical side of things so I could get in to see him and work with him around other areas. When he raised issues with his medication I would be quite empathetic towards him and try and bridge some gaps that way. But ultimately putting out that 'the doctor chooses what medication you're on, I can speak up for you but I can't change his mind per se'.

In doing this, care coordinators seemed to be attempting to protect their engagement with service users by ensuring medication was not the focal point of their work, but also at times by positioning themselves as advocate and the psychiatrist as the 'enforcer', a classic 'good cop/bad cop' approach.

When care coordinators were successful in advocating for medication changes, it could signal to service users that they had been listened to and supported, thus bolstering the relationship, as this care coordinator explained in relation to a service user who had been angry with her about the imposition of the CTO:

> Recently she wanted a reduction of her depot. In the past I've always agreed with her because it makes her feel tired so she hasn't got a lot

> of quality of life and I do understand that. I've always advocated for her, so I thought, this will either go one way or the other. If she does get a reduction and it doesn't go right we're going to be back where we started, but I'm going to have to show her that I trust her, how she feels and what she's saying to me. So I did, managed to talk the doctor into reducing it and she was quite grateful and so after that she's been alright.

However, even if practitioners understood service users' feelings about medication, worked with service users to find a dosage that was therapeutically viable and distanced themselves from the medical aspect of care, very few of them would consider what the majority of service users wanted, which was a move from injections to oral medication. All but one of the service users in the study were on depot injections, despite the majority stating a preference for oral medication. Practitioners' described a symbiotic relationship between the two; the CTO was viewed as difficult to implement in terms of monitoring of treatment adherence if an individual was on oral medication, therefore where possible the use of injections was written into the conditions. If the use of injections was not possible the CTO as a whole might be questioned. Indeed, adherence with medication is central to the control mechanism of the CTO, recall.

Practitioners' use of recall

Recall is a process which while acknowledged by practitioners to appear as simple and clear in the guidance, could be confusing, time-consuming, bureaucratic and unpredictable in practice, often involving skilled coordination and persistence. In one of the teams under study, one care coordinator had six CTOs on his caseload and because those service users regularly refused their treatment, he often spent two days a week coordinating recalls back to hospital. In this sense, care coordinators often undertook work which would usually be carried out by AMHPs when managing a Mental Health Act (MHA) assessment, such as coordinating the Police and the ambulance when necessary, finding and booking a bed, delivering the recall notice and carrying out the recall itself. As we have seen, practical and ethical difficulties in the use of CTOs are often entwined and this is most evident in the use of recall.

Practical and ethical challenges in recall: disjointed services and care

Observations in both teams suggests that bed shortages could cause considerable difficulties in executing timely recalls; often recalls were issued but then not put into action until the following week when a bed became available. More fundamentally, differences in the perceptions of the purpose of inpatient care could hinder the recall process. Inpatient teams saw admissions as being for the provision of acute care rather than for preventative work, the latter being what recall is often aimed at. In the absence of respite or 'halfway' services, this could cause problems, as this care coordinator explained: 'They don't want people on the ward if they're not acutely unwell because there's pressure on the ward, whereas with CTOs we're getting them in to get them back on track, I think that you have to do a bit of pushing for it to happen.' Slow or 'blocked' recalls could negate the perceived protective purposes of the CTO in relation to dealing proactively with relapse and providing a 'short-cut' to inpatient care.

When practitioners discussed the difficulties they had had with recall then, it became clear that the separation of practical and ethical difficulties could at times be a false divide. Another issue where practical problems compounded ethical discomfort was the dislocation that could occur for service users when recalled. Lack of bed space meant that when service users were recalled, this could be to anywhere within the Trust, which created difficulties on discharge for service users in that they could be left far from home with little money and for practitioners who had to subsequently facilitate transport. This points to a process which is system rather than person focused, and indeed unfair if the service user was discharged from recall within a few hours, or did not want or need to be recalled in the first place. More fundamentally, incongruence existed between the theory of recall and its practice, including discontinuity of care and knowledge in the recall process. In theory, recall was seen as an opportunity to find out what needed to happen to support that service user in the community.

It was therefore deemed important by practitioners for inpatient staff to know the individual beyond their case file, in order to be able to conduct a well-founded assessment at recall and for the service user in return to feel able to discuss their circumstances more openly, as this AMHP states:

> It would be a safeguard almost, for them to comfortably explore some of the problems with the care plan, but they go to a different doctor on a ward they don't know and sometimes the recall is just give them the depot and send them back out, so I think it's more superficial.

Blurring boundaries through recall

Such practice dovetails with the unease practitioners expressed earlier about the CTO as a whole encouraging mechanistic and reductive practice. Recall was really at the heart of these concerns, particularly in cases where individuals had got into 'recall cycles', similar to the 'revolving door' problem which CTOs were at least in part meant to alleviate. In one team there were a number of service users who were recalled to hospital on a monthly basis, as they always refused or avoided visits and their injection. One of the characteristics of CTOs across all countries where they are enacted is that none of them 'cross the Rubicon' (Dawson, 2005) of enforced treatment in a community setting – people are always brought back into hospital for enforced medication. We highlighted in the last chapter how for service users this distinction could be meaningless as it is based on a narrow notion of consent to treatment. Further, the cycling of a small group of individuals in and out of hospital on a monthly basis to receive their depot meant that the concept of this threshold loses its potency, as the boundary between community and hospital became porous and enforced treatment in the community happened by proxy:

> Obviously you can't make somebody have the treatment if they don't want it in the community but then the alternative is … they are made to have it when they get recalled to hospital. You've created a new version of revolving door, instead of them coming into hospital for a couple of months and then going out for a year, it's come in for a couple of hours or a couple of days and then out for a month. (AMHP)

None of the practitioners interviewed felt comfortable with CTOs being used in this way; guidance states that recall is 'not expected to be used regularly' (National Institute for Mental Health in England, 2008, 34) and repeat recalls raised concern regarding what the CTO was supposed to be used for. The consequence of using recall in this way was not only related to ethical difficulties around enforced treatment, but also that it may remove the ability of service users, as seen earlier in Sarah's case, to self-manage and use their own strategies to cope:

> I think often people aren't given very much leeway, and people don't have the choice like they maybe used to have to actually say, 'yes well I know actually in 6 months after not taking my depot I'll become really unwell, but actually I feel so rubbish when I'm on that depot that I'd rather have 6 months where I'm enjoying my life and choose to take that risk'. (AMHP)

Furthermore, regular recalls could signify the breakdown of relationships, where active resistance could mean community care becomes an on-going conflict, with recall the 'battle ground'. This care coordinator distinguished between service users thusly:

> It works very well with those people who have traditional respect for the law and authority and they've learnt they don't take their

> medication, they get recalled, they think, 'oh, I can't be bothered with this hassle, I'll just have it'. However, there are others where it doesn't work so well because they've got no respect for it. They don't believe it has any validity in their life.

Even so, recall could be seen as the 'lesser of the two evils' in some cases, particularly those where recall was straightforward and where service users would not have agreed to treatment in any circumstances. Although being caught in a recall cycle was still recognised as disruptive to these service users, it was deemed better that it be used in this way especially if risk was a key concern. A care coordinator explained how he and the psychiatrist had managed what he called their *shared moral ambiguity* about such cases by testing it out at appeal:

> We were asking, 'are we doing this the right way, is this the right thing to do?' If the Tribunal said discharge them we would've had no problem because we're becoming that cleft stick, you know, we're morally muddled up and legally … But then the court said that you're doing the right thing by keeping the CTO running, that's fine.

Gaining legal approval gave repeat recalls legitimacy, particularly in terms of proactively dealing with risk for service users who were deemed as being difficult to manage in the community. Although most practitioners accepted this argument, at the same time some did not only feel service users' right to choose was limited by the use of recall, but that their own discretion could also be restricted by it. The imposition of a CTO could be seen as a defensive decision, and so could the active use of recall, as this care coordinator states: 'The CTO defines the actions that we will have to take. There's always emergencies come up. But recall creates the emergency.' The very presence of recall as an option could make it difficult not to use.

The use of recall thus becomes a strategy for managing uncertainty, as this care coordinator sums up: 'It's just a kind of, very quick, immediate response and a sort of definite response and this is just what we're doing.' Where practitioners were unsure about the nature of the situation and what they could do, recall provided a way to act. One way this manifested was in the 'Catch-22' embedded in the recall process where individuals can be recalled without prior assessment. This meant that if an individual cannot be seen, and the practitioner does not know their status, the response can be to recall them 'just in case', which could result in 'false positives' and unnecessary admissions. In one case, a woman had not been seen for some time as her care coordinator had left the team and there had been little follow-up with her since. Case notes stated that she had 'apparently not been compliant with her medication resulting in disengagement from the team'. However, given that the team had only contacted the woman twice in the preceding two months, it seems that recall was more a way of getting her back in the system rather than being due to non-adherence or her mental state.

Negotiation and mitigation in the recall process

Despite the potential for defensive practice, the use of recall was not always clear-cut. The use of repeat recalls for breach of medication conditions was highly variable. Regardless of the practical and ethical difficulties that recall could raise, it was a broadly held view that recall could be a beneficial preventative intervention for a number of reasons related to protection and risk management. At the same time, some practitioners preferred to use the CTO in a less intrusive way, keeping recall to a minimum. In this sense, and as with their ethical views on the CTO as a whole, practitioners could broadly be separated into those who saw recall as only to be used when necessary relating to a careful consideration of the individual at hand, and those who felt it was a helpful tool which could be used more freely to manage risk in a clear way. Within these categories practitioners displayed varying levels of flexibility about when and how recall was implemented.

The majority of the psychiatrists interviewed had what can be described as a 'black and white' view of recall, where early recall was seen as the best approach: 'Recall is something that you use when the adherence contract is broken. And I think you do that within a week. I think the point is actually to do it early, otherwise what's the point in the CTO?' There was a dual argument here that first, for the CTO to have authority it had to be treated like an enforceable contract and second, that recall could be justified on the assumption that non-adherence to medication would always bring risk of harm to health and safety. Other practitioners were less sure, treating recall as a 'grey area'. A care coordinator who worked across Assertive Outreach and Forensic services believed his exposure to individuals classed as high risk meant he had a more relaxed approach to recall: 'It is about knowing individuals, knowing what the trigger factors are, knowing the risks that they pose, and looking at them realistically and saying "what's the point in recalling someone?"'

Discomfort was expressed about the 'contractual' focus on compliance to conditions and whether injections had been missed, rather than individual circumstances, as this AMHP explains: 'Decisions to recall are made much more around ensuring ongoing medical treatment than "what is the current risk at this time?"' Moreover, some practitioners expressed the concern that using recall in this way could undermine the work they had done to maintain a relationship with service users within the CTO. It was felt that a reactive approach to recall could further embed the superficial compliance that some service users demonstrated because it could lead service users to not be honest and open about what they were experiencing, particularly if they were anxious about the idea of recall. Stuart's care coordinator described such difficulties in relation to their relationship:

> I try to say to Stuart, the more open and honest he can be about what he's experiencing, the less chance there is of him ending up back in hospital. There's no reason no matter what he experiences we can't manage it, because he'll never be in a more supported environment than where he is now. But, at the same time, I think he's scared that, if he says 'the TV started talking to me again' or 'I've started to see the dark shadows' or, you know, 'when I look back at the time when I was the Son of God, actually, I think I might be the Son of God again', but he's never going to say that to me because I think he's terrified that the CTO allows us just to whip him straight back into hospital and he hated it on the ward.

Consequently, and as with the decision to make the CTO in the first place, care coordinators could play a significant mediating role in recall decisions. Psychiatrists filled in and signed off recall papers, but care coordinators were the ones who initially drew attention to whether a recall was needed. Negotiation and 'steps to compulsion' were used as a way of averting recall where possible. For those service users where it was felt there was a chance recall could be avoided, practitioners talked, for example, about giving service users a set number of chances to meet with them before recall was triggered. Practitioners also described 'reminding' service users of the CTO in order to achieve compliance: 'Kid, cajole, jest, bad jokes, whatever. You never argue with anybody anyhow, that's pointless. With other people it might just be literally a blunt statement because you know that's how they respond best' (Care coordinator). A Managers' Hearing Chair, meanwhile, explained the various ways he saw recall being dealt with:

> What happens is they get extra support going in there to maintain or get them back on their medication or change their medication rather than the power of recall and it seems to be the threat of the power of recall, rather than the actual usage. I mean over the past months I've chaired quite a lot and I can remember one actually being recalled although several have not complied with medication, but other methods have been tried rather than the power of recall actually being invoked.

Even once the recall papers had been issued, hospitalisation was not necessarily the result. A Mental Health Act Officer reported regularly seeing paperwork for recalls which did not eventuate, where the recall notice was being used by practitioners only for leverage even though they are legally binding documents. Such actions could be seen as a way of maintaining good relationships and attempting to alleviate the anxiety of service users by being 'true to their word' regarding their explanations of when recall would happen. It should be noted, however, that averting a recall did not necessarily result in lowered feelings of coercion. The leverage sometimes used could reinforce feelings of powerlessness, as seen here in an excerpt from Patrick's case notes written by his care coordinator:

> Patrick was angry that the dose had been increased and refused to take the depot. I reminded him that he is under the Community Treatment Order and he will have to accept the increased dose. I told him that he is free to accept this depot at home and if he doesn't do that then he will be recalled to hospital and given this injection. Patrick was very angry with that and said 'just give me the injection' and didn't want to have any further discussions. I tried to reinforce that, even though my reaction might look punitive I am trying to act on his best interests and don't want him to end up in hospital again.

Connecting back to the psychological impact of CTOs discussed in the last chapter, using the threat of recall to avoid recall could sharpen service users' sense of being in a 'no win' situation, despite practitioners best intentions.

It should also be noted that the narrative of psychiatrists being quick to use recall, and care coordinators' ethical discomfort with this meaning they try to avert recall, was not always the case. Team dynamics played a role in the initial decision to make the CTO and continued to play a role in how CTOs unfolded. In a team where the psychiatrist was very keen on CTOs, recall was used actively, including repeat recalls. In the team where the psychiatrist expressed reluctance about CTOs he was also cautious about using recall, which could cause frustration for many of the care coordinators. The psychiatrist told me that:

> I would not be shaking the remit of the CTO over the patient's head, 'you have to obey me otherwise I will recall you', that's not the way I see it at all. CTO or no CTO I think the care of the patient has to be provided in a respectful way. We need to show some flexibility, we can't follow this rigidly – 'once you breach conditions then that's it, you come to hospital immediately'. We have to remind the patient that 'this is what you agreed on', they might cooperate, or they might have a good reason for not doing it.

His view was that the service user needed to be listened to, and an attempt made at a mutually agreeable solution before recall was triggered. However, the view in the rest of the team was that their professional judgement was being ignored, as this care coordinator explained:

> We say, 'we really need to get them in, let's recall', and then you're met with a brick wall sometimes, and that's frustrating. Because when we say they need to be in, that means they really, really do need to be in. Not yesterday, not tomorrow or next week, now.

Not being able to use recall proactively for protective and risk-related purposes could undercut the value of the CTO for practitioners. However, there were two particular kinds of cases across the field sites where recall was unlikely to be considered by all practitioners.

Distinguishing between 'recallable' and 'non-recallable' cases

The first of these can be described as 'complex cases', where the individual did not only have a primary diagnosis of psychosis but also of substance misuse and/or personality disorder. In these particular cases the individual's circumstances would often not 'fit' the CTO, making it difficult to actively use. For example, it was seen by practitioners as pointless to recall someone with a diagnosis of personality disorder because:

> Our inpatient consultants don't believe in personality disorders as such or, if they do believe in them, they don't believe that an inpatient acute unit is the right place to treat someone with a personality disorder. Because you can't give someone a tablet and settle them down and send them back out again, it's more long-term work. (Manager)

Psychosis by itself can be monitored to a certain extent, whereas deciding whether an individual's behaviour is caused by their psychosis or by substance misuse/personality disorder is a more difficult task. Often practitioners would have to try and differentiate between the two when deciding on recall. As the following manager's account of an appeal discussion suggests, recall was therefore not always used when significant risk was present; for recall to occur the risk also had to be related to a mental state that could be treated immediately with medication in hospital:

> The panel were concerned about the potential risk that client posed and whether management in the community with a CTO was the appropriate way or whether he should be actually back in hospital as an inpatient. And the client, he's quite a complex client because he's got the paranoid personality behaviours as well. I was trying to explain to them that the CTO is in place for the voices he hears in terms of

compliance with medication. But he's making threats against people and it's not linked to his voices, it's his personality and we can't recall him because of that really. The panel really struggled to get to grips with that.

As seen here, the purpose of the CTO could be questioned if risk was not being seen as dealt with. This questioning also arose in multi-agency working, with other agencies struggling to understand why an individual was not being recalled when behaving riskily and the team making the argument that risky behaviour not caused by deterioration in mental health was outside the remit of the recall function. In this sense, practitioners were making a similar argument to the one they made against the use of 'soft' conditions such as drug/alcohol abstention; that it was not the role of mental health services to 'police' behaviour that fell more into the social rather than the medical realm. A care coordinator recounted a meeting about Nick, where probation services were pushing for recall due to a spike in Nick's amphetamine use which caused aggressive behaviour, but the team had assessed his mental health as stable and so the psychiatrist had refused. Therefore, while risk was one strong criterion for recall, it was still carefully delineated as being in or outside the boundaries of the CTO.

Practitioners also felt that for some individuals with a diagnosis of personality disorder, the CTO, and specifically the recall function, reinforced negative interactions with the team. In one professionals meeting about a service user who had made threats against members of staff it was noted that the CTO had resulted in: 'an escalation in his behaviour towards our team. The threatening behaviour is increasing, the threats to staff are becoming more significant. He's doing everything that he possibly can to sabotage the treatment that we've given him.' Although the individual was breaching his conditions, recall was viewed as unfeasible because bringing him to the hospital site would increase the risk for staff. Furthermore, with the CTO in place, law enforcement agencies were less likely to deal with such behaviour. Not only did the CTO mean other agencies placed pressure on mental health services to act in regards to risk, it could also mean they did not act themselves. One practitioner said the CTO meant agencies such as the police felt they could 'wash their hands' of individuals. In this case the care coordinator commented: 'Because of the CTO, the CPS didn't charge him when he breached his harassment order against us. Apparently I should understand as a healthcare professional that I'm fair game.' CTOs could thus shift the burden of responsibility for 'risky' individuals onto mental health teams and individual practitioners, rather than maintaining a shared responsibility across agencies; instead of managing risk the CTO could therefore exacerbate it. Such individuals could be seen as 'impossible' cases, with no resolution in sight, and with the CTO muddying what was already a complex and challenging situation. As this service user's care coordinator said to me after the meeting: 'As a case study, he's really fascinating, because he's got us beaten so far.'

The second kind of case where recall would not usually be considered was where the service user was deemed to be attempting to use the recall function for their own purposes, which did not chime with the purposes of the team. As noted earlier, individuals who used hospital admission as a coping strategy for various reasons would try and trigger recalls when they felt it necessary, for example by refusing their medication. Simon was a good example of someone who had done this with varying success while on the CTO in order to escape social pressures such as difficulties with housing. As Simon's CTO went on, it became increasingly difficult for him to be recalled; in his case notes it was requested that practitioners no longer initiate recall unless absolutely necessary, and in an appeal report it was noted: 'His social worker felt that the CTO was not necessary since if anything Simon was too demanding of support.' There was a potential dichotomy at work here; practitioners talked about recall in protective terms, and indeed understood why service users might act in this way, as a natural response to changes to and subsequent limitations of services: 'We don't have respite care anymore … so the only way he can get respite is by becoming non-compliant, deteriorating and getting into hospital that way, where he feels safe' (Care coordinator).

However, that sense of protection and reciprocity could be limited when it came to service users' self-perceived welfare needs, partly because it was felt that inpatient services were likely to immediately discharge a service user who was recalled for these reasons. In such cases differentiating between when recall should or should not be used was also framed in terms of 'breaking the cycle' of dependence. As was observed at Simon's appeal, the care coordinator explained how they weighed up such decisions:

> I think if it was psychosis we'd be looking at recall, not voluntary admission, that's what the CTO is for. So you have to separate out the two things, his psychosis and his risks with that and his ability to cope and live independently. We've been trying to treat him at home when he's feeling like this, trying to break the cycle of him coming in when he feels that he can't cope.

As with personality disorder and substance misuse, recall here was seen as only feasible for psychosis related behaviour. Service user actions that reflected problems with well-being or emotional distress were not deemed liable. Again, this raises broader questions about what the limits of CTO usage might be and the ways that service user actions muddied the operation of control, a point that we will return to.

Conclusion

In this chapter we have drawn out the main themes that underpin practitioner ethical reasoning and acting on CTOs, as well as touching on the various contextual factors which constrain practitioner agency. The ethical debates that practitioners engaged in about the CTO in conceptual terms also played out in CTO practice, demonstrated by how much practitioners were willing to live with uncertainty, which influenced both the approach to medication practitioners were willing to take under the CTO, and their use of recall. This variation was related to the ethical stance practitioners took towards the CTO, which could be either taking a 'hard and fast' approach to activating the CTO to ensure treatment and thus risk management, or a more flexible approach to allow for self-efficacy and realisation.

Practical–ethical beliefs on feasibility and autonomy meant that many practitioners engaged in sustained work to try and maintain a space where flexible and negotiated engagement could take place within the framework of compulsion. Furthermore, practitioners held the narrative and the empirical in tension regarding how CTOs 'should' work and how they 'do' work, as can be seen particularly with concerns about the lack of care and continuity in the recall process, the use of repeat recalls and the blurring of boundaries on consent and compelled medication in the community. Altogether this points to an underpinning tension along a spectrum of power relations, between what can be described as 'surface' practice where the CTO is used routinely and superficially to maintain compliance and in turn manage a very particular kind of risk, or 'depth' practice where the use of the CTO is tailored to individual circumstance and to encourage meaningful interaction and positive change.

We should note here that we are not necessarily suggesting that one kind of practice is more valid than the other. How engagement plays out within the CTO is a mutual undertaking between practitioners and service users. It needs to be acknowledged that with some individuals, 'surface' practice was all that could be managed, and indeed could be seen as an attempt to limit coercion, first by making it possible for such individuals to be in the community in the first place and second, by respecting their wishes for minimal involvement. Equally, attempts to avert unnecessary compulsion such as using the threat of recall as leverage could lead to increased feelings of coercion. Furthermore, routinised practice under the CTO framework should not automatically be seen as encouraging reductive and 'surface' interaction. The controlling nature of CTOs – based on rules and sanctions – could in some cases encourage better relationships through providing space and clarity for engagement. Indeed, given that risk-oriented work is often critically aligned with proceduralised approaches (Webb, 2006; Hardy, 2015), it is interesting to note that risk management could be enhanced within a relational context. Conversely, a more stereotypical approach to risk in terms of monitoring and surveillance could be seen as hampering effective risk management. Indeed, it should be recognised that the CTO could exacerbate risk rather than control it, by aggravating service user behaviour, and by signalling to other agencies that they could take a step back in active risk management. In this sense, there were particular individuals and circumstances where the CTO was deemed not 'workable'. For service users who were particularly resistant to the CTO, it could become an emotionally draining experience for practitioners and could render the recall mechanism difficult to operate. In a more fundamental sense, for particularly 'complex cases' the limitations of what practitioners felt was the responsibility of mental health services and the unintended consequences of activating recall, had the potential to effectively nullify the CTO.

The implicit logic of CTOs also meant that their implementation was sometimes beyond the control of practitioners highlighting the operation of power in systemic as well as relational terms. The broad criteria for CTOs could make their initial application difficult to challenge, and once in place they could hold a logic of their own, whereby the easily applicable nature of recall and the pressure to avoid costly mistakes could make it difficult not to use. Paradoxically, the legal discretion integral to CTOs could narrow the choices practitioners might make, thus encouraging defensive practice. Contextual factors also played a significant mediating role. Team dynamics did not always play out as would be expected; it could be assumed that the team psychiatrist would be an advocate for the CTO, driving its imposition and active use. While this was often the case, the psychiatrist could also hamper the CTO, thus leading care coordinators to question its purpose if they were not able to put it into action. Similarly, the broader institutional relationships the CTO operated within – between inpatient and community services and between community services and other agencies – could constrain practitioner autonomy in CTO use and undermine their perceived purpose. The impossibility of CTOs for some people and in some circumstances points to a more fundamental question on when to end compulsion, which we explore in the next chapter.

6

Sense of an ending: deciding when to relinquish control

Thus far we have traced the 'story' of community treatment orders (CTOs) from policy-level formation, through service user and practitioner conceptualisations and experiences, the means by which CTOs are put into practice and the factors that influence that process. This chapter reports on what can be a particularly problematic aspect of social work practice – the decision to remove a statutory mandate and change an individual's status from 'involuntary' to 'voluntary'. The focus of the chapter will be on when practitioners place limits on the legal exercise of control and how they decide when a CTO should end. Decision-making in these circumstances can be highly complex with an inherent quality of unpredictability and risk-taking. The broad and therefore largely discretionary remit for statutory interventions such as CTOs means that they can be easy to apply, but that much rests on the judgement of practitioners in deciding whether to remove them. Through data taken from observations and interviews, we draw out the power dynamics present in discharge decision-making forums and the varying ways both practitioners and service users utilise accounts of change, stasis, risk, responsibility and relational knowledge to support their arguments for and against discharge. These arguments bring to the surface deeper foundational concerns regarding how change can be known and interpreted, particularly in relation to evidence, causality and the effectiveness of CTOs.

We begin by exploring decision-making at CTO reviews, where there is room for debate, contestation and negotiation in discharge decisions, including discussion of the differing stances practitioners may take to 'risk-taking' in coming to discharge decisions together while also accounting for service user narratives. This leads on to a broader analysis of the dual and reinforcing roles of trust and evidence-gathering in deciding whether to relinquish legal control. Broadly 'objective' and 'subjective' approaches to decision-making are shown to converge in a process which relies on the capacities of service users to persuade practitioners of change. As we note, if service users are perceived to 'step outside' this assigned role of responsibility post-discharge, then the result may be the formation of a 'CTO cycle'; discharge from the CTO can be difficult to achieve, but taking that further, once having been on a CTO escaping entirely from legal forms of compulsion can be just as challenging.

We will also explore ways in which discharge decisions are not only influenced by evidence-based judgements of risk but also incorporate more subjective positive and negative effects of the CTO for individual service users. These were not 'hard' effects such as hospitalisation rates but 'soft' effects related to the tipping points between dependency and responsibility, and therapeutic engagement and alienation as they play out in individual service users' responses to the CTO. Such responses also highlight the potential perverse consequences of CTOs, whereby discharge from the CTO can encourage the very attitudes and responses the CTO is supposed to stimulate. Furthermore, not all service users wish to be removed from the CTO. We note the counter-intuitive responses compulsion can produce. Compulsion and coercion are often closely linked; what we suggest is that coercive experiences can also be related to the removal of compulsion through proposed discharge of the CTO.

Negotiating discharge

It appears that there are two kinds of CTO discharge scenarios that practitioners have to deal with:

- Those individuals who were resistant to the CTO and whether to maintain the CTO as the framework necessary to contain such difficulties, or to take a risk and discharge on the basis that support and treatment could be provided more effectively in a less coercive way.
- Those individuals who were adhering to the CTO and whether to maintain the CTO because it was believed that the individual would not maintain progress without it; or to take a risk and discharge on the basis that the individual has a moral right to that opportunity.

CTO reviews brought to the surface such dilemmas through debates between different practitioners, and practitioners and service users. Here we explore how such dilemmas manifested in reviews, beginning with a description of practitioners differing attitudes to risk, and the effect on service users of these attitudes. We then look at how practitioners worked out whether discharge from the CTO should happen or not in reviews, specifically in relation to the influence of service user testimony. The section concludes with a discussion of the difficulties of escaping the CTO for service users, even post-discharge.

Reviews typically occurred in the weeks before the CTO was up for renewal. They were more informal arenas than appeal hearings, and usually included the care coordinator, the Responsible Clinician, the Approved Mental Health Professional (AMHP) who had seconded the initial CTO decision and the service user. Nearest Relatives and other key family members could also attend. Reviews tended to be more discursive than appeal hearings (see Jobling, 2019 for an analysis of appeal decision-making). At appeals, the main participants aside from the panel have already 'made up their minds' so to speak. In reviews, there was more room for negotiation and persuasion. While none of the participants in this study was discharged at appeal, 6 out of 18 were discharged at the review stage. The pattern of discharge followed the team dynamics presented earlier. For example in the team where the psychiatrist was not a proponent of CTOs, five out of ten of the service users included in the study were discharged. He always used current engagement as a basis for his decision. In the team where the psychiatrist was an advocate for CTOs, one out of eight of the service users included in the study was discharged (and only after much persuasion from the care coordinator). He always used potential future engagement as a basis for his decision, that is forecasting what the service user would do post-discharge, hence making the possibility of discharge much more difficult.

Holding on or giving hope

Where practitioners differed in their views it was around how best to manage the uncertainty and risk inherent in the discharge decision. In Christine's case, the psychiatrist felt it was time for the CTO to be discharged whereas the AMHP felt strongly that it should be maintained due to her knowledge of Christine's history. The care coordinator (who remained neutral during the review) commented afterwards:

> Thing is, I know Jenny [the AMHP] has known Christine for a long time, but you can get things wrong sometimes. And with Christine, she has to have a chance. We can always bring her in under the Mental Health Act if needs be. Is it really worth it in the balance if she feels unhappy about it? I mean who is it for, her or us? At the end of the day, it's Dr Stokes' decision. Though Jenny probably won't like it.

The care coordinator illustrates the role of positive risk taking in CTO decisions, whereby defensive decision-making can be challenged and where the potential for individual change would be respected. Practitioners talked about the need for hope and proving their trustworthiness to service users by not 'shifting the goalposts' when discharge would happen. This psychiatrist explained that preparation for discharge should start from the beginning of the CTO:

> So being clear from the start about what would constitute success of the CTO, and for how long that CTO would have to be successful,

> or what other conditions would have to be met for you to consider removing it. They need a little bit of hope, if they're not happy about it.

This was not the case for all service users however. For service user participants where professionals had not got to the stage of discussing discharge as a possibility with them, it could seem like a far-off prospect. This meant some participants described holding a rather fatalistic attitude to discharge from the CTO, with Andrew stating: 'It's just down to time to elapse, time to run its course, that's what I have to do with the CTO, keep out of trouble and all that.' This in turn could engender a sense that the CTO was 'never-ending', as illustrated by Michael, who expressed uncertainty about when the CTO could end: 'I'm not sure how long a CTO can last for, if it's a lifetime event for instance or if the CTO is just like a six month investigation into a person who is not well.' Trying to 'read' professional intentions could be difficult, particularly when professionals were uncertain themselves. Sheila described how she had tried and failed to get a clear answer from her psychiatrist:

> I did ask him point blank, I said 'how many more years do you think I will have to be under the Mental Health Act?' and he said 'about another two years'. Well two years is nearly up with but I bet if I asked him he'd say something different. You never know where you are with them you see.

Retaining optimism about coming off the CTO could be difficult in such circumstances, as Patrick illustrated when asked what would have to happen for him to be discharged, and he answered: 'I don't know, a miracle.'

Evidence and trust

Despite this, it was interesting to observe the differences between how service users were positioned (and positioned themselves) in discharge discussions, as compared to when they were first placed on the CTO. We saw earlier that very few participants reported being meaningfully involved in discussions when they were placed on the CTO. However, being discharged from the CTO was a different matter, with service users taking centre stage in discussions about whether to continue the CTO or not. Because discharging an individual from a CTO was seen as taking a risk, the ability of participants to persuade professionals of their intentions was an important factor in the process, as Graham illustrates when asked how he had been discharged:

> He [the psychiatrist] just says 'I don't know whether to take you off it', but I just said 'I'm ready to volunteer now. I've been on medication a

> long time, different ones, and this one works, so it's medication I need. They'll [his family] make sure I take it anyway'. So he said 'I'm not going to extend the Order'. For him to do that, he would have kept me on it if I'd said no to medication.

Invoking the dual elements of evidence and trust were necessary for service users to secure discharge. Trust has been referred to earlier in relation to service user trust in services and practitioners, yet trust in service users also figured in practitioner decision-making, particularly on discharge. The presence of the CTO may make it difficult for practitioners to judge whether an individual's actions are representative of internal or external drivers and therefore likely to be consistent over time, or only responsive to compulsion. For the majority of participants therefore, they had to persuade the psychiatrist of their intentions to work collaboratively and honestly with the team, as Irene describes: 'If there were any changes in the way I was feeling, I would definitely tell him, and as long as he was happy about that he was happy to take me off the treatment order.'

Observation of CTO reviews illustrated the different ways service users went about this persuasion to reinforce trust, including: contrasting the past and present, appeals to the strength of relationships with practitioners, presentation of coping strategies and dealing with practitioner doubt. The following exchange in Christine's review illustrates all of these elements of persuasion:

Psychiatrist:	Have you had any issues with taking your meds?
Christine:	No, I know they keep me well
Psychiatrist:	So do you think the CTO … without it you'd take your meds?
Christine:	Yeah …
Psychiatrist:	That wasn't a strong yes [smiling]
Christine:	It *is* a strong yes [emphatically]. This is the wellest I've been in the last 5, 6, 7 years.
Psychiatrist:	And contact with the team, is it because of the CTO you do it?
Christine:	No, it's helpful. I get on with Naomi [care coordinator] and if she's not there I can always ring Martha [the team secretary].
Psychiatrist:	If we took you off the CTO would you still ask for help if you needed it?
Christine:	Yes, because I'd phone the ward if I was feeling unwell
AMHP:	But you haven't done that in the past have you Christine?
Christine:	Yes, but I'm weller now.

In Christine's case, even though the AMHP was strongly against discharging her from the CTO, the psychiatrist was sufficiently satisfied with Christine's responses to discharge her, as he concludes in the review:

> I think if being freer would be helpful for you, and you could feel more in control of your treatment, I would support the move to remove the section. But if I think the CTO was making you have contact and take medication then it would be different. But you've said it's your wish to take medication so I'm quite happy to take you off the section.

Sometimes, practitioners did not feel they could get a sense of what was going on 'under the surface' with a service user, either because of a lack of relationship or because the service user was not 'enacting' enthusiastic compliance but instead doing the 'bare minimum'. As noted previously, such behaviour could be deliberate as a way of retaining some control while simultaneously doing what was needed in order to secure discharge. However, acting in this way could also make discharge decisions less certain, as the following example demonstrates:

> I had one case, where I didn't know him that well, he was on a CTO and I did think 'now then, I'm not sure if he's going to comply or not'. And he really was a man of very few words so I wasn't sure what was happening. You wouldn't get anything from him. and you could never get underneath to see, well is he masking stuff or is he just very blunted, or is he getting on fine and he just doesn't want us knocking on his door every fortnight? And I thought 'I think we'll get this renewed' and we did renew it and I thought 'do you know what, I think there really wasn't a need for that but it's done now'. And then it was coming up to lapse, we let it, and it was fine in the end, but it was because I didn't have a feeling either way of what would happen. (Care coordinator)

Practitioners also talked about 'testing out' service users' trustworthiness by progressively lessening the level of intervention while still on the CTO and gauging the service user response to increased freedom before deciding on discharge. This could take the form of 'bargaining' with service users about expectations. For example, in an observation of a home visit, a care coordinator told the service user: 'make the right changes in your life then when the next review comes up we'll look at it seriously about whether we need this CTO or not'. More often, the 'testing out' was in relation to moving from injections to oral medication. The CTO in such cases could be seen as a way of meeting service user goals within a controlled environment, as this care coordinator commented in relation to an upcoming Tribunal:

> I'm thinking of changing my view to the tribunal to say we could try a phased self-medication with his current medication, to show we're using the CTO in a positive way, to try and reach his goals. We might not have shared goals about what's wrong with him, but we can have shared goals for plans for the future.

In this sense, service users had to do more than 'talk the talk' in terms of persuading practitioners of their readiness for discharge.

CTO cycles

Such enactments of responsibility did not necessarily end when the CTO ended. The 'threat' of future compulsion could act as a way of binding service users to standards of behaviour in the future, even when they were no longer on the CTO. Although Irene believed her relationship with the team and in particular her care coordinator was much improved due to the lifting of the CTO, she also described taking her medication under some pressure: 'They said if I get unwell, I'd end up put back on the Community Treatment Order, so I decided to take it.' Irene's care coordinator explained to me that she had tried to talk about the CTO discharge in positive terms with Irene, as a chance for them to work together, but that the psychiatrist had taken the opposite tack at the discharge meeting: 'He said to her "this doesn't change anything, you need to keep taking your meds, because I hate to say it but if you don't the whole thing will start again and you'll be on the CTO for a very, very long time".'

This meant that when service users did relapse they could become caught in CTO cycles, whereby relapse once the CTO ended was seen by practitioners as a result of coming off the CTO and 'proof' that it worked. An AMHP remarked that:

> Very often it is that, 'well I told you so', and that fits in with the risk-averse culture and way of working, because it might have had bugger all to do with the CTO the fact they've relapsed and they've come back in, but then that massive unscientific link is made, 'it's because we've taken them off the CTO that this has happened'. It's quite a useful leap of faith for a consultant to make if he wants to put them back on the CTO without any questions for a long time again.

Consequently, once an individual had been placed on a CTO it could colour any further treatment and intervention; if an individual was placed on a CTO more than once, it could become increasingly difficult to be discharged from it. Patrick had been on the CTO for over two years without a relapse by that point, the longest time he had been well for a number of years, and he felt he had done everything that could be asked of him: 'I don't know what they want. I don't know what they expect. Two years. I would've thought that after two years they would've discharged me.' The CTO therefore could act as an encompassing form of compulsion, facilitating movement between levels of compulsion, but making it difficult for individuals to be entirely free of it. In this regard being taken off the CTO could also be seen in resigned terms, as Patrick stated: 'It's just swings and roundabouts.'

Discharge dilemmas and balancing acts

For practitioners, discharge dilemmas were not only related to making judgements based on service user presentation and their trust in the service user. They also talked about balancing the potential positive and negative consequences of maintaining or discharging the CTO dependent on the individual in question. In this sense, the ethical balancing acts that practitioners maintained carried forward into decisions to discharge. The two balancing acts that practitioners considered at this point can be related to first weighing up dependency and responsibility, and second weighing up engagement and alienation.

Dependency vs responsibility

The rationale that CTOs could foster a sense of responsibility was widely held by practitioners. The provision of boundaries and 'contractual' obligations via the CTO could be seen as a way of generating behaviour change through sanctions (recall) and incentives (staying out of hospital) over time. An ideal scenario was if such behaviour change led to stability, recovery and eventual attitude change, with the service user not only adhering to desired ways of interacting and being but actively pursuing self-care and adherence. Nevertheless, practitioners generally held the view that some individuals would never reach this final stage. For service users who had been in the system for a long time and who were deemed institutionalised, the very reason the CTO was perceived to be effective was because of their conditioned attitude to authority, and it was difficult to see how the CTO would be removed in such cases:

> The moment we take them off the CTO, they've stopped being compliant again … that's just about boundaries and the way people respond to them … Some people just do really well with boundaries in place, and the moment they don't have them anymore they just don't know how to function ultimately. And that's probably true of a few clients … who have spent long periods of time in secure environments

> ... they just become accustomed to having those boundaries and having to deal with them. (Care coordinator)

There was an acceptance here of the need for dependency in some cases. At the same time, however, some practitioners had concerns that a 'tipping point' might be reached on lengthy CTOs, whereby they would foster a sense of dependency and undermine self-efficacy. In this way, the CTO could be framed as a continuation of institutionalisation. Practitioners wondered about the fairness of on-going community compulsion simply because it was less restrictive than detainment in hospital, as this AMHP points out:

> The temptation would be just to keep something that's keeping the person stable in place ad infinitum and gloss over the fact that it is actually still a section of the Mental Health Act and having some impact on their liberty. There's not that many people who would have been on section three for the same length of time.

These potential 'soft' negative outcomes of CTOs have typically been neglected in research and policy discussions, but a number of practitioners expressed the view that: 'There is a big risk in taking away somebody's autonomy and how that makes you feel as a person and how that affects your long term development.' The decision to remove a CTO is usually seen as taking a risk, whereas in this light, retaining the CTO is viewed as the potentially harmful option, albeit less direct.

Furthermore, it was felt by some practitioners that the CTO could discourage accountability and unfairly shift responsibility onto practitioners, as one care coordinator talked about in reference to a service user where criminal charges of assault had been dropped because he was on a CTO:

> So now he takes no personal responsibility for his actions because he knows that we'll monitor him, we'll make decisions for him and if anything goes wrong again, it's not his fault. So, for me, him not being on a CTO and having some responsibility might be better, a CTO makes it my responsibility.

Indeed, removing the CTO could encourage the 'responsibilised' response it was hoped that the CTO would elicit, as this psychiatrist explains:

> There have been times where the patient was under the CTO and engagement had been a problem. With one we decided to give him a try to see how he'd cope without the CTO because he'd been on it for three years, and actually engagement has improved, the patient is taking more responsibility for his problems. We must have done at

> least ten recalls for him in those three years for his depot, but now he's off the CTO for a few months, and he's been happy to have his depot without any problems. He knows he's not obliged to engage with the team so he's happy to see us, and he's more involved in his own care.

This was especially the case when service users were believed to be subverting the CTO for their own purposes. Earlier we noted that where service users had absorbed the CTO into their coping strategies, the CTO could be deemed first as meaningless as the recall function became undermined, and second as reinforcing dependency through the engraining of patterns of behaviour. Other service user responses to the CTO could also influence discharge decisions, as described next.

Engagement vs alienation

Some practitioners held the view that in cases where individuals on CTOs were resentful of them, continuous CTOs would negate any therapeutic work that could be done: 'I always try and get them off the CTO within 12 months. As a therapy move, because you can only work against somebody's liberties so long before you alienate yourself from them because you keep on renewing it.' Again, a 'tipping point' could be reached. While the contact the CTO ensured could support the building of an initial relationship, in the longer-term the CTO could get in the way of sustaining these relationships. Alternatively, where service users resented the CTO from the beginning, it could damage any pre-existing positive relationships or worsen an already difficult relationship.

The challenges caused by this kind of response were not only limited to damage to the therapeutic relationship. As described in the last chapter, in particularly complex cases, where personality disorder and/or substance misuse were present alongside psychosis, the CTO could not only be ineffectual in managing the risks that arose but could also exacerbate conflict and consequently risk. The CTO might be kept on in such cases as an overt practice of defensive decision-making, as a care coordinator commented in a CTO review on such a case: 'I'm just thinking about the unknown. To take it off now with the increased risks, we'll be hung out to dry.' In this sense it is ironic that while it might heighten risky behaviour, the CTO could be kept on solely in order to give the impression risk was being managed.

More broadly, individuals who were actively resistant to the CTO could undergo significant 'battles' with practitioners to regain a sense of control, either through working within the system, by using every appeal possibility to challenge the CTO, or working outside the system, by acting like the CTO did not exist (avoiding appointments and disregarding notices of recall to hospital). In Craig's case, he used both routes, with the problems the

CTO caused between him and his care coordinator leading to the decision to remove it:

> I'd say the biggest factor to take Craig off the CTO … when I visited him, he sat with a notebook and a pen while we were having a conversation and I thought I can't, how on earth do you work with someone when they're sat with a notebook and a pen recording every element of your conversation ready for the next tribunal … you can't work with someone like that, can you? It's impossible … so that for me was the–, this is nuts … he's got to come off it. (Care coordinator)

During follow-up interviews with service users post-discharge, it became clear that despite the continuing presence of leverage and the potential 'threat' of a further CTO, its removal could be a step towards repairing the service user-practitioner relationship and enabling more effective support. Rebuilding a mutual sense of trust and moving the relationship away from a focus on monitoring and compliance necessitated practitioners disassociating themselves from the CTO. Irene, when talking about the post-CTO changes to her relationship with her care coordinator said: 'We've got a lot closer now. I'm more free, I've got more choice now. I feel she helps me more now. Because they know I want help now.' The CTO is designed to encourage individuals into engaging with practitioners, but what these participants' experiences suggest is that feeling compelled into accepting help can sometimes undermine more meaningful engagement. Moreover, in Irene's view, having to accept support meant that practitioners 'had' to provide it; being taken off the CTO represented more freedom on both sides of the relationship, and in turn she felt more valued by her care coordinator. Discharging the CTO could act as a way for practitioners and resistant service users to find a 'mutual account' within which they could work together.

However, a significant minority of service users who were happy to be on the CTO wanted it to be a long-term presence in their lives, which could bring its own set of challenges for practitioners. Service users could closely align their sense of self and what they subsequently felt they needed in terms of support and external authority with the CTO. For these service users who appreciated the boundaries the CTO provided, the idea of the CTO being removed could generate similar feelings associated with coercion such as not having their view respected, anxiety and a lack of control. Nick expressed considerable anxiety about the thought of being discharged: 'I'd like to stay on it for the rest of my life, if I could. I wish they'd done this years ago to us. Maybe things wouldn't have turned out the way they have turned out.' In such cases, a pattern of uncertainty surfaced in practitioner discussion of individuals, in terms of how and if to bring about CTO discharge. On one hand, practitioners often thought the service user was more than ready to be taken off the CTO, on the other they were aware of the distress such a decision would cause and recognised that the CTO offered meaningful security to the service user. A psychiatrist talked about the difficulties these situations could bring:

> There are cases where the CTO has to be continued at the insistence of the patients themselves. Very surprising. There is one particular patient, she is so adamant to remain on the CTO, so that makes the decision-making very difficult. Myself and the other people involved really strongly feel the CTO has run its course and she could function extremely well and engagement is not an issue. But I think it would be unwise to go against the express wishes of the patient. It would definitely affect the therapeutic relationship, we'd definitely be blamed if it goes wrong. It's going to be quite a battle to convince her really.

As one AMHP commented, if it were an inpatient section, there could be gradual discharge from hospital to acclimatise the individual, but 'you can't do a gradual discharge for a CTO'. The service user in this kind of situation thus has a substantial amount of control over discharge decision-making. 'Never-ending' CTOs are usually presented as generated by the nature of the CTO framework and by practitioners, but in these cases it is the service user who drives sustained compulsion. This highlights both the variety of responses the CTO can provoke and the complexity of discharge decision-making in relation to such responses.

Conclusion

Given that CTO reviews allow for contestation and shifts in decision-making, how service users presented their progress took a more significant role than it had at other decision-making points in the CTO process. In order to overcome practitioner qualms about risk-taking and alleviate their sense of uncertainty, service users who had managed the CTO well then had to persuade practitioners that they would continue to engage with services and to make progress in their lives. To do this, service users called on evidence of their progress and the trust that they had built up with practitioners. Where practitioners believed they really knew and trusted the individual in question and witnessed adherence through different phases of the CTO, a decision to discharge was more likely. In turn, practitioners were more likely to elicit such a response from service users if they were clear and honest about when and why the CTO would end. Hence the agency service users displayed in acting on CTOs, together with the mediating influence of the service user-practitioner relationship on the CTO, continued to be present in its final stage as they had throughout. Equally, a reliance by practitioners on particular kinds of proof and conceptualisations of causality could make it difficult for service users to entirely escape the CTO. While individuals who have been within the mental health system for a long time tend to be consistently subjected to various kinds of formal and informal leverage, the very fact that a CTO had been in place could frame future service user actions and service responses in a way which meant the CTO could not entirely be escaped.

For service users who had not adhered to the CTO, practitioners also had to decide whether to take a risk in discharging. Such dilemmas were framed in ethical terms and continued the balancing acts practitioners had taken over the course of the CTO about whether it could be deemed morally proper and relatedly the effect it had both on individual service users and their actions towards the CTO. In this sense the practical and the ethical remained entwined; practitioners expressed qualms about the impact on service users of reaching a 'tipping point' in dependency and alienation but also about the responses such effects could engender and the difficulties they might bring for service provision and practice. Given the nature of such cases, deciding to take this risk was not based on active persuasion on the part of service users, but instead whether maintaining the CTO was worth the ethical discomfort and associated difficulties it had brought or exacerbated. Here we can see the unintended consequences of the CTO as a whole in terms of the outcomes it might produce, and indeed how removing the CTO could elicit the outcomes it was hoped that the CTO would bring in relation to relationship-building and inculcating responsibility. Conversely, not all service users struggled against the CTO, and those service users who felt strongly that the CTO met a need for them that could not be met in other ways might experience anxiety and disenfranchisement about the idea of being 'forced off' the CTO. In sum, the CTO may be least effective for those for whom it is supposed to work – those who resist compulsion – and in a sense too effective for those where it is not deemed necessary – those who are willing to engage.

7

Practice paradoxes and (perverse) consequences

In this penultimate chapter, we distil the themes we have identified in this book relating to the self-work service users displayed while on the community treatment order (CTO) and the disparate consequences for the 'ends' of CTOs this generated. In Chapter 3 we noted that service users pushed the boundaries of the CTO in various ways, finding space for actions beyond the intended remit of the CTO; 'a genuine room for play that provides strategic opportunities' (Han, 2019, 20). In Chapters 4 and 5 we touched on, via 'impossible' practice and decision-making 'tipping points', the ways that practitioners managed (or indeed did not manage) the anomalies and contradictions these service user actions produced in CTOs. Accordingly, there is no straightforward account of what the implications of CTOs might be and how they might unfold. How we think about variable conducts and counter-conducts relates to how the consequences of control work are framed. If an individual responds in unexpected ways to compulsion, the benefit versus harm balance becomes complicated due to unanticipated and unintended effects. How do we give weight to some consequences over others? Where does the primacy lie in perceptions of whether consequences are 'good' or 'bad'?

CTO 'ends': self-work, change and consequences

We ground these questions in a reflection on six specific service user participants. Service users' sense of self and self in ethical relation to others led to complex and ambiguous responses to compulsion which are not always easily categorised into binary forms of compliance and resistance to the CTO. Revisiting Foucault's (1997a) dimensions of ethical self-work, we can see that they relate to: external impetus for change, the means by which we act upon ourselves to bring about such change and the end person we seek to become through these means. In formulating forms of conduct and counter-conduct, the CTO cannot be understood as transformative in and of itself but instead as the external catalyst. The task is to delineate how the means and ends service users have conceived for themselves relate to the means and ends of the CTO. Service users can be placed along a spectrum from acceptance to resistance, and the cases referred to in this study can be located at different points on this spectrum.

Acceptance of CTO means and ends: the contrasting cases of Nick and James

Nick and James can be described as the two service users who most wholeheartedly accepted the CTO and both expressed strong respect for the authority of the professionals who worked with them. Neither of them had experienced recall, as they had adhered to the CTO and practitioners saw the role of the CTO in their cases being for boundary-setting rather than active intervention. In a superficial sense, they both can be seen as CTO 'success' stories, particularly regarding behaviour change. However, there are interesting contrasts that can be drawn between them which are not quite as clear-cut, beginning with how the CTO related to the changes they wanted to see in themselves. Nick and James aligned themselves with different aspects of the CTO agenda, each corresponding to how they saw themselves and their relationships to others. For some service users, self-conception was refracted through a 'risk' identity and Nick was one of those individuals who expressed extreme anxiety about what he thought he was capable of in relation to harming others, particularly those who he was close to. The CTO for him was a way of externalising the control he did not feel able to exert over himself and therefore he accepted one particular 'end' of the CTO – risk management – as it related to the kind of individual he wanted to become. As such, Nick was also one of the individuals who did not want to be discharged from the CTO, and talked about it as being necessary for the safety of others as well as his continuing and relative autonomy in the community. James, conversely, had taken on board the messages about responsibility inculcated in the CTO. He saw himself very much in relation to the broader mental health system and network of support he received from practitioners, family and friends. In this sense he felt it his 'duty' and responsibility to use the CTO to recover and live what he viewed as a productive and independent life. James did not see the CTO as a permanent proposition but trusted that the changes he was making in his life would demonstrate to practitioners that he was ready to move on from the CTO when ready.

Nick's compliance with the CTO and insistent dependence on its continuation can, however, also be seen as a form of resistance to practitioners' attempts to 'move people on' to independence. James, although he spoke in a particular way about authority, took some control from his treating team by making his own autonomous decision on how and where he should receive medication, and thus acted on his own volition to make the CTO process fit his perception of what it should be. In making this choice, James also reduced his treating team's ability to monitor his medication and consequently created some 'space' for himself within compulsion. Although Nick and James orientated themselves respectively to the risk and recovery aims of the CTO, they were therefore not entirely 'exemplars' of conduct. In this sense Nick and James encapsulated the tensions that can exist between differing control ends.

Resistance to CTO means but acceptance of ends: Irene

Irene held much resentment about being under the CTO, related to a sense of what 'normality' should be for her and the anxiety the CTO caused as a framework for potential intervention at any time. However, much of her resentment was ironically yet strongly related to her acceptance of the potential ends of the CTO. By forcing her to engage, she felt the CTO had taken away her ability to engage on her own terms, which was very important to her. For Irene, the CTO reinforced barriers between her and professionals, blocking the ability for relational work and meaningful engagement while at the same time magnifying an adversarial focus on the negation of her rights. Irene wanted to be able to collaborate with professionals, a view which reflected her belief on what the service user-practitioner relationship should be. In this sense, Irene believed in the potential 'first-level' aim of the CTO – consistent engagement with services – while at the same time disliking the CTO as the means to get there. While the CTO ensured superficial compliance on Irene's part, it was only when it was lifted that she and her care coordinator felt she was able to fully engage with treatment and support. Consequently, it can be argued that in cases like Irene's, where the 'norms' the CTO is supposed to be promoting are accepted but the use of the CTO in itself is not, coming off the CTO might encourage the responsibilised response that its use is supposed to facilitate.

Resistance to CTO ends but acceptance of means: Simon

Resistance to CTO ends but acceptance of its means meant in Simon's case 'playing the CTO game' for his own ends, which did not cohere with the CTO drivers of risk or recovery. Simon regularly attempted (and at least initially succeeded) in triggering recall by refusing his medication and avoiding contact with services. He explained this as a way for him to get admitted to hospital, which he saw as a significant safety net when he needed 'time out'. Simon had developed a pattern over the years of seeking admission to a respite facility as a coping strategy, but with the closure of this service and increasingly limited access to beds in acute services, his coping strategy had been disrupted. In one sense placing Simon on the CTO had further removed his ability to decide when he needed additional help. However, by subverting the key component of the CTO, Simon had found a way of meeting his self-prescribed needs and retaining some kind of agency. Simon's care coordinator was sympathetic to Simon seeking to maintain his much-needed dependency on services in this way, understanding it as a protective factor, but at the same time his actions did not fit with the mandated use of recall. Simon had effectively undermined the use of the CTO by making it difficult for practitioners to decide when *they* thought he 'needed' recall and consequently his CTO was eventually discharged.

Resistance to CTO ends and means: the contrasting cases of Andrew and Craig

At the furthest end of the spectrum were those individuals who rejected both the CTO and what it stood for. Resistance to CTO ends and means meant a complete rejection of the 'service user role', and Andrew and Craig provide interesting insights into how this might play out. Neither Andrew or Craig felt the CTO had any place in their lives – they resented both the compulsion it placed them under and the sense that it was aimed at shaping their attitude and behaviour, when they wanted to be 'left alone' by services. They articulated this resistance in different ways, however. Andrew would continue to have occasional meetings with his care coordinator, but avoided medication where possible and refused to meet his psychiatrist. Craig also avoided appointments but would, in addition, resist recall by disappearing for days at a time when it was instigated and regularly fight the CTO legally through the appeals system, thus in a way using the system against itself. A combination of Andrew's forensic history and a tendency to acquiesce to recall meant that his treating team had decided the CTO on balance was worth maintaining even though it had a significant negative effect on him personally. In contrast, although it was felt unlikely Craig would consistently engage with services once the CTO was lifted, he was deemed to pose little risk. This, along with the additional problems the CTO was causing both practically and ethically meant that on balance the decision was made to stop his CTO.

Conclusion

These cases have illustrated the non-binary forms conduct and counter-conduct can take. Conduct and counter-conduct are two sides of the same coin and mutually constitutive – neither involves 'stepping outside' of existing power structures, but instead responding to disciplinary power in different ways, as related to both individual and social means and ends. Removing this 'either/or' distinction from discussions of power and resistance means that such responses can be seen in a more variegated sense, which does not look 'beyond government' (Rose, 1999, 281) but at how individual action plays out *within* the strategies and techniques of government. As Death (2010, 236, emphasis in original) comments, forms of conduct 'have the potential to reinforce and bolster, as well as *and at the same time as,* undermining and challenging dominant forms of … governance'. With CTOs, it is possible to see where conduct and counter-conduct contain continuity and movement between them: with Nick who although compliant in every sense to the CTO highlights the challenges practitioners might face when individuals resist the lifting of compulsion; Irene, whose personal 'ends' aligned with those of the CTO even if she resented the CTO in itself; Simon who took the means of the CTO to achieve his own ends; and even with Craig, who used the oversight system integral to the CTO as a form of resistance to the CTO.

Moving on to how we might think about CTO consequences, these six cases also point to the way that complex responses can lead to complex and sometimes perverse consequences. Furthermore, they highlight how these consequences can be weighed up by practitioners in different ways depending on the individual and their circumstances, thus leading to differentiated decisions on when the CTO might be continued or not. For example, in Irene's case it was recognised that the unintended consequence of the CTO was to further alienate her from the therapeutic relationship, and the consequence of removing it was to increase her sense of having some kind of responsibility for her treatment in partnership with practitioners, thus furthering her engagement with services. Or as in Simon's case, his subversion of the recall function meant that the CTO was rendered useless and thus deemed by practitioners as pointless to continue. A similar story can be told about those individuals believed to be high risk, where the very presence of the CTO could further exacerbate 'risky' behaviour, inverting the intended purpose of the CTO as a way of managing risk in the community.

Hence, although the underlying premise of recall is to compel individuals to behave in a certain way, such compulsion can work least well for many of those who are deemed to need the CTO most. However, CTOs were more often than not viewed in terms of success *and* failure by practitioners. For those individuals like Andrew whose resistance to the CTO regularly triggered recall, practitioners might think of it as a 'failed CTO' because it has exacerbated rather than mitigated the 'revolving door' cycle, leaving individuals with less stability in the community, damaging the therapeutic relationship and costing time and resources. An alternative view is that if repeat recalls means service users are regularly taking medication and subsequently staying relatively well, then the CTO is working in lowering their risk to others and ensuring they are protected from the worst of relapse. By thinking about the implications of control in this way, we are able to both elucidate the variety of consequences that can occur but also consider success and failure in more multifaceted and partial terms, taking into account the varying significance they are given by different actors and the ethical balancing acts practitioners may face when weighing them up.

This latter point is particularly important when considering how control-oriented interventions turn out, as it promotes a discussion of value which does not conflate ethicality with effectiveness. The products of power are unpredictable and therefore difficult to judge. The question of value in control practices will be considered in the concluding chapter.

8

Reconciling control

In this book we have endeavoured to get beneath the surface of community treatment order (CTO) *practice* – to better understand how and why it manifests in particular ways, what drives these manifestations and the implications for service users and practitioners who are invested in them. In doing so, we have built upon the scaffold of the existing body of CTO research to provide a distinctive theorising of CTOs: by exposing the 'ins and outs' of CTO practice; how it keys into both service users' and practitioners' ethical beliefs and sense of self; how it influences and is influenced by the therapeutic relationship; and how it may result in mixed and unexpected responses and consequences. Such an account holds significant relevance for social work, in foregrounding the various ways control plays out via different kinds of power within the mental health domain. This final chapter draws together our analysis and considers its implications for control work in community mental health specifically and social work more broadly, exploring the ways that control and ethical social work can be reconciled. We begin with a reflection on the central themes of our analysis.

The thinking and doing of CTOs

In this section we return to the questions we posed at the beginning of the book and consider what our analysis tells us about CTO 'regimes of practice'.

Assembling rationalities for introducing the CTO

Foucault argued that programmes of government include the seeds of their failure, which inevitably leads to on-going mutations in forms of government (Lemke, 2000). The unintended effects of deinstitutionalisation can be seen as a starting point for programmes such as CTOs, which, in turn, are based on specific ways of thinking about the ensuing problems to be solved. A particular assemblage of behavioural and biomedical rationalities was thus called upon in the creation of CTOs. The management of individuals with severe mental difficulties in the community represented a problem that politically, needed to be seen to be dealt with, hence *why* CTOs came to be embedded in policy regimes.

In policy discourse CTOs have been framed as a solution by way of strengthening the surveillance and (primarily medical) control of risky individuals in the community. In the case of CTOs, the group made 'visible' to be worked upon are 'revolving door patients' and a concern with risk can especially be seen in how this group is left undefined in legislation, relying instead on professional discretion, meaning the application of CTOs can be decided preventatively on the prediction of aberrant behaviour patterns. However, a concern with risk can be seen as the mirror to an agenda which encourages the individual to be prudential in managing their own lives. The recovery agenda as it has played out in mental health policy over the last two decades has been largely defined in ways which individualise social problems (Nielsen, Buus and Berring, 2023). Bringing 'irregular citizens' (Zedner, 2010) through recovery and back into the fold thus requires that strong boundaries are put in place in order to overcome internal constraints, so that individuals are able to develop the discipline to comply, maintain stability and eventually operate in the community with a sense of self-efficacy and in a way which coheres with normative rules. From this perspective, CTOs can be seen as a typical governmental practice which is aimed at disciplining what individuals may become; the limitation of negative freedom in the short term encourages individuals' capacity for positive freedom in the longer term.

This tallies with the intensification in recent decades of a behaviourist trend in social policy and an associated turn to 'coercive support' across a range of welfare domains (Brown, 2024). A 'thin' biomedical model was called upon in the policy development of CTOs; non-compliance results from a lack of insight framed as a neurological deficit, and subsequently the prevalent mediating factor for risk and recovery is medication adherence, which will enable self-regulation. There is little acknowledgement in this framework of the complex social and personal reasons why individuals might be non-adherent, their history, hopes and self-conceptions, or the societal and institutional factors which mediate risk and pathways to recovery. Because programmes like CTOs are based on 'thin' assumptions about drivers for behaviours, they can also contain simplistic expectations about the responses of the 'target' group and subsequently what the programme outcomes will be. It seems that both the multifaceted motivations and challenges service users and practitioners bring to CTOs, coupled with the complex ways they interact with CTOs, mean such expectations are not always fulfilled. Policy interventions framed as 'carrots, sticks and sermons' (Bemelmans-Videc, Rist and Vedung, 1998) do not account for such context or the reflexive work it instigates.

Thinking the CTO through

We have noted that practitioners saw a need for CTOs, and that they felt the CTO filled a gap in mental health practice. In this sense, practitioners were aligned both with the policy narrative on CTOs and prior research on practitioner attitudes towards the CTO (DeRidder et al, 2016). Specifically, CTOs were viewed as giving practitioners more control and certainty regarding the oversight of particular individuals in the community. It is noteworthy that practitioners did not only welcome CTOs for practice-oriented reasons but also thought that CTOs represented a 'better deal' for service users too. Indeed, this latter belief points to one particular difference between policy and practice-level theory on CTOs. In contrast to CTOs being theorised as lessening demand on services, practitioners felt that CTOs could be turned to service users' advantage through giving them access to resources via the obligations they held under the CTO. It seems therefore that an element of practitioner reasoning for the CTO was that they framed it in a reciprocal way as a 'true' contract, rather than the relatively one-sided version that had been argued for in policy formulations.

This connects with a practice-level purpose for CTOs that was entirely missing from the policy agenda – that of giving service users' protection of various kinds. Protection was a strong motivator for some practitioners, either through seeing the CTO as an intervention which would mean more coercive experiences could be avoided, or through ensuring relapse was dealt with through access to inpatient services in a timely manner. Thinking in this way brings back a categorisation which is missing from the dual risk/responsibility narrative for CTOs – that of dependency – which does not align easily with disciplinary 'practices of government … which have come to rely on the agency of the governed themselves' (Dean, 2010, 82). As one practitioner put it: 'What's wrong with just caring for people when they're unwell? Everyone seems obsessed with moving people on, why can't we just accept that some people aren't going to move on, and need our support?' As illustrated in the last chapter, some service users also valued the CTO in similar terms, as a signifier of care, enduring and reliable support, such that they felt they were being coerced into having it removed. For those individuals, control did not equate to coercion; instead the opposite – potential freedom from the CTO – was experienced as coercive. The public positioning of policy programmes aimed at behavioural change as premised on control can hide the provision of enhanced support such programmes may provide to the individuals made subject to them, particularly when more universal provision is becoming increasingly restricted.

Furthermore, given the longstanding arguments that mental health services are focused on an instrumentalist process of risk minimisation (Szmukler and Rose, 2013; Stanford et al, 2017), it is worth pointing out that protection was as or more important for many practitioners than risk management. Of course, some service users prefer the 'short, sharp shock' of intermittent compulsion rather than the sense of 'never-ending' compulsion of the CTO. Accordingly, a paternalistic form of protection – typified by practitioners believing they are acting in the best interests of service users even if against their wishes – can be as central to the defence of restricting autonomy as risk management, yet a preoccupation with risk to others in mental health discourse means that this aspect of control can arguably be overlooked.

Given practitioners' involvement with the everyday reality of service users' lives, there was little support for the idea that risk 'events' could be understood or managed in the simplistic way presented in CTO policy debates, with emphasis instead placed on the compound elements which made such events unpredictable. Nevertheless, by ensuring medication compliance, practitioners felt that CTOs helped to manage *certain* kinds of risk for *certain* kinds of individuals, and therefore were better present in such cases than not. Campbell and Davidson (2009) note the deep-seated personal and emotional responses practitioners might have to service users, including fear, which can influence the use of compulsory intervention. The emotional toll of working with individuals in the community deemed as high risk due to a history of violence cannot be underestimated, and defensive practice was not simply about 'back-covering' – CTOs could give practitioners psychological ballast in feeling they were controlling what risks they could.

While practitioners did not take a straightforward view of CTOs or their purposes, more often than not referring to more than one, a general difference could still be drawn between those who referred to CTOs meeting risk and protective purposes, and those who saw them more as a vehicle for recovery. Accordingly, recovery could not only be in tension with risk management but also with the protective notions of care and dependence discussed earlier. It could be difficult for practitioners to reconcile these different theorisations for CTOs, and how they went about this appeared to be premised on the 'web of beliefs' (Bevir, 2010) they held about practice and what it is to be a 'good' practitioner (Evans, 2012). Such difficulties were at the heart of the ethical dilemmas and balancing acts many of them experienced in CTO practice. For those practitioners who saw their work as based more on a recovery model, the CTO should be used only when necessary and then only in a 'light-touch' way in order to both counter potential coercion and to discourage dependency. In recovery terms then, the imposition of the CTO would be seen as only worthwhile if it was not actually activated once in place, providing an 'invisible' guide for service users. It is with recovery that we can see practitioners perhaps most aligned with policy-level drivers for CTOs, theorising CTOs as providing a foundation for maintenance, subsequent behavioural change and even service user 'enlightenment' on the best way forward, leading to autonomy and responsibility in the community.

In this sense, the notion of recovery was viewed by practitioners as being most relevant when service users were deemed 'ready' to recover. The concept of insight can be seen therefore as one particularly significant manifestation of expert knowledge that practitioners drew upon in formulating CTO practice.

As we have seen, insight is a difficult concept to pin down, containing 'a multiplicity of meanings within, and across, discourses' (Diesfeld and Sjostrom, 2006, 90). Nevertheless, presented as an 'objective' state, insight is a central facet of how CTOs are theorised as a way of inculcating particular norms and ways of being. Used clinically to direct when CTOs are needed, and to decide if they are 'working' in recovery-oriented terms, insight thus provides a significant foundation for the 'conduct of conduct' through the CTO. In contrast, service user understanding of responsibility through the CTO was integrated with their description of recovery as a precarious journey, reliant on the care and aid of others. Such a view suggests a broader conception of recovery, more aligned with its original user-led formulation than the individualised form discussed thus far. As Trnka and Trundle (2014, 139) point out, the notion of responsibilisation does not account for the fact that 'descriptions of the self-managing individual frequently reveal a subject entangled within widespread ties … and duties to others'.

Interaction and influence in CTO practice

A key way therefore in which policy programmes such as CTOs illustrate the multifaceted operation of power is that even though they are based on compulsion, for certain purposes to be met they depend at least partly on the choices and actions of the subjects of intervention, but that these choices are made via a form of 'bonded agency' (Burkitt, 2016). Control can generate potent psychological effects; for service users who experienced feelings of stigma because of the CTO, it magnified their pre-existing sense of being 'outsiders' and, in turn, the limitations on what was possible and hoped for in life. Here we can see a reflection on self and self in relation to others as an articulation of belonging. Such feelings translated into how the CTO framework was interpreted, and the most obvious indicator of this was the way that the CTO was perceived to pervade various aspects of life even if this was not the case. Control then can be experienced coercively in ways that overspill the boundary of a discrete intervention, which reinforces distrust in services in general, and the actions and motivations of practitioners in particular. This process of internalisation of CTO 'messages' and binding them to pre-existing notions of self did not only apply to those service users who saw the CTO in a negative light. The CTO could play into beliefs on vulnerability and fragility, but also could trigger ambivalence through underscoring tensions between where individuals saw themselves in the present versus where they wanted to be in the future and accordingly between what they might need but also want in terms of service involvement.

How practitioners attempted (and sometimes failed) to work with such self-conceptions reiterates that processes of subjectification via governmental means are complicated by how people are 'made up' from below via communicative action, the application of lay normativity, as well as from above through discourse (Hacking, 2004; Haugaard, 2022).

The connection practitioners and service users did or did not make with each other was a central generative driver of why the CTO manifested in the way that it did. The work practitioners carried out in countering powerful narratives of stigma the CTO could engender while still holding the boundary of the CTO thus aligns with Barnett et al's (2008, 632) argument that 'rationalities which govern strategic interactions are not [solely] the pre-existing properties of the different actors involved, but are an emergent dimension of ongoing interaction itself'. It seems from the findings that there were two related aspects to this interactional activity. First, when and how service users are informed about the CTO and involved in its implementation and second how the CTO is framed in various ways which might fit with the underlying beliefs service users hold about their lives in the past, present and future. It appears that where early 'groundwork' was undertaken with service users, and careful negotiation took place – particularly on medication – the potential negative experience of coercion was more likely to be alleviated. Such findings reflect the body of research (see Newton-Howes, 2010) on how the experience of coercion can be alleviated by creative approaches to control work.

In this way, practitioner theories on how CTOs might work are 'muddied' by what they know about the circumstances and standpoints of individual service users. Indeed, it seems that in their persuasive discussions with service users, many practitioners held in critical abeyance their own perspectives on explanations and solutions for the mental distress experienced by service users. With skilled work, practitioners and service users could construct a mutually conducive narrative of how the CTO might meet shared goals. So, while practitioners utilised insight in CTO decision-making, this was not necessarily reflected in their day-to-day practice with service users. The invocation of insight could act to distance practitioners from service users and hamper the development of such mutual goal-setting. Instead we observed a rather complex interplay between the strong influence of insight on CTO formulations and ensuing decisions, and the everyday reality of CTO practice where obligations were negotiated when possible and practitioners often attempted to shape CTOs to 'fit' service user perspectives. Similarly, practitioners believed that placing service users on an injection as part of their conditions was central to making the CTO 'work'. However, for service users, actively accepting the CTO and making it 'work' in their terms could depend on medication choices remaining broad and practitioners acting in concordance with them in working toward wider goals, instead of expecting compliance. Equally, if practitioners gave a sensitive explanation of the CTO and their intentions in using it based on prior knowledge of the service user and their self-beliefs, then service users were more able to accept its imposition and operate within its bounds. Various compromises thus resulted in a version of the CTO which was 'good enough' for both parties. It needs to be acknowledged that for some practitioners, their view of what made the CTO 'work' could take precedence over co-constructing its purpose and remit, and this meant they reinforced rather than countering coercion through their failure to correct service user misconceptions on the boundaries of the CTO. As can be expected, while observed by us and referred to in the practice of others, this remained unspoken by practitioners in relation to their own practice, perhaps denoting a recognition that such strategies moved beyond ethical balancing acts to the crossing of ethical lines.

It also needs to be emphasised that careful and ethically boundaried work carried out between practitioners and service users could be constrained by institutional and cultural factors. Specifically, the tensions that exist between inpatient and community services due to resource constraints, fragmented communication and differing beliefs on the role of inpatient care, made it difficult at times for CTOs to be implemented in ways conducive to mitigation of coercion. In cases where the CTO was deemed inappropriate by community practitioners and yet was still imposed, it could have a damaging knock-on effect on the ongoing relationship they held with service users and consequently on the provision of services to those individuals. AMHPs acted as gatekeepers to a certain extent, by ensuring that the initial process was carried out thoroughly and that the CTO was reasonable and ethical in its scope. However, none of the AMHPs recollected ever disagreeing to a CTO, suggesting they would find it hard to do so given the wide remit of the legal criteria and the pressures inherent to group decision-making.

This illustrates a broader theme regarding the implicit logic of the CTO and the difficulties practitioners sometimes faced in contesting such logic, even when they felt the CTO should not be imposed in a particular case, or should be used differently than it was being used once in place, for example in the activation of recall. Foucault (1990, 94–5) acknowledges this problem for relational forms of power when he states:

> Power relations are both intentional and non-subjective … there is no power that is exercised without a series of aims and objectives. But this does not mean it results from the choice or decision of an individual subject, let us not look for a headquarters that presides over its rationality.

Evans and Harris (2004) make the point that an increase in rules and bureaucracy can ironically lead to more space becoming available for practitioners to operate with discretion. Here, however, the breadth of latitude present in CTO criteria and operation meant practitioners could feel their range of choices became restricted and consequently their ability to act with discretion limited. The interaction of structural with relational and reflexive forms of power meant CTOs could take on a momentum of their own which was in some ways distinct to the motivations and ethical beliefs of the actors involved in their use.

The pluralistic unfolding of surface-level practice

The evolution of CTO practice in particular directions – the most obvious example being the creation of recall 'cycles' – also highlights the relationship that runs throughout the findings between what can be constituted as 'surface' and 'depth' level practice as denoted in the last section (Howe, 1996; Parton, 2008). These forms of practice cohered with practitioners' normative ideals regarding what practice 'should' be like and what was possible under the CTO in relation to risk, protection or recovery. The mechanistic, reductive and authoritarian use of CTOs, involving fast and definite responses to infractions of the CTO 'contract' to solely contain risk, was viewed as necessary in a small number of cases by some practitioners, even when it caused significant ethical unease. As such, this practice is the closest illustrative example of CTOs as functions of repressive, causal power we encountered.

Even so, the kinds of CTO practice we witnessed were not always straightforwardly 'superficial' or 'deep' in application or effect. Surface and depth practice cannot only be characterised by a tension between external mandates on practice and practitioners' preferred ways of working. Instead, the way they manifested here was in less hierarchical and more interactional ways. Surface and depth practice was influenced by surface and depth responses, and it was the case that superficial engagement via the CTO could be a way for both service users to maintain some sense of control, and practitioners to lessen coercion by maintaining a minimal presence. Alternatively, attempts to mitigate the CTO framework by demonstrating flexibility and working with service users could exacerbate coercive experiences by sharpening service users' sense of the compulsion they were under, as with the circumvention of recall by practitioners. Furthermore, the structure and routine the CTO framework offers can enable as well as constrain deeper levels of engagement. The use of conditions, particularly in ensuring regular contact, could help to build trust and acceptance of support where previously it had not been possible. Having a contract to work to could also clarify the boundaries of intervention for service users and give practitioners a starting point for 'difficult' and reflective conversations, particularly on risk. Boardman and Roberts (2014) note that there has been little attention paid in mental health research or practice to service users' views on risk and risk management, and they comment that risk planning and assessment is often carried out without the service user's knowledge or involvement. While CTOs have been criticised for being ostensibly another 'top-down' tool for risk management it appears that they can act to make concerns around risk explicit and become a co-constructed risk management endeavour, embedded within relational practice.

Indeed, it seems that this relational work was important for effective risk management within the CTO. Building trust can help mitigate risk concerns by curtailing hazardous events through increased access, disclosure and cooperation by service users (Blumenthal, Wood and Williams, 2018). The interplay between a lack of trust in practitioners and the fear that the CTO brought for those service users who viewed it coercively could result in an unwillingness to disclose sensitive information, thus making it more challenging for practitioners to pre-empt difficulties. In more complex cases, particularly where signifiers of risk such as a forensic history, substance misuse and a diagnosis of personality disorder were present, it seems that the CTO had the potential to stimulate risk. A combination of the negative response of the service user to additional control, a lack of ability to use recall as a safeguard in such cases, a reluctance on the part of practitioners to manage 'social' causes of risky behaviour, and the CTO giving other agencies the opportunity to divest their responsibilities, meant that contrary to policy formulations, a possible perverse consequence of the CTO was further entrenchment of what might be deemed the 'riskiest' of cases. It seems therefore that considering the CTO as a standalone risk management tool is not enough. Szmukler and Rose (2013) argue that risk management is all-encompassing in mental health services. However, the limits the CTO can be put to and the delineation of different kinds of risks by practitioners mean that this might not always be the case.

Weighing up change

For the majority of cases however, CTOs could be perceived as working too well given the multiple theories of practice they encompassed combined with practitioner notions of causality. Research suggests that the average length of CTOs in England is three years (Barkhuizen et al, 2020), much longer than was predicted by the Government when CTOs were first introduced into legislation and our analysis of decision-making at the point of CTO renewal/discharge highlights why this might be the case. CTOs were seen to not only be difficult to discharge but also difficult to escape entirely with initial application of the CTO making its reimposition more likely further down the line. It seems that a wider-reaching consequence of CTOs is that rather than replace the 'revolving door' it may supplement it with other forms of institutionalisation. Such a theorisation moves beyond simply comparing hospitalisation to community compulsion, by complicating what may be considered the 'least restrictive' approach. It also highlights a second strand of practitioner decision-making considered in this study, and that is how different kinds of knowledge are weighed up. In this sense, it is not just a case of practical–moral concerns about the consequences of the CTO as considered in the last chapter but also how practitioners think about change, both internal and external, when making decisions about ending the CTO. Practitioners took different approaches and had different comfort levels when managing uncertainty, but central to the decision to discharge was the evidence the service user presented – how convincing they were that 'true' change had been achieved – combined with the trust practitioners held in them. In this sense, we turned from the more common way trust is considered – service users' trust in practitioners and services – to the ways that trust plays out in practitioner decisions. Brown and Calnan (2012) argue that a false dichotomy between rationality and irrationality underpins thinking on decision-making, and that choosing to trust is a necessary and effective way of managing uncertainty. They separate trust from notions of familiarity and confidence; describing the conditions in which it becomes relevant, such as where an individual is vulnerable amidst uncertainty, leading to an interaction of dependence with choice; and defining the process of trust formation as active and relational. As Ramsay (2009) states, the ability to reassure is necessary for individuals to move out from control frameworks and for practitioners, being dependent on service users' narratives means taking a 'leap of faith'.

Implications for social work practice

CTOs are now an embedded and seemingly durable feature of English mental health policy and practice. At the same time however, continuing bed shortages, changes to commissioning and provision, the ongoing disparity between health and mental health funding and in a more fundamental sense deepening societal inequalities continue to influence the use of CTOs and compulsion more broadly. In this sense, it is important to keep track of how CTOs are being used within the wider policy and practice context, as it seems likely that further pressures on services will make it harder for practitioners to use CTOs in the more individually tailored ways that this study has highlighted. Nevertheless, we can still consider the messages the conclusions reached hold for social work practice, particularly within the mental health field. As Shaw and Gould (2001, 195) suggest 'all situations are different to some extent' and so reasonable comparison between contexts based on 'thick description' is of particular value for 'real world' practice settings. Flyvbjerg (2006) problematises predictive theory in the social sciences, arguing that 'context-dependent knowledge' allows for 'deep' experiential learning in a way that 'rules-based' knowledge does not. At the same time, research often has more of an indirect and cumulative influence than a direct impact on policy and practice. It is also necessary to acknowledge that the study findings do not foster a straightforward, non-contradictory narrative on what can be said about practicing within frameworks of control within mental health. We are mindful of Foucault's (1988, 197) position 'that it is not up to us to propose. What we have to present are instruments and tools that people might find useful … this is how, in the end, possibilities open up.' Consequently, these findings should be considered as starting points for discussion and debate rather than definitive proclamations and dependent on taking into account constraints on practice alongside the diversity of situations, needs, perspectives and responses of practitioners and service users alike.

The interplay between (and within) policy, practitioner and service user 'ends'

CTOs cannot be seen as premised on a single policy aim but instead on the interplay of different goals – namely risk, recovery and resources – which can both support and be in tension with each other. These goals have been modified and mediated by practitioners in line with their own priorities, and also led to protection/reciprocity appearing as drivers in practitioner accounts. In turn, service users hold their own purposes and anti-purposes for CTOs, which interact in various ways with policy/practitioner expectations, and disrupt the 'thin' theorisation of thought and behaviour that CTOs are based on. The challenges these different configurations bring for CTO 'ends' are manifold. From a policy perspective, the tensions present in policy formulations have been translated to practice, and although many practitioners tried to uphold recovery as an end result, there are strong constraining factors, including the very nature of the CTO framework which counteract this agenda. This is not to suggest that recovery is necessarily preferable to other purposes in all circumstances. Indeed, risk management, recovery and protection were important for different service users; the individualised version of recovery that dominates in policy/practice did not fit with many service users' conceptions of what recovery is; and considerations of risk and protection had their place – albeit within their own sets of constraints – as part of the practice of CTOs, particularly considering the relational risk management that occurred. However, given suggestions that CTOs should be reconsidered because they have proven ineffective for 'revolving door' and recovery purposes, there is potentially a misalignment between policy/practice and the way that CTOs have been judged thus far. For practitioners, the challenges are related to first balancing and prioritising competing goals for individuals service users at different points in the CTO and second demonstrating awareness and sensitivity towards the role service users see CTOs playing in their lives, so they can where possible, orientate CTOs to a shared purpose for service users' treatment and support. In this way it seems more likely that outcomes will be reached that are acceptable and meaningful to both practitioners and service users.

The role of relationship in mediating coercion under the CTO

A large part of managing this challenge for practitioners is mediating the potentially coercive effects of CTOs for those service users who are not enamoured with their use. Early discussion and explanation of the CTO with service users in a way that was relevant to them as individuals made a significant difference to shifting views and perspectives and alleviating potential difficulties further down the line. In addition, practitioners talking about the aim of the CTO from the beginning, and developing with service users a clear idea of what success would look like for them could help mitigate feelings of hopelessness and uncertainty. While the conditions of CTOs are automatically documented, it may also be helpful, perhaps as part of the care plan, for practitioners to document what the CTO is being used *for* with that particular service user, which can be revisited as a guide throughout the process. It also should be acknowledged that with some service users, such an approach was not possible due to engrained mistrust in services and practitioners. In these cases, however, 'working round' the CTO by adapting it to the service user, negotiating and arbitrating medication, and focusing on wider emotional, social and practical needs could support the continuation of helpful collaborative work. In addition, while service user beliefs about the CTO were more fixed and less amenable to external influence once it was in place and active, practitioners being honest and clear about how the CTO would work for individual service users at particular points could at times help to alleviate anxiety about its use. In a broader sense, it seems that an important 'bridge' that could be built is for practitioners to understand, accept and acknowledge this anxiety as connected to service users' felt stigma and coercion, their sense of self and their hopes and fears, rather than invalidate it because there were no concrete adverse implications of the CTO.

Questioning the conflation of control and coercion

The discussion also points to where the received wisdom on mitigating coercion may not always hold true. Using the CTO to protect from 'harsher' compulsion may have its place for some individuals, but simply comparing community compulsion favourably to hospitalisation is not always enough. For some service users, what feels like the unending presence of the CTO combined with not being able to make a choice on how they live in the community and 'take a chance' on being admitted, meant that this favourable comparison did not always stand. More specifically, attempts to circumvent or soften the functions of the CTO could have the effect of enhancing service users' sense of coercion. There is no easy way of resolving such paradoxical eventualities, and as we pointed out in the discussion of 'surface' and 'depth' practice, practitioners might draw on approaches from both 'types' of practice in ways that are adapted to the individual service user they are working with, without assumptions being made about one approach necessarily being more fitting, effective or ethical than the other. Further, it seemed important for care coordinators in particular to know when the CTO was a hindrance more than a help and be given the opportunity by other professionals to 'let go' of control via rescinding the CTO in those cases in order to bring about a more sustainable relationship.

The role of institutional and cultural factors

The work practitioners carried out with service users cannot be seen in isolation – institutional and cultural factors were significant in shaping CTO processes and consequences. There have been significant differences between rates and patterns of CTO use in different parts of the country (Weich et al, 2020), and while the institutional pressures in both field sites were similar to national policy and service trends, team-level cultural influences appeared to contribute more to differences in use. Professional roles could lead to team-level tensions on CTO use, most evidently between psychiatrists and care coordinators, and psychiatrists and AMHPs. In addition, group decision-making on CTOs demonstrates that given the wide parameters of their criteria they can be difficult for practitioners to challenge, unless there is a team mandate to do so. It is ironic that the room for manoeuvre that practitioners have with CTOs means that they can feel that their options in decision-making are limited to agreement on the imposition and active use of CTOs. In their post-legislative scrutiny of the 2007 Mental Health Act, the Health Committee stated that they were 'surprised by the extent of variation between clinicians' when using CTOs and that this should not 'be permitted to continue without serious professional challenge' (HC Health Committee, July 2013, HC 584, para 92). It should not be surprising given how CTOs have been set up to begin with that this variation has occurred. However, it is difficult to say what 'serious professional challenge' might mean. It seems that where CTOs were actively questioned and challenged there had been open discussion about them, which had meant the team coming to a general agreement on how they would be used irrespective of organisational role. Perhaps this says something about the potential usefulness of such forums for incubating a shared understanding of CTOs.

In a broader sense, inter-agency communication on the role and remit of the CTO is also of importance. Criminal justice agencies such as the police and probation could see the CTO as almost akin or as a substitute to any involvement they might have with a service user, which could leave mental health practitioners sometimes feeling that they had been left without support and under pressure to 'do something' even if they justifiably did not regard it as entirely their responsibility in complex and high-risk cases. Although the pressures on inpatient services are qualitatively different, differing expectations of the CTO between inpatient and community services could adversely affect continuity of care. These are longstanding issues in mental health and unlikely to be resolved soon. However, it seems important to acknowledge the significant role they play, particularly in contributing to the complex consequences that can result from CTOs.

Balancing the varying consequences of CTOs in decision-making

The part intangible factors play in CTO decisions needs to be considered, in particular the roles that ideas and forms of knowledge take. In particular, we have noted the central place a consideration of insight takes in CTO decision-making and how it is put to use in a flexible way. It seems that practitioners who retained some critical distance from the concept of insight were able to come to an understanding of service user actions and motivations which meant they were more likely to demonstrate an adaptable and situational response to both the use of the CTO and when it should be discharged. Practitioners' consideration of insight can be seen to be working with as well as against relational knowledge in decision-making however, specifically when deciding whether to trust service user accounts of change. More broadly, the connections between the ethical frameworks that practitioners espoused and the way they responded to uncertainty and enacted risk-taking should also be highlighted. Practitioner beliefs about good practice mostly played out in terms of the parameters of control they were prepared to work within. We have highlighted throughout the practical–ethical nature of practice and how practitioners navigate between what they think is *ideal*, what is *possible* and indeed what is *necessary* when using CTOs. Indeed, taking account of the reactions of service users to the CTO and the subsequent effects that arose in terms of patterns of CTO use, levels of engagement represented a skilled endeavour which entailed looking beyond what 'types' of service users CTOs 'should' be used for. Instead, it involved practitioners sorting through a constellation of factors, both evidential and ethical, and making decisions at the various critical junctures in the life span of the CTO on that basis in relation to implications for the individual in question, as well as the community they live within. Emphasis is typically placed on the longevity of CTOs and the difficulty in bringing them to an end. By illuminating *why* this might be the case, and more significantly when practitioners *do* feel able to discharge CTOs, it is possible to see a starting point for thinking and acting critically in relation to 'CTO cycles', specifically the continuous re-imposition of CTOs.

Conclusion

We began this book by highlighting controversies regarding the role of power in social work and how the operation of power has garnered both sophisticated and inelegant criticism from observers who highlight the consequences for individuals where practitioners use forms of control ineffectively, heavy handedly or in unethical ways. Despite Foucault's assertion that the characterisation of power as a top-down form of sovereignty is limited, professional power is still largely visualised via this lens as a primary instrument of domination through which the state controls its populations.

These controversies remain current across the 'psy' disciplines, whether psychiatry, psychology, nursing or social work, manifesting in debates regarding the appropriate balance between care and control (Payne, 2008; Hardy, 2015). More specifically, they are central to discussions regarding if, when and how control mandates which operate via coercion can and should be used, if at all (Hemmington and Vicary, 2023). The consensus seems to be that such practice retains the potential for unethical acts particularly where decisions are undertaken within risk averse contexts. For some, compulsion represents a last possible resort which is best avoided and only to be contemplated within certain circumstances and under the strictest scrutiny. At worst it is portrayed as an unjust and illegitimate strategy that subjects people to involuntary treatment, undermines trust and integrity in and of mental health professionals, and strips service users of freedom, self-determination and the right to decide for themselves how best to live their lives.

The findings presented in this book however, suggest that this account is one sided. As we have seen, service users themselves have different ideas and perspectives regarding the purpose and experience of control, as do practitioners. Although bound by law, practice is varied, driven by ambiguous mandates, hard to predict and has multiple (often conflicting) consequences. And yet both service users and practitioners refer to various aspects of process, practice and consequences in positive terms, and indeed refer to life changing positive effects. On the other hand, the potential for and reality of ineffective and unethical practice is also recognised. The picture painted is one in which there is no way of knowing in advance how the use of control will play out. Subsequently we cannot presume what consequences may result from control work, or indeed from attempts to mitigate the negative effects of control.

Following on from this analysis, our study suggests that there would be benefits in considering alternative models to make sense of the ethics of power in mental health, which recognise the interplay between sovereign, disciplinary, consensual and reflexive forms of power. The continued emphasis within mental health law and practice on involuntary compulsion in its various guises reflects the predominant view that sometimes, people experiencing mental distress pose a risk to themselves or others and that the state has a responsibility to intervene to prevent such harm from occurring. Although this perspective has faced sustained criticism, nevertheless it remains a predominant concern within the politics of mental health and therefore within related health and welfare organisations (Burns, 2011). Despite various progressive shifts in how we think and talk about mental health, fear remains a significant factor in legal and policy development, and the mental health apparatus embodies this concern via the various statutory instruments by which practitioners can exercise power to remedy such concern. In social work in particular, practitioners are used to their work being criticised by various stakeholders as either ineffective or unethical. Both positions are evident in the study data. However, a distinctive theme also emerged regarding practitioner decision-making which is worth emphasising. Practitioners repeatedly reported making judgements within a framework of situated ethics. This change-oriented approach reflects the reality of complex and messy contexts for practice, and is necessarily less rooted in value based models. Instead, it is action oriented and more focused on pragmatic ends than idealised frameworks for decision-making. This should not be too surprising. Many authors (for example, Polkinghorne, 2004; Brendel, 2006; Hardy, 2015) have emphasised how practice realities challenge idealised models in ways that can be revealing. Thus, it is not a case of evaluating whether or not practitioners adhere to particular values that ought to determine whether practice is deemed ethical, but the experientially diverse ends – medical, emotional, social, psychological – experienced by multiple stakeholders, which are themselves messy and unpredictable. This is not to suggest that we adopt a sanguine perspective on power. Given that the data in this study highlights both positive and negative effects of control oriented practice, we should retain an ambivalent stance regarding the ethics of professional practice. However, a less idealist, more realist approach, enables a space for us to explore in more depth and detail the ways in which positive and negative consequences emerge in situated settings characterised by complexity. Ultimately, judgements regarding whether or not power has been used ethically can only be made on a case by case basis in full awareness of the limits to wider applicability and the implications of this that therefore accrue.

This book, then, has enabled some movement beyond the dichotomous perspectives that have emerged on CTOs since they were formulated. Governmental analysis of *how* practitioners and service users think and act in response to differential forms of power has implications for *why* CTOs follow particular pathways, and in introducing an ethical dimension to policy-practice evaluation broadens analysis beyond asking what factors make CTOs 'effective' or not. Conversely, exploring why CTOs play out as they do through various configurations has highlighted the ways that a governmental analysis, which can emphasise the 'strategic games' (Foucault, 2000) individuals play out in response to reformatory forces, may be complicated by accounts of agency and interaction which situate such responses as also co-constructed and 'embedded in broader practices of self-making and personhood' (Barnett et al, 2008, 644). Interpreting this normative dimension of everyday life is necessary to avoid a representation of 'bloodless figures who seemingly drift through life, behaving in ways which bear the marks of their social position and relations of wider discourses, disciplining themselves only because it is required of them, but as if nothing mattered to them' (Sayer, 2005, 51).

Taking a view of the operation of power as plural and micro-political in nature has enabled the CTO to be understood as a complex, diversely realised intervention positioned within the social and ethical world of service users and practitioners. The connections that can be made between forms of conduct and counter-conduct in the face of CTO means and ends demonstrate that the operation of power does not fit neatly into categories of 'power and powerlessness, consent and constraint, subjectivity and subjection' (Dean, 2010, 84). CTOs do not align simply or only with the more authoritarian arguments for their use. It seems therefore that the criticisms CTOs engender have perhaps overshadowed those elements of the policy that may result in positive practice and empowering outcomes. At the same time, CTOs cannot be said to always or only reach the more 'Utopian' goals also put forward by advocates of their use; the consequences we have highlighted suggest that CTOs are not always without adverse implications, particularly in the way of coercive effects. In this sense, 'taking a side' on CTOs does not allow for the contradictions that lie within such rationalities to begin with, nor with how there are continuities and breaks between these rationalities and practice which appear in sometimes unexpected ways.

Ambivalence regarding the operation and effects of power requires critical engagement with evidence of its effects. Consequently, while we have discussed the evaluative judgements made as part of CTO practice, we have been careful to not place ourselves as researchers within a strong value position on CTOs, while at the same not advocating a value free position. As Dean (2010, 46) puts it 'a stance that is neither enamoured with the "will to govern" nor utterly opposed to the practice of governing' is well placed to encompass the intersections and interactions of multiple logics of government. It may be that research on the use of control via CTOs cannot resolve the ethical and political conflict they present. However, research *can* shed light on ethical dilemmas and the ensuing evaluative judgements that occur in relation to control practices, in a way that refers to both the multiple and overlapping implications they hold and what matters to practitioners and service users in their use. A genuinely critical approach involves exploring how power may cause both avoidable suffering as well as flourishing in society (Sayer, 2009), and we have tried to impart the relationship of CTOs to both states of being and consequently distil what messages can be carried forward into future CTO policy and practice.

Appendix: How the study was conducted

We utilised a loosely ethnographic approach in this study. Ethnography typically draws upon an eclectic mix of methods, 'in fact gathering whatever data are available to throw light on the issues … that are the focus of inquiry' (Hammersley and Atkinson, 2007, 3). This, in turn, was embedded within a multiple case study design. In this appendix we sketch out this methodological approach and also explain how the ethical issues which arose in undertaking the study were managed.

Research design

Ethnography, 'focuses on people's ordinary activities in naturally occurring settings, uses … flexible methods of data collection, requires the researcher to be … involved in the field … and explores the meanings which … human activity has for … people themselves and wider society' (Brewer, 2000, 20) so as to gain an 'intimate familiarity' (Brewer, 2000, 11) with the participant experience. It entails the unstructured, naturalistic gathering of data, the use of relatively few small-scale cases and an analysis of data that focuses on the 'meanings, functions and consequences of human actions and institutional practices, and how these are implicated in … wider contexts' (Hammersley and Atkinson, 2007, 3). In being guided by ethnographic principles, the study enables an insight into community treatment order (CTO) practice from the 'inside'.

By undertaking a multiple case ethnography, this study combines the depth of ethnography with the comparative potential of a multiple case design, thus enabling the tracking of CTOs across settings and time. Both Mental Health Trusts ('Trusts') where the research was based had a relatively large number of CTOs. As the study progressed both similarities and contrasts between the sites emerged.

Fieldwork lasted for a period of eight months, with time being split equally between Assertive Outreach Teams (AOTs) in each Trust. Because the main purpose of AOTs is to work with 'difficult to engage' service users, these teams can attract a high volume of CTOs, and thus were selected on the basis that they would provide ample opportunity to observe CTO practice. Eighteen CTO cases were tracked over the fieldwork period; this enabled CTO cases to be followed as they unfolded in different ways. The core of the study data derived from these cases, including observations of key meetings, notes from case files and semi-structured interviews with service users, care coordinators and Approved Mental Health Professionals (AMHPs), and case-holding psychiatrists. Contextual information was also collected via key informant interviews with relevant stakeholders, field notes of daily team practice, observations of team meetings and attendance at Trust training and research events.

Methods

Combining different kinds of data collection, especially interviews and observations, is especially beneficial when exploring professional practice. Interviews allow for individual cases to be explored in depth and to develop a timeline of events. Observations capture actors coming together at a particular time and place, and a sense of how particular processes and people play out and interact. Document analysis ensures an unmediated data source is included to gain a sense of how actions are accounted for. By undertaking analysis of CTO policy making, the study also sheds light on macro level decision-making. Table A.1 maps how these methods link to the guiding research questions for this study.

Interviews

Interviews were semi-structured, using a topic guide to help explore participants' thoughts, feelings, perceptions and experiences of CTOs. Following Patton (2002, 359) questions were open-ended, neutral, singular and clear. Interviews with service user participants covered the significance of the CTO to them; the effect it may have had on relationships; their understanding of what the CTO meant; their involvement in the process

Table A.1: Research questions and associated methods

Research question	Methods
How have problems been framed for the CTO to solve?	Document analysis (macro-level)
In what ways are CTOs conceptualised by practitioners and service users? For practitioners, how do they formulate CTO practice based on these conceptualisations?	Semi-structured interviews
How do CTOs work to regulate behaviour and what factors – inclusive of participant action – influence why they work in those particular ways?	Observations; interviews; document analysis (micro-level)
What are the varying consequences of the CTO that result from these practices and how are these consequences thought about by practitioners and service users? How do CTOs work to produce change in service user identities and conduct, and in what ways are the transformational potentials of CTOs realised or resisted?	Observations; interviews document analysis (micro-level)

and decision-making; compliance with the CTO; their understanding and experiences of the key mechanisms of the CTO; and their hopes for the future. Interviews with practitioner participants covered their experiences of using CTOs, drawing on the case in question as well as other cases; the effect practitioners believed CTOs had on their practice; decision-making processes and factors; and their views on the CTO more generally.

The interviews with service users mainly took place in participants' homes. Careful consideration of the impact of the process for the respondent was undertaken. Trust staff were present for some of the interviews, either because it was not felt lone working was appropriate or because the service user requested their presence. This may have affected what service users said.

Interviews with practitioners took place within the workplace and were flexible to suit respondent needs Although a semi-structured guide was used, many of the interviews had a narrative flavour, with practitioners providing in-depth accounts of the CTO cases they had dealt with.

The legal oversight of CTOs is maintained via an appeals process, where Tribunals or Managers' Hearings hear evidence on whether the CTO should be discharged or not. The perspectives of these decision-makers have only rarely been explored in the literature. To develop a more rounded picture of CTO decision-making, group interviews with Managers' Hearing Chairs within the Mental Health Act offices of the respective Trusts took place.

Observations

Observation entails watching and listening to what people say and do, which enables the researcher to get closer to everyday practice. In this study, observation generated data on decision-making in action, including what factors were prevalent in decision-making and how practitioners and service users engaged with each other in relation to the CTO. Observed meeting included:

- A selection of team and handover meetings within each team
- CTO review meetings
- Managers' Hearing and Tribunal appeals
- Informal meetings between service users and practitioners

Fieldwork was scheduled as follows:

First phase (two months): Mostly broad-based observation with little participation, spending time getting to know the environment, systems within community mental health services and relationships building with participants.

Second phase (five months): Increasingly, more active participation within the teams allowing for more consistent discussion of CTO-related

Table A.2: The number of each type of case-related observation

Reviews	Managers' hearings	Tribunals	Hospital discharge meetings	Miscellaneous*
12	8	2	3	7

Note: * AMHP interviews with service users, AMHP interviews with family and the general weekly visit between the care coordinator and the service user.

events and took on a more focused character. It also led to an increase in the undertaking of informal 'interviews', which further enabled the development of our understanding of the detail of CTO practice.

Third phase (one month): This phase was largely taken up with managing a shift back to observation rather than participation.

Where possible, verbatim notes were taken during or immediately after observations. After formal observations, contextual notes were also completed. Informal observations were incorporated into written up field notes, giving detail of what happened on a day to day basis within teams. Care was taken when developing fieldnotes to distinguish as far as possible between descriptions and analytical/evaluatory considerations. The keeping of fieldwork diaries also enabled the processing of sometimes contradictory thoughts and feelings on how CTOs were being used. Table A.2 shows the kinds and number of case-related observations taken.

Document analysis

Using documents as data can 'provide a new and unfiltered perspective on the field and its processes' (Flick, 2009, 261) as they have not been created specifically for the study. Documents provided information on the development and eventual form of CTO policy itself, thus enabling a review of the policy-making process to occur. They also give an insight into how CTOs are written about by practitioner communities and, more broadly, the decision-making process of CTOs.

For the policy review, searches of Hansard and associated parliamentary papers were conducted. Alongside this, policy analyses by bodies such as the Mental Health Alliance, and academic papers on the formation of the Mental Health Act and the history of mental health policy, provided valuable historical knowledge. Finally, the international context was accounted for, by drawing on academic, policy and legislative sources to help construct a picture of how CTOs have developed globally over time.

For the case file review, the hard files and electronic records of 17 of the 18 service user participants were investigated. These included details of formal decision-making on CTOs and copies of the reports made by practitioners for appeals. Spending time within the Mental Health Act offices of both Trusts while completing this task provided a serendipitous alternative perspective on CTO use, as it enabled the widening of observations to include informal comings and goings of practitioners for legal advice.

Analysis

Analysis was based on transcriptions from the interviews, document analysis and on detailed field notes and memos generated through observation. A combination of thematic and narrative analysis was employed and enabled CTO 'storylines' to become apparent, from participant conceptualisation through active use of the CTO and finally decision-making on whether to discharge. McCracken (1988) suggests close line by line reading of texts to understand first order concepts before moving on to develop second order concepts. These second order concepts were then developed into a thematic framework, made up of concept groups, each of which included detailed accounts. The process began with analysing service user interviews. Once a foundational framework had been developed from this data, the process was repeated with practitioner interviews, followed by observations, and finally with the documents, thus moving from first person viewpoints through to enactments and recording of the CTO process.

Once the analytical frameworks were developed, a bespoke software programme was utilised to sort and separate out the respective data into discrete categories. These were then compared and contrasted to establish further sub-categories. Conceptual frameworks from the different data sources were integrated, highlighting connections and distinctions.

With time, data driven configurational 'maps' of CTO concepts and stories were created (Sayer, 1992). By moving between data and sources the links between the thematic analysis crystallised in the process of individuals interacting with CTO components, enabling developing understanding of the different paths a CTO might take. In turn, following the narratives highlighted interactional outcomes. Just as importantly, returning to the interview data shed light on how those outcomes were perceived in partial and differential ways by practitioners and service users.

Fieldwork considerations: participants

A total of 62 participants were involved in the study; 18 were service users, 20 were practitioners working with those service users, 16 were practitioners recruited as additional key informants and 8 were Managers' Hearing Chairs.

Trusts and teams: recruitment, selection and characteristics

Initial approaches to NHS Mental Health Trusts entailed writing to the senior management (typically at Director or Chief Executive level) of ten Trusts in the North of England. Selection was pragmatic, based on which Trusts showed active interest. The two trusts selected also fitted into a theoretical model where a comparison could be made between different local practice regimes and cultures. Both covered areas with a high level of poverty and deprivation. However, the contrast between their approaches to mental health service provision is marked. Table A.3 gives an overview of their key differentiating characteristics.

The senior managers of the two Trusts responded positively because they believed that the use of CTOs in their Trusts was an issue worth investigating. One of the Trusts had higher usage of CTOs than the national average, and they were concerned about overuse; the other Trust had recently taken over services in an area where the use of CTOs was very different to the rest of the Trust and management wanted to find out how CTOs were being practiced locally.

Practitioner participants: recruitment, selection and characteristics

Once an arrangement was made with the AOT Manager, a visit was arranged to present to practitioners. Staff were then contacted individually to go through the information sheet/consent form and gain consent.

Table A.3: Characteristics of the two Trusts

Characteristics	Trust 1	Trust 2
Geographical and socio-economic	Large urban area with high levels of unemployment, poverty and deprivation.	A small urban centre and a large semi-rural hinterland. High levels of unemployment, poverty and deprivation.
Mental health service provision	Strong community focus with a large number of 'satellite' team offices. Little inpatient provision. Outreach approach with few visits by service users to the office.	Strong hospital site focus with most teams based within the hospital grounds. Relatively high number of inpatient beds. Office-based approach with many appointments taking place on site.
Structure	Large centralised Mental Health Act Office. 'Traditional' model of tiered services with Community Mental Health Teams, Assertive Outreach Teams, Crisis Teams, Early Intervention Teams.	Dispersed administrative support through small localised Mental Health Act staff teams. 'New' model of services based on Care Clusters, including Recovery Team (psychosis, complex needs), Social Inclusion Team (psychosis and mood disorders, low-level needs) as well as Assertive Outreach.
CTO use	Greater numbers of CTOs. Average length of CTO > 1 year.	Fewer CTOs. Average length of CTO 8 months.

Table A.4: Practitioner participants by role and profession

	Care coordinator	Psychiatrist	AMHP	Manager	Total
Nurses	11			1	12
Social workers	5		8	3	16
Occupational therapists	1			1	2
Psychiatrists		6			6
Total	17	6	8	5	

In addition to the 'case-specific' practitioners recruited from the two AOTs, 16 practitioners were included as key informant interviewees only, either because they were able to provide an overview on the use of CTOs (three clinical leads/managers) or because they were able to answer interesting questions that were raised during the fieldwork period. Similarly, some care coordinators were interviewed from other types of teams, where CTO use was lower, including two 'typical' Community Mental Health Teams and an Early Intervention in Psychosis Team. This was to explore the differences in practice and perspectives that might occur in settings where CTOs were rarer. Table A.4 shows practitioner participants by role and professional background.

Of the 36 practitioners, 20 were female and 16 male, and gender was weighted towards women among all professional groupings, except for the psychiatrists. The majority (32) were White British with the remaining four participants being British Asian or Black African, again represented more in the psychiatrist grouping. Experience in practice varied from one to 40 years. Longer serving practitioners were able to reflect on changes in services over time.

The largest professional group represented was social work (16), with nurses making up the majority of the remainder of participants (12), differing from previous research which tended to focus more on psychiatrists. It has been suggested that social work brings a distinctive set of values to multidisciplinary mental health practice (Allen, 2014). However, there was little evidence of this in the field sites. Rather, there was a range of value perspectives within all professions who took on the role of care coordination. Differences in perspectives were generally premised on *role* rather than *profession*. Hence, although the AMHPs were all social workers, the distinctive perspective they took was related to their legal mandate rather than their profession.

Service user participants: recruitment, selection and characteristics

Service users were initially approached via their care coordinator, who provided information regarding the research and asked their permission for

Table A.5: Service users who were not recruited

Declined	7
Risk	8
Capacity	10
Care coordinator not recruited	5
Gatekeeping*	9
Miscellaneous**	3

Notes: *This is related to the care coordinator stating they did not feel the person would agree to take part as they were deemed too hostile to services in general.

** There was a small group who had agreed to meet, but for one reason or another, such as a change in circumstances or missed appointments, the initial contact didn't go ahead.

direct contact. Meetings were then scheduled, in order to answer questions and check capacity to understand, retain and assimilate the information given, and communicate choice in regards to the research (Appelbaum, 1998). Service users at different CTO stages were specifically recruited to ensure a range of experiences. Service users were not included if their care coordinator did not think they would be able to make an informed decision in regards to participation in the research; had a learning disability or a diagnosis of dementia; did not speak English; or were under 18. The reasons for not being able to recruit are outlined in Table A.5.

Two thirds (12) of the service users were male, as reflects the national and international trends on gender and CTOs (Churchill et al, 2007; Care Quality Commission, 2011). An effort was made to ensure women were represented in the selection due to the known gender bias of CTO use. Almost all (16) identified as White British, which was indicative of the ethnic makeup of the field sites, but not of the higher than expected (as compared with the general population) national rates of CTOs for people particularly from Black ethnic groups (Care Quality Commission, 2011).

As might be expected, the majority of the participants were socially isolated. All participants received Personal Independence Payments and most were on other benefits of some kind, with three working in a self-employed capacity. Five participants were also on appointeeships, meaning the local authority managed their money for them. Most participants were single (14) and lived on their own in the community, either in supported accommodation or a local authority tenancy.

Most participants (14) were in their forties or fifties and had been involved with services for a number of years (range of 3 to 33 years); all had been diagnosed with some enduring form of psychosis. However, this picture is complicated as the majority of participants had also been given a number of different diagnoses with half having secondary diagnoses of personality disorder and/or substance misuse. Not all participants saw their own experiences as fitting with their diagnosis and indeed some were resentful of the labelling and subsequent stigma attached to it.

During their time in services, all participants had had at least one involuntary admission to hospital, with the most experienced by a participant as over 30. Consequently, some but by no means all participants fitted the criteria for the 'revolving door' patient. Additionally, risk of harm to others was a documented issue in almost half of the cases (8).

Most participants had only been on one CTO, although a sizeable minority had experienced two or more. These experiences meant they were able to describe their experiences in some depth. The length of CTOs ranged from three months to just over two years. Just over half of participants could be described as stable on their CTO, with only five having experienced one or more recalls to hospital, either on their current or on previous CTOs, and another three having been admitted voluntarily to hospital on their current CTO. Approximately one third of participants were discharged from their CTO during the course of the fieldwork period and another was discharged shortly before it began, but still included in the research due to the perspective they were able to give on their experience.

Fieldwork considerations: ethics

Given the study's focus on the ethical dilemmas and consequences of mental health policy and practice, it was important to pay close attention to ethics when making decisions on research design. Attaining ethics approval involved a rigorous ethical process and in order to provide a framework for ethical research to take place, a number of procedures and safeguards were implemented. Additionally, undertaking qualitative research also involves a continuous consideration of ethics throughout the research process, by consciously being a 'moral researcher' when making reflexive decisions in the field.

Ethical reflexivity in fieldwork

Professionally qualified researchers have been described as on the 'inside 'out' (White, 2001, 104), and previous researcher practice experience meant it was easy to become engaged in familiar tropes of practice language and activity. It took a number of careful preparatory meetings with service users before enough trust was built to ask them to participate in the research. With practitioners, sometimes the discussion slipped into 'coded language and communication' culturally common to participants (Kanuha, 2000, 443), which required conscious reflexivity to question what was held as self-evident. This made it difficult to remain in the position of 'acceptable incompetent' (Lofland, 1971) and also to retain a marginal position with appropriate distance between researcher and participants. Being in the teams over time meant sometimes being asked to contribute by field members in unexpected ways, which disrupted this sense of distance. Quirk (2008) notes that conducting ethnography within an institutional setting can be distinctively destabilising due to researchers having ambiguous institutional roles. For example, following an interview, one service user asked research staff to write a letter for her upcoming Tribunal stating that she did not need to be on a CTO. It was explained that researchers could not intervene in cases. At the next meeting she withdrew from the study; the researcher had misjudged how this service user understood the research process and, in turn, the service user had misunderstood the researcher's role.

Qualitative research involves the analysis of participant narratives beyond their initial descriptive meaning and can create tension between researcher and participant understanding and ownership. Finch (1986) argues that within qualitative research with its traditionally small sample sizes, it is important to not 'betray' individual participants by representing their group in ways which can reinforce public stereotypes. In presenting the research, we tried to remain sensitive to original meanings and in how individuals may 'look' to various audiences. In this way, the study was informed by a relational 'ethics of care' that 'ground principles such as respect, integrity and justice in the concrete relationships of actual research' (Hugman, 2010, 162).

Relatedly, respecting practitioner perspectives while maintaining research integrity required careful consideration. It is important that the research experience is perceived as generally positive by participants and gatekeepers, for intrinsic moral reasons, but also so that attitudes towards research and researchers in general are not adversely affected, thus affecting potential future access. Familiarity derived from team embeddedness sharpened the sense of responsibility regarding how findings were presented and what was included. Although there are no straightforward methods of eliminating ethical dilemmas in research, we have tried to strike a balance between competing factors in an honest and open way that has maintained good relationships with research participants along with ensuring the findings are presented with integrity.

Summary

In taking a case-based approach the study has been able to follow CTOs as they develop over time, gain access to a range of perspectives on their use, and enable interesting and original configurations of data and analysis. Combining interviews with observations and document analysis has allowed for an analysis of participant reflection on CTOs, the everyday practice of CTOs and an unmediated timeline of CTO decision-making, as well as a macro-perspective of CTO policy making. Analysis of this data has attempted to do justice to the complexity and diversity of materials generated. By providing a detailed account of how the research was carried out, including by giving a sense of the participants and their circumstances, readers have an account which enables them to approach the findings presented in this book with a good understanding of the methodological frameworks which support the study as a whole.

References

Alexander, J. (2010) *The Performance of Politics: Obama's Victory and the Democratic Struggle for Power*. Oxford University Press.

Alfandari, R., Davidson, G., Khoury, J., Ramon, S., Shankman, M. and Tuck, E. (2022) Social work, care and control: An international perspective. *International Social Work*, 65(4), 487–502.

Allen, R. (2014) *The Role of the Social Worker in Adult Mental Health Services*. The College of Social Work.

Anthony, W.A. (1993) Recovery from mental illness: The guiding vision of the mental health service system in the 1990s. *Psychosocial Rehabilitation Journal*, 16(4), 11–23.

Appelbaum, P.S. (1998) Missing the boat: Competence and consent in psychiatric research. *American Journal of Psychiatry*, 155(11), 1486–8.

Appelbaum, P. and Gutheil, T. (1979) Rotting with their rights on: Constitutional theory and clinical reality in drug refusal by psychiatric patients. *Bulletin of the American Academy on Psychiatry and Law*, 7, 308–17.

Arango, C. and Amador, X. (2011) Lessons learned about poor insight. *Schizophrenia Bulletin*, 37(1), 27–8.

Arendt, H. (1970) *On Violence*. Harcourt Brace & World.

Asgarian, L. (2023) Abolishing social work: A call for revolutionary change. *Critical Social Work*, 24(1), 15–30.

Bar El, Y.C., Durst, R., Rabinowitz, J., Kalian, M., Teitelbaum, A. and Shlafman, M. (1998) Implementation of order of compulsory ambulatory treatment in Jerusalem. *International Journal of Law and Psychiatry*, 21(1), 65–71.

Barkhuizen, W., Cullen, A.E., Shetty, H., Pritchard, M., Stewart, R., McGuire, P. et al (2020) Community treatment orders and associations with readmission rates and duration of psychiatric hospital admission: A controlled electronic case register study. *BMJ Open*, 10(3), e035121.

Barnett, C., Clarke, N., Cloke, P. and Malpass, A. (2008) The elusive subjects of neo-liberalism. *Cultural Studies*, 22(5), 624–53.

Bartlett, P. and Sandland, R. (2007) *Mental Health Law: Policy and Practice* (3rd edn). Oxford University Press.

Bemelmans-Videc, M., Rist, R. and Vedung, E. (1998) *Carrots, Sticks and Sermons: Policy Instruments and Their Evaluation*. Transaction Publishers.

Bentall, R. (2004) *Madness Explained: Psychosis and Human Nature*. Penguin.

Beresford, P. and Rose, D. (2023) Decolonising global mental health: The role of mad studies. *Cambridge Prisms: Global Mental Health*, 10, e30.

Berlin, I. (1969) *Four Essays on Liberty*. Oxford University Press.

Bevir, M. (2010) Rethinking governmentality: Towards genealogies of governance. *European Journal of Social Work Theory*, 13(4), 423–41.

Bevir, M. (2016) Governmentality after neoliberalism. In *Governmentality after Neoliberalism* (pp 1–15). Routledge.

Blom-Cooper, L., Hally, H. and Murphy, E. (1995) *The Falling Shadow: One Patient's Mental Health Care 1978–1993*. Gerald Duckworth & Co. Ltd.

Blumenthal, S., Wood, J. and Williams, J. (2018) Relational approaches to risk management in forensic social work. *Journal of Forensic Social Work*, 8(2), 123–45.

Boardman, J. and Roberts, G. (2014) *Risk, Safety and Recovery*. Briefing paper, Centre for Mental Health.

Bracken, P. and Thomas, P. (2005) *Postpsychiatry: Mental Health in a Postmodern World*. Oxford University Press.

Brendel, D.H. (2006) *Healing Psychiatry: Bridging the Science/Humanism Divide*. MIT Press.

Brewer, J. (2000) *Ethnography*. McGraw-Hill Education.

Brockmann, J. and Garrett, P.M. (2022) Social work and the neoliberal project: Critical reflections on power and resistance. *Critical Social Policy*, 42(3), 401–20.

Brophy, L. (2009) *Using the Emancipatory Values of Social Work as a Guide to the Investigation: What Processes and Principles Represent Good Practice with People on Community Treatment Orders*. Doctoral dissertation, University of Melbourne.

Brophy, L. and Ring, D. (2004) The efficacy of involuntary treatment in the community: Consumer and service provider perspectives. *Social Work in Mental Health*, 2(2–3), 157–74.

Brown, K. (2024) Vulnerability and the intersection of welfare and penal mechanisms. *Social Policy & Administration*, 58(2), 234–51.

Brown, P. and Calnan, M. (2012) *Trusting on the Edge: Managing Uncertainty and Vulnerability in the midst of Serious Mental Health Problems*. Policy Press.

Burkitt, I. (2016) Relational agency: Relational sociology, agency and interaction. *European Journal of Social Theory*, 19(3), 322–39.

Burns, T. (2011) *Our Necessary Shadow: The Nature and Meaning of Psychiatry*. Penguin.

Cairney, P. (2009) The British policy style and mental health: Beyond the headlines. *Journal of Social Policy*, 38(4), 671–88.

Calton, T. and Spandler, H. (2009) Minimal-medication approaches to treating schizophrenia. *Advances in Psychiatric Treatment*, 15(3), 209–17.

Campbell, J. and Davidson, G. (2009) Coercion in the community: A situated approach to the examination of ethical challenges for mental health social workers. *Ethics and Social Welfare*, 3(3), 249–63.

Campbell, J., Davidson, G., McCusker, P., Jobling, H. and Slater, T. (2019) Community treatment orders and mental health social work: issues for policy and practice in the UK and Ireland. *International Journal of Law and Psychiatry*, 64, 230–7.

Canvin, K., Bartlett, A. and Pinfold, V. (2002) A 'bittersweet pill to swallow': learning from mental health service users' responses to compulsory community care in England. *Health & Social Care in the Community*, 10(5), 361–9.

Care Quality Commission (2010) *Monitoring the Use of the Mental Health Act in 2009/10*. Care Quality Commission.

Care Quality Commission (2011) *Monitoring the Use of the Mental Health Act in 2010/11*. Care Quality Commission.

Care Quality Commission (2025) *Monitoring the Mental Health Act in 2023/24*. Care Quality Commission.

Castells, M. (1983) *The City and the Grassroots: A Cross-Cultural Theory of Urban Social Movements*. University of California Press.

Černe Kolarič, J., Plemenitaš Ilješ, A., Kraner, D., Gönc, V., Lorber, M., Mlinar Reljić, N. et al (2024) Long-term impact of community psychiatric care on quality of life amongst people living with schizophrenia: A systematic review. *Healthcare*, 12(17), 1750.

Chakrabarti, S. (2014) What's in a name? Compliance, adherence and concordance in chronic psychiatric disorders. *World Journal of Psychiatry*, 4(2), 30–6.

Churchill, R., Owen, G., Singh, S. and Hotopf, M. (2007) *International Experiences of Using Community Treatment Orders*. Institute of Psychiatry, Kings College London.

Cooper, D. (1967) *Psychiatry and Anti-Psychiatry*. Tavistock Publications.

Corring, D., O'Reilly, R. and Sommerdyk, C. (2017) A systematic review of the views and experiences of subjects of community treatment orders. *International Journal of Law and Psychiatry*, 52, 74–80.

Cossu, G., Kalcev, G., Sancassiani, F., Primavera, D., Gyppaz, D., Zreik, T. et al (2024) The long-term adherence following the end of Community Treatment Order: A systematic review. *Acta Psychiatrica Scandinavica*, 150(2), 78–90.

Darwin, C. (2004) *The Descent of Man, and Selection in Relation to Sex*. Penguin.

David, A.S. (1990) Insight and psychosis. *British Journal of Psychiatry*, 156(6), 798–808.

Dawson, J. (2005) *Community Treatment Orders: International Comparisons*. University of Otago.

Dawson, J. (2009) Concepts of liberty in mental health law. *Otago Law Review*, 12(1), 23–36.

Dawson, J. and Mullen, R. (2008) Insight and use of community treatment orders. *Journal of Mental Health*, 17(3), 269–80.

Dawson, J., Romans, S., Gibbs, A. and Ratter, N. (2003) Ambivalence about community treatment orders. *International Journal of Law and Psychiatry*, 26, 243–55.

de Waardt, D.A., van Melle, A.L., Widdershoven, G.A.M., Bramer, W.M., van der Heijden, F.M.M.A., Rugkåsa, J. et al (2022) Use of compulsory community treatment in mental healthcare: An integrative review of stakeholders' opinions. *Frontiers in Psychiatry*, 13, 1011961.

Dean, M. (1994) *Critical and Effective Histories: Foucault's Methods and Historical Sociology*. Routledge.

Dean, M. (2010) *Governmentality: Power and Rule in Modern Society* (2nd edn). Sage.

Dean, M. (2013) *The Signature of Power: Sovereignty, Governmentality and Biopolitics*. Sage Publications.

Dean, M. (2015) Foucault must not be defended. *History and Theory*, 54, 389–403.

Dean, M. and Villasden, K. (2016) *State Phobia and Civil Society: The Political Legacy of Michel Foucault*. Stanford University Press.

Death, C. (2010) Counter-conducts: A Foucauldian analytics of protest. *Social Movement Studies*, 9(3), 235–51.

Department of Health (1999) Radical changes needed to mental health services, says minister. Press release 1999/0036, 21 January 1999.

Department of Health (2007) *Mental Health Bill 2007, Regulatory Impact Assessment Revised Version*. The Stationary Office.

Department of Health (2008) *Code of Practice: Mental Health Act 1983*. The Stationary Office.

Department of Health (2015) *Code of Practice: Mental Health Act 1983*. The Stationary Office.

Department of Health and Social Care (2018) *Modernising the Mental Health Act: Increasing Choice, Reducing Compulsion*. HMSO.

Department of Health and the Home Office (2000) *Reforming the Mental Health Act* (Cm 5016).

DeRidder, R., Molodynski, A., Manning, C., McCusker, P. and Rugkåsa, J. (2016) Community treatment orders in the UK 5 years on: A repeat national survey of psychiatrists. *BJPsych Bull*, 40(3), 119–23.

Diesfeld, K. and Sjostrom, S. (2006) Interpretive flexibility: Why doesn't insight incite controversy in mental health law? *Behavioral Sciences and the Law*, 25(1), 85–101.

Elbogen, E.B. and Johnson, S.C. (2009) The intricate link between violence and mental disorder: Results from the national epidemiologic survey on alcohol and related conditions. *Archives of General Psychiatry*, 66(2), 152–61.

Evans, T. (2012) *Professional Discretion in Welfare Services*. Ashgate.

Evans, T. (2014) The moral economy of street-level policy work. *Croatian and Comparative Public Administration*, 14(2), 381–99.

Evans, T. and Harris, J. (2004) Street-level bureaucracy, social work and the (exaggerated) death of discretion. *British Journal of Social Work*, 34(6), 871–95.

Fazel, S., Långström, N., Hjern, A., Grann, M. and Lichtenstein, P. (2009) Schizophrenia, substance abuse, and violent crime. *JAMA*, 301(19), 2016–23.

Fazel, S., Lichtenstein, P., Grann, M., Goodwin, G. and Långström, N. (2010) Bipolar disorder and violent crime: New evidence from population-based longitudinal studies and systematic review. *Archives of General Psychiatry*, 67(9), 931–8.

Finch, J. (1986) *Research and Policy: The Use of Qualitative Methods in Social and Educational Research*. Falmer Press.

Fistein, E.C., Holland, A.J., Clare, I.C.H. and Gunn, M.J. (2009) A comparison of mental health legislation from diverse Commonwealth jurisdictions. *International Journal of Law and Psychiatry*, 32(3), 147–55.

Flick, U. (2009) *An Introduction to Qualitative Research* (4th edn). Sage.

Flyvbjerg, B. (2006) Five misunderstandings about case-study research. *Qualitative Inquiry*, 12(2), 219–45.

Foucault, M. (1977) *Discipline and Punish: The Birth of the Prison*. Pantheon.

Foucault, M. (1980) Two lectures. In C. Gordon (ed) *Power/Knowledge: Selected Interviews and other Writings 1972–1977* (pp 78–109). Pantheon Books.

Foucault, M. (1983) The subject and power. In H. Dreyfus and P. Rabinow (eds) *Michel Foucault: Beyond Reason and Hermeneutics* (2nd edn) (pp 777–95). The University of Chicago Press.

Foucault, M. (1988) *Politics, Philosophy, Culture*. Routledge.

Foucault, M. (1990) *The History of Sexuality. Volume 1: An Introduction*. Vintage.

Foucault, M. (1997a) The ethics of the concern of the self as a practice of freedom. In P. Rabinow (ed) *The Essential Works of Michel Foucault, vol. 1: Ethics: Subjectivity and Truth* (pp 281–301). The New Press.

Foucault, M. (1997b) Polemics, politics and problematization: An interview. In P. Rabinow (ed) *The Essential Works of Michel Foucault, vol. 1: Ethics: Subjectivity and Truth* (pp 111–20). The New Press.

Foucault, M. (2000) Omnes et singulatum: Towards a critique of political reason. In J. Faubion (ed) *Power* (pp 298–327). The New Press.

Foucault, M. (2006) *Madness and Civilisation: A History of Insanity in the Age of Reason*. Vintage Books.

Foucault, M. (2007) *Security, Territory, Population*. Palgrave.

Foucault, M. (2011) *The Government of Self and Others: Lectures at the College de France, 1982–1983*. Edited by F. Gros. Picador.

Fox, J. (2025) Twin births, twin abolitions: Abolishing the capitalist, carceral state and the liberal individual – and, with them, conventional social work. In I. Hyslop and B. Pease (eds) *Abolition in Social Work and Human Services: Visions, Possibilities and Challenges* (pp 284–98). Policy Press.

Garret, P.M. (2020) 'Faulty tools?' Why social work scholarship needs to take a more critical approach to Michel Foucault. *Journal of Social Work*, 20(4), 483–500.

Gaventa, J. (2003) *Power After Lukes: An Overview of Theories of Power Since Lukes and Their Application to Development* [unpublished briefing paper].

Gaventa, J. (2010) *Power and Powerlessness: Quiescence and Rebellion in an Appalachian Valley*. University of Illinois Press.
George, M. (2011) Community treatment orders: Locating a social worker's space. *Social Work in Mental Health*, 9(3), 206–21.
Gibbs, A., Dawson, J. and Mullen, R. (2006) Community treatment orders for people with serious mental illness: A New Zealand study. *British Journal of Social Work*, 36(7), 1085–100.
Gibbs, A., Dawson, J., Ansley, C. and Mullen, R. (2005) How patients in New Zealand view community treatment orders. *Journal of Mental Health*, 14(4), 357–68.
Gilburt, H. and Mallorie, S. (2024) *Mental Health 360: Acute Mental Health Care for Adults*. The King's Fund.
Goffman, E. (1961) *Asylums: Essays on the Social Situation of Mental Patients and Other Inmates*. Anchor Books.
Graley-Wetherell, R. and Morgan, S. (2001) *Active Outreach: An Independent Service User Evaluation of a Model of Assertive Outreach Practice*. Sainsbury Centre for Mental Health.
Gramsci, A. (1971) *Selections from the Prison Notebooks*. Q. Hoare and G. Nowell Smith (eds). Lawrence and Wishart.
Hacking, I. (2004) Between Michel Foucault and Erving Goffman: Between discourse in the abstract and face-to-face interaction. *Economy and Society*, 33(3), 277–302.
Haglund, K., von Knorring, L. and von Essen, L. (2003) Forced medication in psychiatric care: Patient experiences and nurse perceptions. *Journal of Psychiatric and Mental Health Nursing*, 10(1), 65–72.
Hall, P.A. (1993) Policy paradigms, social learning, and the states: The case of economic policymaking in Britain. *Comparative Politics*, 25(3), 275–96.
Hammersley, M. (2009) Why critical realism fails to justify critical social research. *Methodological Innovations Online*, 4(2), 1–11.
Hammersley, M. and Atkinson, P. (2007) *Ethnography: Principles in Practice*. Routledge.
Han, B.-C. (2019) *What Is Power?* Polity Press.
Hansard, House of Commons Debates (18 June 2007) vol. 461, col. 1193.
Hansard, House of Lords Debates (28 November 2006) vol. 687, col. 656.
Hansard, House of Lords Debates (2 July 2007) vol. 693, col. 842.
Hansard, House of Lords Debates (2 July 2007) vol. 693, col 843.
Hardy, M. (2015) 'Depoliticisation and the transformation of social work'. *Critical Social Policy*, 35(2), 244–64.
Hood, R. (2018) *Complexity in Social Work*. Sage.
Haugaard, M. (2022) Foucault and power: A critique and retheorization. *Critical Review*, 34(3–4), 341–71.
Haugaard, M. and Cooke, M. (2010) Power and critical theory. *Journal of Power*, 3(1), 1–5. https://doi.org/10.1080/17540291003647530

Haugaard, M. and Ryan, K. (2012) *Power and Political Theory*. Manchester University Press.

Healy, K. (2000) *Social Work Practices: Contemporary Perspectives on Change*. Sage Publications.

Hemmington, J. and Vicary, S. (2023) *Making Decisions in Compulsory Mental Health Work: Boundaries, Frames and Perspectives*. Policy Press.

Hiday, V.A. (2003) Outpatient commitment: The state of empirical research on its outcomes. *Psychology, Public Policy & Law*, 9(1–2), 8–32.

HM Government (1983) *The Mental Health Act 1983*.

HM Government (2007) *The Mental Health Act 2007*.

Hodges, I. (2002) Moving beyond words: Therapeutic discourse and ethical problematization. *Discourse Studies*, 4(4), 455–79.

House of Commons Health Committee (2013) *Post-legislative scrutiny of the Mental Health Act 2007*. Session 2013–14, HC Paper 584.

Howe, D. (1996) Surface and depth in social-work practice. In N. Parton (ed) *Social Theory, Social Change and Social Work* (pp 77–97). Routledge.

Hugman, R. (2010) *Understanding International Social Work: A Critical Analysis*. Palgrave Macmillan.

Hunter, S. (2003) A critical analysis of approaches to the concept of social identity in social policy. *Critical Social Policy*, 23(3), 322–44.

Ingram, G., Muirhead, D. and Harvey, C. (2009) Effectiveness of community treatment orders: A systematic review. *Australian and New Zealand Journal of Psychiatry*, 43(5), 384–92.

Jansson, S. and Fridlund, B. (2016) Perceptions among psychiatric staff of creating a therapeutic alliance with patients on community treatment orders. *Issues in Mental Health Nursing*, 37(10), 701–7.

Jessop, B. (2010) Cultural political economy and critical policy studies. *Critical Policy Studies*, 3(3–4), 336–56.

Jobling, H. (2019) The legal oversight of community treatment orders: A qualitative analysis of tribunal decision-making. *International Journal of Law & Psychiatry*, 62, 95–103.

Joint Committee on the Draft Mental Health Bill (2005) *Draft Mental Health Bill Volume 1 Report*. Session 2004–5, HL Paper 79-1, HC Paper 95-1.

Kanuha, V.K. (2000) 'Being' native versus 'going native': Conducting social work research as an insider. *Social Work*, 45(5), 439–47.

Kinderman, P. and Tai, S. (2008) Psychological models of mental disorder, human rights, and compulsory mental health care in the community. *International Journal of Law and Psychiatry*, 31(6), 479–86.

Kisely, S.R., Campbell, L.A. and O'Reilly, R. (2017) Compulsory community and involuntary outpatient treatment for people with severe mental disorders. *Cochrane Database of Systematic Reviews*, (3), Art. No.: CD004408. https://doi.org/10.1002/14651858.CD004408.pub5

Kisely, S., Preston, N.J., Xiao, J., Lawrence, D., Louise, S., Crowe, E. et al (2013) An eleven-year evaluation of the effect of community treatment orders on changes in mental health service use. *Journal of Psychiatric Research*, 47(5), 650–6.

Kortrijk, H.E., Mulder, C.L., Roosenschoon, B.J. and Wiersma, D. (2010) Treatment outcome in patients receiving assertive community treatment. *Community Mental Health Journal*, 46(4), 330–6.

Lambert, T.J., Singh, B.S. and Patel, M.X. (2009) Community treatment orders and antipsychotic long-acting injections. *The British Journal of Psychiatry*, 195(52), S57–S62.

Laing, R.D. (1960) *The Divided Self: An Existential Study in Sanity and Madness*. Tavistock Publications.

Lawn, S., Delany, T., Pulvirenti, M., Smith, A. and McMillan, J. (2015) The experience of community treatment orders for clients, family members and mental health professionals: A qualitative study. *International Journal of Nursing Studies*, 52(6), 1010–17.

Lawn, S., Delany, T., Pulvirenti, M., Smith, A. and McMillan, J. (2016) Examining the use of metaphors to understand the experience of community treatment orders for patients and mental health workers. *BMC Psychiatry*, 31(16), 82.

Lawton-Smith, S. (2005) *A Question of Numbers: The Potential Impact of Community-Based Treatment Orders in England and Wales*. King's Fund.

Leichsenring, F., Steinert, C., Rabung, S. and Ioannidis, J.P.A. (2022) The efficacy of psychotherapies and pharmacotherapies for mental disorders in adults: an umbrella review and meta-analytic evaluation of recent meta-analyses. *World Psychiatry: Official Journal of the World Psychiatric Association (WPA)*, 21(1), 133–45.

Lemke, T. (2000) Foucault, governmentality and critique. Paper presented at the *Rethinking Marxism Conference,* University of Amherst (MA), 21–24 September 2000.

Lepping, P. and Malik, M. (2013) Community treatment orders: Current practice and a framework to aid clinicians. *The Psychiatrist*, 37, 54–7.

Lessard-Deschênes, C., Pariseau-Legault, P. and Goulet, M.H. (2024) Does mental health practice benefit from procedural justice theory? A critical analysis on the opportunities and pitfalls of procedural justice to address coercion and human rights issues in psychiatry. *Aporia*, 16(1), 8–20.

Leucht, S., Leucht, C., Huhn, M., Chaimani, A., Mavridis, D., Helfer, B. et al (2017) Sixty years of placebo-controlled antipsychotic drug trials in acute schizophrenia: Systematic review, Bayesian meta-analysis, and meta-regression of efficacy predictors. *The American Journal of Psychiatry*, 174(10), 927–42.

Li, I.H., Hsieh, W.L. and Liu, W.I. (2023) A systematic review and meta-analysis of the effectiveness of adherence therapy and its treatment duration in patients with schizophrenia spectrum disorders. *Patient Preference and Adherence*, 17, 769–80.

Light, E. (2014) The epistemic challenges of CTOs: Commentary on … Community Treatment Orders. *Psychiatric Bulletin*, 38, 6–8.

Lippert, R. and Stenson, K. (2010) Advancing governmentality studies: Lessons from social constructionism. *Theoretical Criminology*, 14(4), 473–94.

Lofland, J. (1971) *Analyzing Social Settings*. Wadsworth Publishing Company.

Lukes, S. (1974) *Power: A Radical View*. Macmillan.

Luxon, N. (2019) Foucault's genealogy of power and resistance. *Philosophy Compass*, 14(8), 315–25.

Madden, A. (2003) Rethinking risk assessment: The MacArthur study of mental disorder and violence by J. Monahan, H.J. Steadman, E. Silver, P.S. Appelbaum et al. *The Psychiatric Bulletin*, 27(6), 237–8. https://doi.org/10.1192/pb.27.6.237

Manning, C., Molodynski, A., Rugkåsa, J., Dawson, J. and Burns, T. (2011) Community treatment orders in England and Wales: national survey of clinicians' views and use. *The Psychiatrist*, 35(9), 328–33.

Marston, G. and McDonald, C. (eds) (2006) *Analysing Social Policy: A Governmental Approach*. Edward Elgar Publishing.

Maxwell, J.A. (2012) *A Realist Approach for Qualitative Research*. Sage.

Maylea, C. (2021) The end of social work. *Critical Social Policy*, 41(4), 769–88.

Maylea, C., Zirnsak, T.M., Edan, V., Armitage, P., Robert, H. and Brophy, L. (2025) Ensuring compulsory treatment is used as a last resort: a narrative review of the knowledge about community treatment orders. *Psychiatry, Psychology and Law* [Advance online publication], 1–20.

McCracken, G. (1988) *The Long Interview* (Qualitative Research Methods Series 13). Sage.

McGregor, C. and Dolan, P. (2021) *Support and Protection Across the Lifecourse: A Practical Approach for Social Workers*. Policy Press. https://doi.org/10.56687/9781447360568

McKee, K. (2009) Post-Foucauldian governmentality: What does it offer critical social policy analysis?. *Critical Social Policy*, 29(3), 465–86.

McMillan, J., Lawn, S. and Delany-Crowe, T. (2019) Trust and community treatment orders. *Frontiers in Psychiatry*, 10, 349.

Mfoafo-M'Carthy, M. (2014) Community treatment orders and the experiences of ethnic minority individuals diagnosed with serious mental illness in the Canadian mental health system. *Int J Equity Health*, 13(1), 69.

Monahan, J., Lidz, C., Hoge, S.K., Mulvey, E.P., Eisenberg, M.M., Roth, L.H. et al (1999) Coercion in the provision of mental health services: The MacArthur studies. *Research in Community and Mental Health*, 10, 13–30.

Monahan, J., Steadman, H., Silver, E., Appelbaum, P., Robbins, P., Mulvey, E. et al (2001) *Rethinking Risk Assessment: The Macarthur Study of Mental Disorder and Violence*. Oxford University Press.

Moynihan, P. (1996) An analysis of the current literature on human rights and psychiatry. In P. Moynihan and B. Healy (eds) *Advocacy in Psychiatric Services*. La Trobe University.

Mullen, R., Dawson, J. and Gibbs, A. (2006) Dilemmas for clinicians in use of community treatment orders. *International Journal of Law and Psychiatry*, 29(6), 535–50.

Munetz, M.R. and Frese, F.J. (2001) Getting ready for recovery: Reconciling mandatory treatment with the recovery vision. *Psychiatric Rehabilitation Journal*, 25(1), 35–42.

Murphy, D. (2021) Social work and the neoliberal agenda: Challenges and responses. *British Journal of Social Work*, 51(3), 789–805.

National Institute for Clinical Excellence (2014) *Psychosis and Schizophrenia in Adults: Treatment and Management*. NICE clinical guidelines 178.

National Institute for Mental Health in England (2008) *Supervised Community Treatment: A Guide for Practitioners*. NIMHE.

Newton-Howes, G. (2010) Coercion in psychiatric care: Where are we now, what do we know, where do we go? *The Psychiatrist*, 34, 217–20.

Nielsen, J.M., Buus, N. and Berring, L.L. (2023) Mental health recovery in social psychiatric policies: A reflexive thematic analysis. *International Journal of Environmental Research and Public Health*, 20(12), 6094.

NHS Benchmarking and ADASS (2018) *AMHPs, Mental Health Act Assessments and the Mental Health Social Care Workforce*. Department of Health and Social Care.

NHS England (2025) *Mental Health Act Statistics, Annual Figures, 2024–25*. https://digital.nhs.uk/data-and-information/publications/statistical/mental-health-act-statistics-annual-figures/2024-25-annual-figures

Novella, E.J. (2010) Mental health care and the politics of inclusion: A social systems account of psychiatric deinstitutionalisation. *Theoretical Medicine and Bioethics*, 31(6), 411–27.

Olofsson, B. and Jacobsson, L. (2001) A plea for respect: involuntarily hospitalized psychiatric patients' narratives about being subjected to coercion. *Journal of Psychiatric and Mental Health Nursing*, 8(4), 357–66. https://doi.org/10.1046/j.1365-2850.2001.00404.x

Olssen, M. (2010) Politics and the philosophy of life: towards a normative framework. In J. Yorke (ed) *The Right to Life and the Value of Life: Orientation in Law, Politics and Ethics* (pp 39–64). Ashgate.

O'Neill, J. (1995) *The Poverty of Post-Modernism*. Routledge.

O'Reilly, R.L., Keegan, D.L., Corring, D., Shrikhande, S. and Natarajan, D. (2006) A qualitative analysis of the use of community treatment orders in Saskatchewan. *International Journal of Law and Psychiatry*, 29(6), 516–24.

Parr, S. (2009) Confronting the reality of anti-social behaviour. *Theoretical Criminology*, 13(3), 363–81.

Parton, N. (2008) Changes in the form of knowledge in social work: From the 'social' to the 'informational'?. *The British Journal of Social Work*, 38(2), 253–69. https://doi.org/10.1093/bjsw/bcl337

Patel, M.X., Matonhodze, J., Baig, M.K., Gilleen, J., Boydell, J., Holloway, F. et al (2011) Increased use of antipsychotic long-acting injections with community treatment orders. *Therapeutic Advances in Psychopharmacology*, 1(2), 37–45.

Patel, M.X., Robson, D., Rance, J., Ramirez, N.M., Memon, T.C., Bressington, D. et al (2009) Attitudes regarding mental health nurse prescribing among psychiatrists and nurses: A cross-sectional questionnaire study. *International Journal of Nursing Studies*, 46(11), 1467–74.

Patton M.Q. (2002) *Qualitative Research and Evaluation Methods* (3rd edn). Sage

Pawson, R. (2006) *Evidence-based Policy: A Realist Perspective*. Sage.

Pawson, R. and Manzano-Santaella, A. (2012) A realist diagnostic workshop. *Evaluation*, 18(2), 176–91.

Payne, M. (2008) *Modern Social Work Theory* (3rd edn). Palgrave Macmillan.

Pease, B. (2002) Rethinking empowerment: a postmodern reappraisal for emancipatory practice. *British Journal of Social Work*, 32(2), 135–47.

Perkins, A.J., Khandker, R., Overley, A. Solid, C.A., Chekani, F., Roberts, A. et al (2023) The impact of antipsychotic adherence on acute care utilization. *BMC Psychiatry*, 23, 64.

Pescosolido, B.A., Manago, B. and Monahan, J. (2019) Evolving public views on the likelihood of violence from people with mental illness: stigma and its consequences. *Health Affairs*, 38(10), 1735–43.

Philp, M. (1979) Notes on the form of knowledge in social work. *Sociological Review*, 27, 83–111.

Pilgrim, D. (2007) New 'mental health' legislation for England and Wales: Some aspects of consensus and conflict. *Journal of Social Policy*, 36(1), 79–95.

Pilgrim, D. and Ramon, S. (2009) English mental health policy under New Labour. *Policy & Politics*, 37(2), 273–88.

Polkinghorne, D.E. (2004) *Practice and the Human Sciences: The Case for a Judgment-Based Practice of Care*. State University of New York Press.

Povall, C. (2006) Policy ethnography: exploring the local processes of public policy implementation. *Current Developments in Ethnographic Research in the Social and Management Sciences Symposium*, 20–35.

Power, P. (1999) Community treatment orders: the Australian experience. *The Journal of Forensic Psychiatry*,10(1), 9–15.

Pridham, K.M., Berntson, A., Simpson, A.I., Law, S.F., Stergiopoulos, V. and Nakhost, A. (2015) Perception of coercion among patients with a psychiatric community treatment order: A literature review. *Psychiatric Services*, 67(1), 16–28.

Quirk, A. (2008) *Obstacles to Shared Decision-Making in Psychiatric Practice: Findings from Three Observational Studies.* Unpublished Doctoral dissertation, Brunel University.

Ramsay, P. (2009) The theory of vulnerable autonomy and the legitimacy of civil preventative orders. In B. McSherry, A. Norrie and S. Bronitt (eds) *Regulating Deviance: The Redirection of Criminalisation and the Futures of Criminal Law* (pp 109–40). Hart Publishing.

Riley, H., Hoyer, G. and Lorem, G.F. (2014) 'When coercion moves into your home': A qualitative study of patient experiences with outpatient commitment in Norway. *Health Soc Care Community*, 22(5), 506–14. https://doi.org/10.1111/hsc.12107

Rissmiller, D.J. (2006) *The Evolution of Mental Health Care: From Asylum to Community*. Praeger Publishers.

Rolfe, T., Sheehan, B. and Davidson, R. (2008) Are consumers on community treatment orders informed of their legal and human rights? A West Australian study. *International Journal of Mental Health Nursing*, 17(1), 36–43.

Roll, J. and Whittaker, M. (2007) *The Mental Health Bill [HL]*, House of Commons Library Research Paper 07/33, 30 March.

Rose, N. (1996) Psychiatry as political science: Advanced liberalism and the administration of risk. *History of the Human Sciences*, 9(2), 1–23.

Rose, N. (1999) *Powers of Freedom: Reframing Political Thought.* Cambridge University Press.

Rose, N. (2002a) At risk of madness. In T. Baker and J. Simon (eds) *Embracing Risk: The Changing Culture of Insurance and Responsibility* (pp 210–37). Chicago University Press.

Rose, N. (2002b) Society, madness and control. In A. Buchanan (ed) *The Care of the Mentally Disordered Offender in the Community* (pp 3–25). Oxford University Press.

Rose, N. (2007) *The Politics of Life Itself: Biomedicine, Power, and Subjectivity in the Twenty-First Century*. Princeton University Press.

Sayer, A. (1992) *Method in Social Science: A Realist Approach* (2nd edn). Routledge.

Sayer, A. (2000) *Realism and Social Science*. Sage.

Sayer, A. (2005) *The Moral Significance of Class,* Cambridge University Press.

Sayer, A. (2009) Who's afraid of critical social science? *Current Sociology*, 57(6), 767–86.

Sayer, A. (2012) Power, causality and normativity: A critical realist critique of Foucault. *Journal of Political Power*, 5(2), 179–94.

Scheff, T.J. (1966) *Being Mentally Ill: A Sociological Theory*. Aldine Publishing Company.

Segal, S.P. (2022) Community treatment orders: Effectiveness and ethical considerations. *Psychiatric Services*, 73(8), 901–8.

Shaw, I. and Gould, N. (2001) *Qualitative Research in Social Work*. Sage.

Shaw, I., Hardy, M. and Sommerfield, P. (2024) Case study research in social work. In P. Rule and J.M. Vaughn (eds) *Handbook of Case Study Research in the Social Sciences* (pp 231–47). Edward Elgar.

Sheppard, D. (1997) *Mental Health Inquiries Published During 1997*. Institute of Mental Health Law.

Sjöström, S., Zetterberg, L. and Markström, U. (2011) Why community compulsion became the solution: Reforming mental health law in Sweden. *International Journal of Law and Psychiatry*, 34(6), 419–28.

Skills for Care (2025) *The Approved Mental Health Professional Workforce in the Social Care Sector*. Skills for Care.

Smith, M., Branton, T. and Cardno, A. (2014) Is the bark worse than the bite? Additional conditions used within community treatment orders. *The Psychiatric Bulletin*, 38, 9–12.

Stanford, S., Sharland, E., Heller, N.R. and Warner, J. (2017) *Beyond the Risk Paradigm in Mental Health Policy and Practice*. Palgrave Macmillan.

Stenson, K. (2005) Sovereignty, biopolitics and the local government of crime in Britain. *Theoretical Criminology*, 9(3), 265–87.

Stenson, K. (2008) Governing the local: Sovereignty, social governance and community safety. *Social Work & Society*, 6(1), 2–14.

Stensrud, B., Høyer, G., Granerud, A. and Landheim, A.S. (2015) 'Life on hold': a qualitative study of patient experiences with outpatient commitment in two Norwegian counties. *Issues in Mental Health Nursing*, 36(3), 209–16.

Stone, K., McCusker, P., Davidson, G. and Vicary, S. (2021) An exploratory survey of mental health social work in Europe. *International Journal of Environmental Research and Public Health*, 18(19), 10462. https://doi.org/10.3390/ijerph181910462

Stroud, J., Doughty, K. and Banks, M.L. (2013) *An Exploration of Service User and Practitioner Experiences of Community Treatment Orders*. National Institute for Health Research.

Stuart, H. (2003) Violence and mental illness: An overview. *World Psychiatry*, 2(2), 121.

Stuen, H.K., Landheim, A. and Rugkåsa, J. (2018) How clinicians make decisions about CTOs in ACT: A qualitative study. *International Journal of Mental Health Systems*, 12, 51.

Swanson J. (2009) What would Mary Douglas do? A commentary on Kahan et al, 'Cultural cognition and public policy: The case of outpatient commitment laws'. *Law & Human Behaviour*, 34(3), 176–85.

Swanson, J.W. and Swartz, M.S. (2014) Why the evidence for outpatient commitment is good enough. *Psychiatric Services*, 65, 808–11.

Swartz, M.S., Swanson, J.W. and Monahan, J. (2003) Endorsement of personal benefit of outpatient commitment among persons with severe mental illness. *Psychology, Public Policy and Law*, 9(1–2), 70–93.

Swartz., M.S., Wagner, H.R., Swanson, J.W. and Elbogen, E.B. (2004) Consumers' perceptions of the fairness and effectiveness of mandated community treatment and related pressures. *Psychiatric Services*, 55(7), 780–5.

Sweeney, A., Davies, J., McLaren, S., Whittock, M., Lemma, F., Belling, R. et al (2016) Defining continuity of care from the perspectives of mental health service users and professionals: An exploratory, comparative study. *Health Expect*, 19, 973–87.

Szasz, T.S. (1961) *The Myth of Mental Illness: Foundations of a Theory of Personal Conduct*. Hoeber-Harper.

Szmukler, G. and Rose, N. (2013) Risk assessment in mental health care: values and costs. *Behavioral Sciences and the Law*, 31, 125–40.

Taylor, D. (2010) Antipsychotic polypharmacy – confusion reigns. *The Psychiatrist*, 34, 41–3.

Tew, J. (2006) Understanding power and powerlessness: Towards a framework for emancipatory practice in social work. *Journal of Social Work*, 6(1), 33–51.

Tew, J., Ramon, S., Slade, M., Bird, V., Melton, J. and Le Boutillier, C. (2012) Social factors and recovery from mental health difficulties: A review of the evidence. *British Journal of Social Work*, 42(3), 443–60.

Timor-Shelvin, N., Hermans, K. and Roose, R. (2023) Social workers as agents of the state: Critical perspectives on professional identity. *European Journal of Social Work*, 26(2), 234–47.

Torrey, E.F. and Kaplan, R.J. (1995) A national survey of the use of outpatient commitment. *Psychiatric Services*, 46(8), 778–84.

Trnka, S. and Trundle, C. (2014) Competing responsibilities: Moving beyond neoliberal responsibilisation. *Anthropological Forum: A Journal of Social Anthropology and Comparative Sociology*, 24(2), 136–53.

Tseris, E. (2025) Beyond 'doing harm' and 'doing nothing': Creating generative alternatives to psychiatric carcerality. In I. Hyslop and B. Pease (eds) *Abolition in Social Work and Human Services: Visions, Possibilities and Challenges* (pp 270–83). Policy Press.

Van Dorn, R.A, Elbogen, E.B., Redlich, A.D., Swanson, J.W., Swartz, M.S. and Mustillo, S. (2006) The relationship between mandated community treatment and perceived barriers to care in persons with severe mental illness. *International Journal of Law and Psychiatry*, 29(6), 495–506.

Van Dorn, R.A., Swanson, J.W., Swartz, M.S., Wilder, C.M., Moser, L.L., Gilbert, A.R. et al (2010) Continuing medication and hospitalization outcomes after assisted outpatient treatment in New York. *Psychiatric Services*, 61(10), 982–7.

Vicary, S., Young, A. and Hicks, S. (2019) 'Role over' or roll over? Dirty work, shift, and Mental Health Act Assessments. *British Journal of Social Work*, 49(8), 2187–206. https://doi.org/10.1093/bjsw/bcz014

Villasden, M. (2024) Power, resistance and social transformation: A Foucauldian analysis. *Theory, Culture & Society*, 41(3), 87–105.

Wade, M., Tai, S., Awenat, Y. and Haddock, G. (2017) A systematic review of service-user reasons for adherence and nonadherence to neuroleptic medication in psychosis. *Clinical Psychology Review*, 51, 75–95.

Wales, H.W. and Hiday, V.A. (2006) PLC or TLC: Is outpatient commitment the/an answer? *International Journal of Law and Psychiatry*, 29(6), 451–68.

Watts, J. and Priebe, S. (2002) A phenomenological account of users' experiences of assertive community treatment. *Bioethics*, 16(5), 439–54.

Webb, S. (2006) *Social Work in a Risk Society: Social and Political Perspectives*. Palgrave Macmillan.

Weber, M. (1978) *Economy and Society: An Outline of Interpretive Sociology*. University of California Press.

Weich, S., Duncan, C., Twigg, L., McBride, O., Parsons, H., Moon, G. et al (2020) Use of community treatment orders and their outcomes: An observational study. *NIHR Journals Library*, 8(9). https://doi.org/10.3310/hsdr08090

White, S. (2001) Auto-ethnography as reflexive inquiry: The research act as self-surveillance. In I. Shaw and N. Gould (eds) *Qualitative Research in Social Work* (pp 100–15). Sage.

Whiting, D., Gulati, G., Geddes, J.R. and Fazel, S. (2022) Association of schizophrenia spectrum disorders and violence perpetration in adults and adolescents from 15 countries: A systematic review and meta-analysis. *JAMA Psychiatry*, 79(2), 120–32.

Wilson, T.E. (2017) Repairing what's left in social work, or, when knowledge no longer cuts. *British Journal of Social Work*, 47, 1310–25.

Youn, S., Watson, A.E., Guadagno, B.L., Murrihy, S., Byrne, L.K., Cheng, N. et al (2025) Systematic review and meta-analysis: Risk factors of violence during first-episode psychosis. *Trauma, Violence, & Abuse*, 27(1), 256–70. https://doi.org/10.1177/15248380241309297

Zedner, L. (2010) Security, the state, and the citizen: The changing architecture of crime control. *New Criminal Law Review*, 13, 379–403.

Index

References to figures appear in *italic* type; those in **bold** refer to tables. References to endnotes show both the page number and the note number (18n1).

W